On the Moral Nature of the Universe

THEOLOGY AND THE SCIENCES

Kevin Sharpe, Series Editor

BOARD OF ADVISORS

Ian Barbour
Emeritus Professor of Physics and Religion
Carleton College, Northfield, Minnesota

Philip Hefner
Director, Chicago Center for Religion and Science
Professor, Lutheran School of Theology at Chicago

Sallie McFague
Carpenter Professor of Theology
The Divinity School, Vanderbilt University, Nashville

Arthur Peacocke, S.O.Sc.
Saint Cross College
Oxford, England

John Polkinghorne, F.R.S.
President, Queens College
Cambridge, England

Robert John Russell
Director, Center for Theology and the Natural Sciences
Professor, Graduate Theological Union, Berkeley

TITLES IN THE SERIES

Nature, Reality, and the Sacred
The Nexus of Science and Religion
Langdon Gilkey

The Human Factor
Evolution, Culture, and Religion
Philip Hefner

On the Moral Nature of the Universe
Nancey Murphy and George F. R. Ellis

Theology for a Scientific Age
Being and Becoming—Natural and Divine
Arthur Peacocke

The Faith of a Physicist
John Polkinghorne

The Travail of Nature
The Ambiguous Ecological Promise of Christian Theology
H. Paul Santmire

God, Creation, and Contemporary Physics
Mark William Worthing

On the Moral Nature of the Universe

Theology, Cosmology, and Ethics

Nancey Murphy
George F. R. Ellis

FORTRESS PRESS   MINNEAPOLIS

ON THE MORAL NATURE OF THE UNIVERSE
Theology, Cosmology, and Ethics

Library of Congress Cataloging-in-Publication Data

Murphy, Nancey C.
    On the moral nature of the universe : theology, cosmology, and ethics / Nancey
Murphy and George F. R. Ellis.
        p.   cm. — (Theology and the sciences)
    Includes bibliographical references and index.
    ISBN 0-8006-2983-3 (alk. paper)
    1. Cosmology.   2. Ethics.   3. Theology.   4. Social sciences.
I. Ellis, George Francis Rayner.   II. Title.   III. Series.
BD511.M85   1996
149'.2—dc20   96-38384
                                                              CIP

The paper used in this publication meets the minimum requirements of American National Standard for Information Sciences—Permanence of Paper for Printed Library Materials, ANSI Z329.48-1984. ♾

Manufactured in the U.S.A.   AF1-2983

00   99   98   97   96   1   2   3   4   5   6   7   8   9   10

To

Mary Roberts

and

James Wm. McClendon Jr.

Contents

List of Figures

Preface

The idea for this book began to germinate in the fall of 1991. We had just participated in a conference at the Vatican Observatory on quantum cosmology, the Anthropic Principle, and theology. At conference end, our thoughts turned to our respective political situations at home—the anti-apartheid struggle in South Africa and the build-up to the Gulf War in the United States—and we asked one another what, if anything, the work of the conference had to do with these life-and-death issues.

In the following months we began to see connections between scientific cosmology (and particularly the anthropic issue), theology, and ethics; the latter discipline, in our view, is too often omitted from the usual theology-and-science discussions. We were eventually able to arrive, at least in outline, at a broad synthesis of these themes; this book presents that synthesis.

Our thesis in brief: The (apparent) fine-tuning of the cosmological constants to produce a life-bearing universe (the anthropic issue) seems to call for explanation. A *theistic* explanation allows for a more coherent account of reality—as we know it from the perspective of both natural and human sciences, and from other spheres of experience such as the moral sphere—than does a non-theistic account. However, not all accounts of the divine nature are consistent with the patterns of divine action we seem to perceive in the natural world. God appears to work in concert with nature, never overriding or violating the very processes that God has created. This account of the character of divine action as refusal to do violence to creation, whatever the cost to God, has direct implications for human morality; it implies a "kenotic" or self-renunciatory ethic, according to which one must renounce self-interest for the sake of the other, *no matter what the cost to oneself.* Such an ethic, however, is very much at variance with ethical presuppositions embedded in current social science. Hence, new research programs are called for in these fields, exploring the possibilities for human sociality in the light of a vision modeled on God's own self-sacrificing love.

So this book is an attempt to synthesize knowledge from a variety of disparate fields, as well as to provide a program for future research. As such, it is necessarily schematic; each chapter deserves to be expanded at least to book length. However, we hope to repay our readers' patience with the inadequacy of our treatment of some issues by providing not only a coherent view of divine purposes displayed in the natural and human worlds, but also a basis for approaching pressing moral and political issues of our day.

Much of the book is a synthesis and development of the work of others. We employ the philosophy of science and epistemology of Carl Hempel, Imre Lakatos, and Alasdair MacIntyre to understand the forms of reasoning that we need in order to justify our claims. Arthur Peacocke has developed a model for relating theology and the sciences that employs the idea of a "hierarchy of sciences"; he suggests that theology be understood as the science at the top of the hierarchy. What is new in our synthesis is, first, the proposal that the hierarchy be split at the higher levels into natural- and human-science branches, and, second, that the human-science branch should have at its top the "science" of ethics. It is then possible to see theology as the discipline that completes both branches—answering "boundary questions," which arise in both cosmology and ethics, yet go beyond the scope of those disciplines alone. A single account of the divine purposes in creation, then, drawn largely from the work of John Howard Yoder, provides a bridge between the natural sciences and the human sciences.

Living on two continents, we would not have been able to write this book without opportunities to meet. We are grateful to the John Templeton Foundation for a generous travel grant. The Vatican Observatory and the Center for Theology and the Natural Sciences in Berkeley, California, have sponsored conferences on theology and science to which we were both invited. Our participation and interaction with other colleagues who attended have played an important role in the development of our thought. In addition, CTNS appointed George Ellis to the J.K. Russell Fellowship in Berkeley in the Spring of 1993. Our sincere thanks to the directors of each institution: Sir John Templeton, George Coyne, S.J., and Robert John Russell.

We also thank those who have read and commented on parts of our manuscript (we regret that we did not find it within our competence to incorporate all of their suggestions): Ian Barbour, Colin Brown, Arthur Peacocke, William R. Stoeger, S.J., John Howard Yoder, John Gardner and his reading group at the University of Wisconsin, and our editor at Fortress Press, Michael West.

We are also grateful to heroic individuals who have effectively brought good out of evil by noncoercive means; thus, in our view, emulating the very character of God: Mohandas K. Gandhi, Martin Luther King, Jr., and countless others. Most recently, Nelson Mandela has shown in a very dramatic way that an ethic based on the concept of kenosis is more than a utopian dream.

Finally, we thank our spouses, Mary Roberts and James Wm. McClendon, Jr., for help with the writing, but also for the inspiration their lives provide in seeking to enunciate an ethic of self-sacrifice. We dedicate this book to them.

Chapter One

Aim and Scope

1 DESCRIPTION OF THE PROJECT

This book is an essay in what we shall call cosmology in the broad sense, or Cosmology, to distinguish it from the narrower field of scientific cosmology. For a variety of reasons, the time has come to attempt the reconstruction of a unified worldview—one that relates human life to both the natural world and to nature's transcendent ground.[1]

We follow an impressive array of scholars who have made great strides in relating theology and the natural sciences. Equally pressing, however, is the need for an objective grounding for morality; we believe that this can be provided by discovering the proper relations between ethics and theology, on the one hand, and ethics and the sciences on the other. We aim to show that a particular moral vision (a "kenotic" ethic) is supported "from below" by evidence from the social and applied sciences, and "from above" by theology. This ethico-theological position has important implications, in turn, for understanding cosmology and other physical sciences.

1.1 The Separation of Ethics from Science and Theology
Ancient and medieval worldviews tended to provide links between theology, ethics, and natural philosophy—the precursor to modern science. Or perhaps

---

1. See Stephen Toulmin, *The Return to Cosmology: Postmodern Science and the Theology of Nature* (Berkeley: University of California Press, 1982).

it would be more accurate to say that for the ancients and medievals, the distinctions moderns have drawn among these disciplines were not yet in place. Stephen Toulmin describes a worldview such as our medieval predecessors had as a "cosmopolis": an overall harmony between the order of the heavens (the Cosmos) and the order of human affairs (the Polis). The rise of modernity marked the end of the medieval cosmopolis. Toulmin reads the early modern poetry of John Donne as a lament for the disintegration of the synthesis that had been developed in medieval and renaissance thought:

> 'Tis all in pieces, all Cohaerance gone,
> All just supply and all Relation.

The destruction of the political order of Europe in the Thirty Years War, the breakdown of the traditional family structure—all such signs of decay in the social order—corresponded to the decentering of the physical cosmos represented by the Copernican revolution.[2]

One of the most striking features of the modern period (ca. 1650–1950), viewed against this background, has been not only its failure to relate the affairs of the human world to those of the heavens and of the Heavens, but its positive insistence on maintaining a logical gulf between them. Immanuel Kant has been most influential in the modern bifurcation of the intellectual world, in fact arguing for a bifurcation in our very faculties of knowing. The natural world is known by experience and the faculty of pure reason, the moral world by intuition and practical reason.

The fragment of Heavenly reality that Kant was willing to countenance was known by means of practical reason. However, the modern tendency has been to separate religion and ethics as well. Jeffrey Stout describes the modern intellectual project as the "flight from authority," that is, the concerted attempt to free ethics and political thought from entanglements with religious tradition, and to establish them afresh on a "reasonable" foundation.[3]

It takes time for the work of philosophers, theologians, and scientists to make its impact upon culture at large. But by 1959, C. P. Snow could remark on the phenomenon of the "two cultures," scientific and religious, and their remarkable isolation from one another.[4]

A number of contemporary cultural phenomena express hunger for a new cosmopolis. The religious and quasi-religious speculations of scientists, and the great popularity of their books, suggest a hunger to relate our burgeoning

---

2. See *Cosmopolis: The Hidden Agenda of Modernity* (New York: Free Press, 1990), 67–69.

3. See *The Flight from Authority: Religion, Morality, and the Quest for Autonomy* (Notre Dame, Ind.: University of Notre Dame Press, 1981).

4. See *The Two Cultures and the Scientific Revolution* (Cambridge: Cambridge University Press, 1961).

knowledge of the cosmos to the pursuit of human meaning, both in the sense of meaningful, fulfilling ways of life (ethics and politics) and in the sense of the quest for an understanding of ultimate reality (religion). The New Age movement can be read as an attempt to find coherence, beginning from the spiritual and psychological side, but incorporating quasi-scientific paraphernalia and ideas:

> While church leaders have been occupying themselves with the world of secular politics, millions of people have begun to turn once again to religion. They are embarking on a spiritual quest: they want to find the source and meaning of their existence; to regain a sense of transcendent divinity; and to find a way to integrate human beings with one another, with nature, and with the whole of reality. . . .[5]

> At root the human potential movement is seeking a new cosmology, a new grounding for reality. The key to this new cosmology is the innate connection between self and world. It seeks to overcome the dualism of modern mind that separates subject and object, the humanities from the sciences.[6]

Against this historical background, our purpose is to return to the kind of synthesis that relates a conception of the natural order to a conception of the good life. The link between the two is provided by an account of the moral character of God and of God's purposes in creating both the Cosmos and the Polis.

2 OUR PRESUPPOSITIONS

Intellectual disputes abound in any era; ours is complicated by the now-widely recognized transition from modern to postmodern modes of thought. More than authors in more stable times, then, we owe our readers an account of the presuppositions that underlie our writing. Thus, we here set out assumptions we shall make in the arguments that follow—assumptions concerning the current status of scientific knowledge, philosophical theses, and theological orientation. While these are indeed presuppositions, it is important to note that they are not unarguable; in fact, the fruit that they bear in the remainder of this volume testifies, if only weakly, to their reasonableness.

---

5. Ted Peters, *The Cosmic Self: A Penetrating Look at Today's New Age Movements* (San Francisco, Calif.: Harper and Row, 1991), x.

6. Peters, *The Cosmic Self*, 69, summarizing a point by David Toolman, in *Facing West from California's Shores* (New York: Crossroad, 1987).

2.1 The Scientific Setting of the Problem

Aspects of the current understanding of science (regarding both content and interpretation of its significance) that will be important to our argument include the following:

Science 1: Bottom-Up and Top-Down Causation. The fundamental forces of physics underlie chemistry and biology, allowing emergent levels of order in the hierarchical structure of systems. Basic physical laws determine what happens at the microscopic level, and hence underlie functioning at the macroscopic levels, through bottom-up causation. The higher levels in turn, however, affect the processes at work at the lower levels through top-down causation.[7]

Science 2: Evolution of Life. The specific issue of the origin of order (despite the Second Law of Thermodynamics), and specifically the origin of life, is understood in the usual way: complex life forms, including ourselves, have developed through a process of evolution over a long period of time from single living cells. The basic process underlying evolution is Darwinian natural selection; the information resulting from this process, shaping the growth and functioning of all living beings, is stored in the universal genetic code of DNA.[8]

Science 3: The Hot Big Bang. The broad context in which this evolution occurs is the astronomical universe, whose overall structure is now well known: the universe has expanded to its present state from a Hot Big Bang, whose physics is well understood back to the time of element formation but is rather speculative at times earlier than that. The Cosmic Microwave Background Radiation recently examined in detail by the COBE satellite is relic radiation from the hot early phase of the evolution of the universe.[9]

There is, however, something of a mystery in how these two elements, evolution and the overall structure of the universe, relate to each other. This issue can be stated in purely scientific terms:

Science 4: The Anthropic Issue. Significant alteration of either physical laws or boundary conditions at the beginning of the universe would prevent the existence of intelligent life as we know it in the universe. If physical laws were altered by a remarkably small amount, no evolutionary development of living beings would be possible; so these laws *appear* fine-tuned to allow the existence of life.[10]

---

7. See Arthur Peacocke, *Theology for a Scientific Age: Being and Becoming—Natural, Divine, and Human,* 2nd, enlarged ed. (Minneapolis, Minn.: Fortress Press, 1993).

8. See Neil A. Campbell, *Biology,* 2nd ed. (Redwood City, Calif.: Benjamin Cummings, 1990).

9. See Joseph Silk, *The Big Bang: The Creation and Evolution of the Universe* (San Francisco: W. H. Freeman, 1980).

10. See P. C. W. Davies, *The Accidental Universe* (Cambridge: Cambridge University Press, 1982).

It will be our view, however, that adequate resolution of this issue leads to fundamental metaphysical issues that lie outside the competence of science per se, requiring a broader scheme of rational understanding (compatible with, but of wider scope than, science proper). In brief:

Science 5: The issue of metaphysics. Science itself cannot resolve the metaphysical issues raised by questioning the reason for (a) existence of the universe, (b) the existence of any physical laws at all, or (c) the nature of the specific physical laws that actually hold. These "boundary questions" require a different kind of account than a purely scientific approach provides.

These themes[11] will be elaborated as needed in the main text.

2.2 Our Philosophical Stance

The following philosophical positions, including views of ethics, will be important for our arguments in the remainder of this volume:

Philosophy 1: Anti-relativism. While it is now widely recognized that all knowledge—theology, social and natural sciences, even philosophy itself—is historically conditioned, we reject the claim that this implies total relativism. A spectrum of positions exists on the justifiability (reliability, objectivity) of knowledge claims within each of these broad disciplines; in each area there are respectable positions that take into account recent criticisms of Enlightenment objectivism, yet without falling into relativism. These include:

Philosophy 2: The reliability of scientific knowledge. While we recognize the thoroughly human character of scientific knowledge and culturally specific factors in the origin of the scientific enterprise itself, we reject the various sociological critiques that reduce science to culture- or gender-specific factors. We claim that objective, cross-cultural criteria exist for rational justification of scientific research programs.[12]

Ethics 1: Fact-value holism. We reject the so-called fact-value distinction. The very term "value" reflects the modern isolation of evaluative judgments, including moral judgments, from the rest of knowledge. The result is that values are taken to reflect nothing but personal or group choices ("subjective values"). We reject this view and would therefore prefer not to use the term "value"; however, it is so thoroughly woven into contemporary discourse that it would be awkward to try to avoid it. Thus, we occasionally place the

---

11. Summarized in some detail in George F. R. Ellis, *Before the Beginning* (London: Bowerdean/Boyars, 1993).

12. See especially Imre Lakatos, "Falsification and the Methodology of Scientific Research Programmes," first published in *Criticism and the Growth of Knowledge*, Lakatos and A. Musgrave, eds. (Cambridge: Cambridge University Press, 1970), 91–196. Reprinted in *The Methodology of Scientific Research Programmes: Philosophical Papers, Volume I*, J. Worrall and G. Currie, eds. (Cambridge: Cambridge University Press, 1978), 8–101.

word in "scare quotes" to remind the reader that we reject its usual meaning.[13]

Ethics 2: Ethics is tied to science but not reducible to it. We claim that ethical knowledge is logically related to knowledge about the way the world is as well as to knowledge of transcendent reality. Thus, ethical judgments should be affected by developments in scientific knowledge but cannot be determined by scientific knowledge alone. This is the *limited* truth in the fact-value distinction.[14]

Furthermore we claim that the sciences are not "value-free"; the applied and human sciences provide knowledge of means-ends relations, and choice of ends presumes judgments about the good for humankind. Since the natural sciences are dependent on the development of technology (applied science) they too are inevitably tied to the ethical realm.[15]

Ethics 3: The non-relativity of moral knowledge. Two factors in modern thought have led to the view that morality is culturally relative. First is the awareness of the variety of moral codes in different cultures. Second is the failure of the Enlightenment's attempt to base morality on pure reason, detached from religious traditions.

We reject the view that cultural variability entails moral relativism; the *fact* of variation does not imply that cultures *ought* to vary in this way, without the added *moral* premise that all cultures are as they ought to be. In addition, we believe, but cannot argue here, that there is a universal capacity among humans to perceive, even if dimly, clues about a transcendent moral order.

This transcendent moral order is dependent upon a transcendent purpose—and thus a purposer. Ultimately, then, ethics is best understood as having a religious basis.[16] Here we set ourselves against the major tendencies in ethical thought beginning with the Enlightenment and promoted especially by the current Continental philosophical tradition, one of whose major tenets is the rejection of a transcendent basis for morality.

Ethics 4: Free will. For the entire moral sphere to have meaning, the hierarchical structuring of the natural world must be compatible with some version of free will. While we recognize the importance of genetics, culture, and unconscious motives in determining behavior, it must be possible that hu-

---

13. See Alasdair MacIntyre, *After Virtue*, 2nd ed. (Notre Dame, Ind.: University of Notre Dame Press, 1984), for an account of the modern severing of the connections between ethics and worldview. See Hilary Putnam, *Reason, Truth and History* (Cambridge: Cambridge University Press, 1981), on fact-value holism.

14. This is as opposed to programs such as sociobiology, which claim to reduce morality to genetically programmed behavior. For a brief critique, see chap. 10, sec. 3.1.

15. These claims will be elaborated and supported in chaps. 4 and 5.

16. See MacIntyre, *After Virtue*.

mans act freely, at least some of the time. Thus, while we do not find current arguments for freedom of the will to be entirely adequate, we must assume that such arguments will be forthcoming.[17]

2.3 Our Theological Position

Theology 1: Theology provides genuine knowledge of a transcendent reality. It has become common in some theological circles to understand theology and religious awareness to be of a non-noetic (noncognitive) character. That is, religious thought is merely a reflection on human "values" or "meaning."[18] In addition, a common assumption among those who engage in the "scientific study of religion" is that religions are merely human constructs.[19] We presuppose, in contrast, that theology constitutes *knowledge* in exactly the same sense of the term as does science, albeit that the problems of justifying theological knowledge are more difficult than those in the natural sciences.[20]

Theology 2: Anabaptist Heritage. Our denominational perspectives, Quaker and Church of the Brethren, influence the questions we ask and the perspectives we take on theology. However, we do not apologize for this, since we believe that the minority tradition to which we belong, the Anabaptist tradition, has a great deal to offer to the world of theology and to the world in general. Most important here is this tradition's emphasis on the central role of ethics in the religious life, and in particular, its commitment to self-sacrifice and nonviolence.[21]

Theology 3: Other religions. We suspect, but cannot argue here, that there is a strand within many of the major world religions that is analogous to the Anabaptist strand of Christianity with regard to the issues of self-sacrifice and nonviolence. Mohandas Gandhi's development of the Hindu concept of *satyagraha* is but one notable example.

Theology 4: Theological claims as explanatory. Theological claims are confirmed on the basis of their ability to answer questions that arise within science and ethics but go beyond the purview of those disciplines alone. This assumption of a theological reality completes the metaphysical basis for cosmology, the need for which was stated above (Science 5). At the same time it provides an objective basis for ethics (Ethics 3).

This claim raises methodological issues relating to confirmation and expla-

---

17. See chap. 2, sec. 3.

18. See George Lindbeck, *The Nature of Doctrine* (Philadelphia: Westminster Press, 1984), on "experiential-expressivism" in liberal theology.

19. See, e.g., Clifford Geertz, *The Interpretation of Cultures* (New York: Basic Books, 1973).

20. See Nancey Murphy, *Theology in the Age of Scientific Reasoning* (Ithaca, N.Y.: Cornell University Press, 1990).

21. See chap. 8 for an account of Anabaptist thought.

nation. We now turn to an explication of the epistemological theories that underlie the arguments of this volume.

3 THE EPISTEMOLOGICAL BASIS

Our explication of the epistemological theories that guide our work, drawn largely but not exclusively from philosophy of science, will be structured in three stages. We first look at the "fine structure": the question of how particular theories are related to the data that justify them. Despite the fact that the various sciences differ considerably in terms of the kinds of data available to them and in terms of how the data are acquired, the same question arises in each of them: how do these data, logically, support or justify the scientific claims?

We next examine the medium scale: how do scientific theories (or theories in other domains) relate to one another in "research programs" and how are these programs evaluated relative to their competitors?

Finally, we consider the question: how are large-scale traditions to be defined and evaluated?

3.1 Carl Hempel: The Hypothetico-Deductive Method

At the beginning of the modern period, philosophers and scientists debated whether scientific reasoning was inductive (from data to general laws and theories) or deductive (particular conclusions about the world derived by mathematical reasoning from general principles). One of the most important advances in the history of epistemology was the recognition that scientific reasoning is neither purely inductive nor purely deductive; rather it is "hypothetico-deductive." This term, coined by Carl Hempel, well reflects the fact that scientific reasoning moves from an observation (fact, datum, experimental result) to a hypothesized explanation of that observation. The way one is to ascertain that the hypothesis does indeed explain the observation is by showing that a description of the observation can be deduced from the hypothesis (along with statements of initial conditions, etc.).[22]

It is helpful to represent the structure of hypothetico–deductive reasoning as in Figure 1.1

Here O_1 represents the original observation; H the hypothesis. O_2 represents a second observation or experimental result. The problem with hypothetical reasoning is that it is always possible to invent more than one hypothesis that explains a given set of observations (i.e., from which a given set of

---

22. See Hempel's *Aspects of Scientific Explanation* (New York: Free Press, 1965); for a more readable account, see his *Philosophy of Natural Science* (Englewood Cliffs, N.J.: Prentice-Hall, 1966).

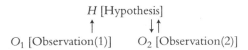

Fig. 1.1. *The basic structure of hypothetico-deductive reasoning.*

observations can be deduced). Therefore, hypotheses must be tested by deducing further observable consequences from them and then checking to see if these predictions are confirmed. The arrows represent the fact that one reasons from O_1 to H, then (deductively) from H to O_2. The arrow returning to H represents the confirmation that results if O_2 turns out to be the case.

Placing H above O_1 and O_2 has a double significance. First, in our usual way of writing a deductive argument, the conclusions that follow from the premises are written below the premises, so this structure indicates that observation statements are deductive consequences of the hypothesis.

Second, the move from observations to hypothesis is always a move to a "higher" epistemological order. At a minimum, it is the move from a limited number of observations to a universal generalization—a "higher" level of generality. For example, Boyle's law explains observations of relative pressures, volumes, and temperatures but goes beyond these observations to make universal claims about the behavior of all (ordinary) gases. In the more interesting cases, however, hypothetico-deductive reasoning moves from one level of description to another. That is, a set of theoretical concepts—a different level of discourse—is invoked to explain phenomena described in lower-level "observational" language. An example here is the move to explain the gas laws by means of the molecular-kinetic theory—a different language that needs to be related to the observations it explains by means of definitions.

This power of hypothetico-deductive reasoning to justify moves to higher-order conceptual schemes is what makes it so important to science—it is the means by which we expand our knowledge of the world beyond what we know from direct observations. We shall see that this "vertical" reasoning not only appears within each of the sciences but also forms the links among the sciences, insofar as they can be organized hierarchically according to the level of complexity they study. In addition, we argue that this kind of reasoning forms the links between the sciences and both ethical and theological accounts of reality developed here. Thus, while it is philosophers of science who have described this form of reasoning, we shall claim that it is essential in most other domains of knowledge, from everyday explanations of events to theology and metaphysics.

We note here one criticism of Hempel's account of scientific reasoning: many now argue that the observations are usually not exact deductive conse-

quences of th hypotheses; we only deduce approximations, and bothersome
additional premises need to be added, such as "all else being equal." In less
rigorous domains of knowledge we are even further from being able to trace
deductive links between hypothesis and observation; the latter follow from
the relevant hypothesis in some looser sense. Our standpoint will be that this
is a problem not with confirmation but with the nature of the conceptual
models that are the basic tools we use to understand reality; they will always
be limited in their domain of applicability, and their use to describe reality
will always be approximate. Thus, there is no way to avoid this problem,
even in the "hard" sciences.

In sum, we extend our knowledge beyond observation by inventing
hypotheses, which, if true, would explain the observed facts (up to a certain
level of accuracy, in some domain of application). The hypotheses are justified
insofar as they provide the "best" available explanation of these observations
and can also be shown to be extensible to other phenomena not already taken
into account (additional criteria for what is "best," to be pursued in the next
subsection, include the criterion of prediction of some new phenomenon not
yet observed, which turns out on investigation to be true of the real world).

3.2 Imre Lakatos: Scientific Research Programs

Recent, historically-oriented philosophers of science such as Imre Lakatos
provide a broader picture of scientific rationality than that of Hempel and
the other neo-positivists. This new account of scientific methodology adds a
number of refinements, based on study of the actual history of science, and
responds to criticisms that had been raised against earlier positions in the
philosophy of science.

Lakatos was responding to at least three problems raised by Thomas Kuhn
for those who would provide a rationalist account of scientific change.[23] The
first was Kuhn's recognition that scientific theories are not commonly subject
to confirmation or falsification on an individual basis, as Hempel's work
would lead one to expect, but rather are embedded in paradigms—scientific
"worldviews" that involve metaphysical assumptions, criteria for good scientific practice, and judgments about relevant domains of phenomena to be
explained. Kuhn noted that while small adjustments are made within the
theoretical structure of a paradigm, paradigms tend to be accepted or rejected
as a whole.

Implicit in Kuhn's account of the paradigm-governed nature of scientific
work are two further problems. First, the data that support scientific theories
are "theory-laden"; that is, far from being pure reports or descriptions of

---

23. See *The Structure of Scientific Revolutions*, 2nd ed. (Chicago: University of Chicago Press, 1970).

observations, scientific data are recognized, described, and interpreted in the light of theoretical assumptions. Second, while there are vague maxims for choosing between competing paradigms that apply across a variety of theoretical perspectives (such as simplicity, empirical fruitfulness), paradigms tend to set their own standards for good science. These two factors call into question the existence of objective rational standards for evaluating competing scientific paradigms.

Lakatos set out to answer the problems recognized by Kuhn, developing his "methodology of scientific research programs."[24] A research program has the following structure: It includes a core theory that unifies the program by providing a general view of the nature of the entities being investigated. The core is surrounded by a "protective belt" of "auxiliary hypotheses." These are lower-level theories, which both define and support the core theory. Also included here are theories of instrumentation and statements of initial conditions. Assorted data support the auxiliary hypotheses.

Since hypothetico-deductive reasoning makes explanation and confirmation symmetrical, the auxiliary hypotheses nearest the edges explain the data; higher-level hypotheses—that is, theories nearer the core or center—explain lower-level theories, and the core theory is the ultimate explanatory principle. The auxiliary hypotheses are referred to as a protective belt, since potentially falsifying data are accounted for by making changes here rather than in the core theory, called the "hard core" since it cannot be abandoned without rejecting the entire research program. It would thus be more accurate to say that a research program is a temporal *series* of networks of theory, along with supporting data, since the core theory stays the same but the belt of auxiliary hypotheses changes over time to account for new data. See Figure 1.2.

A mature program also involves what Lakatos calls a positive heuristic, which is a plan for systematic development of the program in order to take account of an increasingly broad array of data. An important development in recent philosophy of science has been the recognition of the role of models in science. Scientists use a variety of kinds of models, from mathematical models to physical models of various sorts. Another way to describe the positive heuristic is to say that it envisions the development of a series of increasingly accurate and sophisticated models of the process or entities under study.

For example, the hard core of Isaac Newton's program consisted of his three laws of dynamics and the law of gravitation. The auxiliary hypotheses included initial conditions and applications of the laws to specific problems. The positive heuristic included, for example, the plan to work out increas-

---

24. See "Falsification and the Methodology of Scientific Research Programmes," in Worrall and Currie, *Methodology of Scientific Research Programmes*, 8–101.

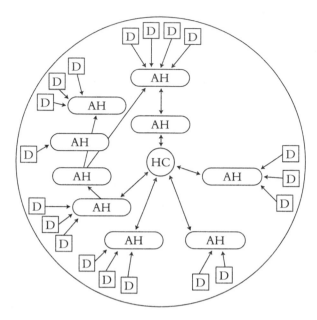

Fig 1.2. Schematic representation of a temporal cross-section of a scientific research program, showing the hard core, auxiliary hypotheses, and data.

ingly sophisticated solutions for the orbits of the planets: first, calculations for a one-planet system with the sun as a point-mass, then solutions for more planets, and so on.

Any account of knowledge that places a high premium on coherence (as all holist theories do) will be open to two charges: (1) that the justification of any belief within the system is ultimately circular, since it is a matter of each part fitting with the others, and (2) that there is no way to judge between two competing and equally coherent systems of belief (the charge of relativism). Lakatos's most important contribution to philosophy of science is his proposal for an external criterion for choosing among two or more competing research programs, each of which has its own domain of theory-laden data and its own internal standards of scientific competence. He recognized, as did Kuhn, that an important factor in assessing a paradigm or research program is how well it can account for anomalies. He also realized, however, that any research program can be made consistent with conflicting data if one adds suitable auxiliary hypotheses. Sometimes these new hypotheses represent genuine improvements in understanding of the subject in question; other times they are mere ad hoc devices to protect the theory from falsification. How to tell the difference? Lakatos proposed that a "progressive" move be defined as one where the new hypothesis not only accounts for the anomaly that led to its inclusion in the program, but also allows for the prediction and corroboration of a "novel fact," that is, one not to be expected in light of the previous version of the research program.[25]

When a research program occasionally makes such content-increasing moves, it is said to be progressive and is to be preferred to one in which all or most of its auxiliary hypotheses are added in an ad hoc manner—called "degenerating." That is, the progressive program's domain of facts increases over time, while the degenerating program's empirical content does not increase to keep pace with the increasing proliferation of theoretical components.

Lakatos claimed not only to be proposing an intuitively plausible answer to the normative question of how scientists ought to decide which research program to work on but also to have found the key to explain *why* scientists in the past abandoned one program in favor of another *when* they did. Subsequent studies in the history of science have gone some way toward establishing the historiographical claim in areas as diverse as economics and high-energy physics.[26]

We have argued elsewhere that the scientific methodology developed by Lakatos can be applied rather directly to theology;[27] and we shall apply it briefly to ethics in chapters 6 and 7. We shall not reproduce those arguments here.

Since the publication of Lakatos's work in the philosophy of science, however, there have been important parallel advances in epistemology generally, somewhat inspired by Lakatos's work but developed specifically to give an account of the structure and justification of broader intellectual traditions. To these we now turn.

3.3 Alasdair MacIntyre: Intellectual Traditions
Alasdair MacIntyre's epistemological concerns grew out of his work in ethics. In *After Virtue* he argued that it is not possible to evaluate an ethical theory apart from the tradition in which it has developed. It was then necessary, in order to avoid moral relativism, to address the question of how moral traditions were to be evaluated. Yet a feature of these larger traditions is that they incorporate their own standards of rationality. Thus, MacIntyre was faced with a problem similar to the one raised in science by Kuhn: how to evaluate

---

25. For a more detailed discussion of the nature of novel facts, see Nancey Murphy, "Another Look at Novel Facts," *Studies in History and Philosophy of Science* 20, no. 3 (1989): 385–88.

26. For a partial list of references, as well as a defense of Lakatos's methodology, see Murphy, *Theology in the Age of Scientific Reasoning*, chap. 3. For criticisms of Lakatos's methodology, see W. H. Newton-Smith, *The Rationality of Science* (London: Routledge and Kegan Paul, 1981).

27. See chap. 8 below; and Murphy, *Theology in the Age of Scientific Reasoning*.

paradigms when the standards of good science are themselves paradigm-dependent.

We shall describe MacIntyre's contributions to epistemology by tracing the development of his thought through several works. In an early article he argued that justification of theories in science depends on our being able to construct a historical narrative that makes the transition from the old theory to the new theory intelligible:

> What the scientific genius, such as Galileo, achieves in his transition, then, is not only a new way of understanding nature, but also and inseparably a new way of understanding the old science's way of understanding nature. It is because only from the standpoint of the new science can the inadequacy of the old science be characterized that the new science is taken to be more adequate than the old. It is from the standpoint of the new science that the continuities of narrative history are re-established.[28]

Thus, he claims, scientific reason turns out to be subordinate to, and intelligible only in terms of, historical reason. This is equivalent to Lakatos's insistence on the historical character of justification in science. Let us call this aspect of justification the diachronic dimension. Here MacIntyre is answering the question of how one justifies a modification within a given tradition.

A second question, however, asks how one justifies the tradition as a whole over against its rivals. MacIntyre takes up this issue in *Whose Justice? Which Rationality?* One aspect of the adjudication between competing traditions is to construct a narrative account of each tradition: of the crises it has encountered (incoherence, new experience that cannot be explained, etc.) and how it has or has not overcome these crises. Has it been possible to reformulate that tradition in such a way as to overcome its crises without losing its identity? Comparison of these traditions may show that one tradition is clearly superior to another: it may become apparent that one tradition is making progress while its rival has become sterile. This aspect of MacIntyre's epistemology resembles Lakatos's distinction between progressive and degenerative research programs.

In addition, if there are participants within the traditions with enough empathy and imagination to understand the rival tradition's point of view in its own terms, then:

> protagonists of each tradition, having considered in what ways their own tradition has by its own standards of achievement in enquiry found it difficult to develop its enquiries beyond a certain point, or has produced

---

28. "Epistemological Crises, Dramatic Narrative, and the Philosophy of Science," in Gary Gutting, ed., *Paradigms and Revolutions* (Notre Dame, Ind.: University of Notre Dame Press, 1980), 54–74; quotation on p. 69.

in some area insoluble antinomies, ask whether the alternative and rival tradition may not be able to provide resources to characterize and to explain the failings and defects of their own tradition more adequately than they, using the resources of that tradition, have been able to do.[29]

Let us refer to this aspect as synchronic justification. Notice that it involves diachronic evaluation of each tradition as an intrinsic element.

Thus, for example, MacIntyre's own reformulation of virtue theory is justified because it solves the problems its predecessors in the virtue tradition of moral reasoning could not solve. But this approach to the justification of an ethical position is an instance of a broader theory of rationality, according to which a tradition is vindicated by the fact that it has managed to solve its own major problems (incoherence, inability to account for experience) while its competitors have failed to do so. This theory itself needs to be justified by showing that it is part of a large-scale epistemological tradition (the Aristotelian-Thomist tradition) and that this large-scale tradition is justified— by MacIntyre's narrative in which he recounts how it has overcome its problems, while its main contemporary competitor, modern Enlightenment reason, has not.

MacIntyre's views have interesting consequences for a broader view of knowledge. In contrast to relativists and pluralists with regard to religion and ethics, he maintains that it is at least sometimes possible to provide a rational justification for accepting one tradition and rejecting its immediate competitors. The overall justification will consist in taking a long-term historical look at how well the conceptual resources of one's tradition have compared with others in resolving intellectual crises. These are the sort of criteria we shall need to employ in order to evaluate our project in chapter 10.

4 OVERVIEW OF THE ARGUMENT

We have now laid enough groundwork that we can present an overview of our argument. We shall start by reviewing the claim that the sciences can be ordered hierarchically in such a way that the higher levels deal with more complex or broadly encompassing wholes; furthermore, the concepts needed for describing and explaining the higher-level entities are not reducible (i.e., translatable without remainder) into concepts of the lower levels. However, we judge that there is no unambiguous way to arrange the sciences above biology; it depends on whether one thinks in terms of more encompassing wholes or in terms of greater complexity. Our solution is to propose a model

---

29. Alasdair MacIntyre, *Whose Justice? Which Rationality?* (Notre Dame, Ind.: University of Notre Dame Press, 1988), 166–67.

of a branching hierarchy, with the natural sciences of ecology, astrophysics, and cosmology forming one branch, and the human sciences (psychology and the social sciences) forming the other. A highly unusual and controversial feature of our approach is the inclusion of ethics as a science at the top of the hierarchy of the social sciences.

It is now becoming widely recognized that in addition to reductionistic or "bottom-up" accounts of causation, it is also necessary to countenance "top-down" causation. That is, reference to phenomena described at the higher levels of the hierarchy of the sciences is sometimes needed to explain phenomena described at lower levels. Questions arise at one level of the hierarchy that can only be answered by reference to entities or processes described at higher levels of the hierarchy. We call these "boundary questions." Thus, there are correspondences between higher ontological (causal) orders and higher epistemological (explanatory) levels.

In the most general terms, the purpose of this book is to argue that when we take into account the full range of human experience, described in terms of such a hierarchical ordering, the generally accepted body of scientific knowledge—the natural and human sciences together—is incomplete. We shall highlight features in contemporary scientific cosmology that call for a higher-level explanation—either metaphysical or theological.

In particular, if one is to give a complete account of "reality" an extremely important phenomenon is the sense of moral obligation. While it could be argued that the experienced sense of moral obligation is an illusion, we claim that it provides important clues to the nature of reality. We shall argue that the human (and applied) sciences, dealing as they do in questions of means-ends relations, are essentially incomplete without an account of the ultimate purpose of human life and human society—a sort of theory that falls within the province of ethics. Furthermore, such an account can only be justified by a metaphysical or theological account of the nature of ultimate reality. Given such a theological account, it is clear that the sense of moral obligation is *not* illusory and that moral relativism is false.

The task of the following chapters, then, is to argue that there is a need for an ethical theory and a theological or metaphysical account of ultimate reality in order to complete the hierarchy of the sciences, and thus to give a complete account of reality.

A second task, however, is to fill in the content of such theories—to describe the purpose of human life and the character of ultimate reality in a particular way. We shall do so by examining some results of science, beginning with cosmology, seeing how far this can lead us; in particular, we note that the so-called fine-tuning, or anthropic character, of the universe raises questions that cannot be answered on the basis of science alone.

We then turn to the human-science branch of the hierarchy of the sciences, taking issue with the standard account of ultimate reality and of ethics presupposed therein. In particular, we reject "the ontology of violence," which implies that selfishness and violent coercion are basic to human nature. In its place we develop a theory of human life as created for self-sacrifice and nonviolence. This "kenotic" ethic—an ethic of self-emptying for the sake of the other—is in turn explained and justified by a correlative theology: the kenotic way of life is objectively the right way of life for all of humankind because it reflects the moral character of God.

This particular theory of ultimate reality—a theory about the *purpose* for which God created the universe—can then be shown to answer the boundary questions raised in cosmology and also, as a bonus, to provide a rationale for phenomena described at lower levels of the natural-science hierarchy: in biology, of the suffering and waste involved in the evolutionary process; and of quantum indeterminacy in physics.

Thus, the same theological theory answers questions (completes the hierarchy of explanation) that arise in both the natural and social sciences. It is noteworthy that the kenotic concept of God, which we develop here, is widely accepted in discussions of the relations between theology and the natural sciences, but the ethical consequences of such a theology are almost universally rejected as impracticable within the sphere of the social sciences. Thus, we bear a heavy burden of argument to counter these social-scientific assumptions. Finally, we use the accounts of rationality summarized above to provide an evaluation of the epistemological status of our system.

In succeeding chapters, then, we propose to accomplish the following:

Chapter 2: Discuss the nature of hierarchies in general and of the hierarchy of sciences in particular, preparatory to arguing later that the hierarchy of the sciences requires higher levels both of an ethical and of a theological or metaphysical nature.

Chapter 3: Review the current status of scientific cosmology, on the one hand aiming to clarify the limits of what can be explained by this discipline, and on the other to see what restrictions are placed on theories of ultimate reality by cosmology alone.

Chapter 4: Elaborate the hierarchy of the sciences to include the social sciences as well as the applied sciences and show the dependence of these sciences on judgments of value.

Chapter 5: Discuss the relations between ethics and the natural and human sciences, and between ethics and conceptions of ultimate reality, showing how they are needed to complete each other.

Chapter 6: Introduce a particular theory of ethics, a "kenotic" ethic, and develop some of its social-ethical consequences for law, economics, and politics.

Chapter 7:   Consider the consequences of our social ethic for research
             programs in the social sciences, along with empirical evidence
             for the possibility of its social embodiment.
Chapter 8:   Show how the kenotic ethic follows from a particular (Ana-
             baptist) theory of the character of God.
Chapter 9:   Show the value of our resulting ethico-theological position
             for answering boundary questions that arise in cosmology and
             other physical sciences.
Chapter 10: Evaluate the overall epistemological status of the proposed
             system, in particular in terms of its relation to what is usually
             regarded as counter-evidence—the problem of evil.

5 SIGNIFICANCE OF THE UNDERTAKING

Presently agreed-upon understandings of the nature of reality are seriously
incomplete—the scientific and the religious standpoints each illuminate certain aspects of reality but are unable to deal with others, and they have not,
since the fragmenting of the medieval cosmopolis, been brought to a satisfactory unity. While various proposals have been made toward their unification,
these have generally lacked essential elements, in particular an objective moral
dimension. We argue that the route to their completion is through tackling
the ethical issues that have so far been inadequately addressed. Our central
contribution to the debate is to present the view that ethics should have a
major role in the theology-science dialogue. Our aim will be to show that
this move can be justified within the context of the best available epistemological and scientific understandings.

   We shall develop details of the argument in a specific Christian context,
enabling us to make the case in a stronger form than if pursued in a universal-
istic way. This does not solve the issue of religious pluralism, which we do
not tackle here. Rather it shows that at least one consistent scientific-religious
viewpoint of the type we envisage can be constructed in a satisfactory way
and related in depth to existing traditions. Thus, this project provides an
outline of one consistent worldview of adequate scope and with substantial
evidential support. Further investigation would be needed to develop the
outline presented here to a proper apologetic position, which we will not
attempt. That project can only be undertaken when alternative views with
similar wide scope have been developed to sufficient depth. We hope the
present essay will help stimulate such development.

Chapter Two

The Hierarchy of the Sciences

1 INTRODUCTION: THE INCOMPLETE HIERARCHY

It has long been recognized that the physical universe can be understood in terms of a hierarchy of systems, organized according to level of complexity, from the inorganic, to the organic, the conscious, and the social. Thus, the natural and human sciences can be ordered hierarchically as well, according to the levels of complexity they study. The lower parts, at least, of the hierarchy can be ordered unambiguously as in Figure 2.1.

We shall argue in the following chapters that such a view of reality, provided by the sciences alone (including the social sciences), is incomplete. Arthur Peacocke has claimed that the hierarchy needs to be completed by considering theology to be the topmost science. Stimulated by this suggestion, we shall claim that theories of a theological or of a metaphysical nature (or both) must be added at the top of the hierarchy in order to give a complete account of reality. In addition, we claim that the hierarchy needs to be

Psychology
Botany/Zoology/Physiology
Biochemistry
Chemistry
Physics

Fig. 2.1. The hierarchical relations among the sciences.

represented as branching above the biological level, giving over one branch to the human and applied sciences, including psychology, and the other to the sciences dealing with nonhuman reality.

In this chapter we consider the essential features of hierarchical systems in general, considering in particular the nature of bottom-up and top-down causation. We pursue the issue of the branching hierarchy in chapter 4, where we argue that, for a satisfactory understanding, the human-science branch needs to be supplemented by ethics, considered as a science.[1] We make proposals for the completion of the hierarchy in chapters 5 through 8, where we argue, first, that both branches need completion by a metaphysical or theological layer of *some* kind and, second, that the same theological account suffices for completion of both branches, answering questions that arise in cosmology on the natural-science side, and ethics on the human-science side.

1.1 Arthur Peacocke on the Hierarchy of the Sciences

It was the dream of the logical positivists, beginning in the 1920s, to reduce all higher sciences ultimately to physics, and the possibility of such reduction has been fiercely debated ever since. It is now becoming widely recognized, however, that analysis and reduction provide only a partial understanding of complex entities, which can only be fully described by employing concepts peculiar to their own level in the hierarchy and by considering causal influences exerted on those entities by their environments. Thus, there is "bottom-up causation"—constraints provided on the whole by the laws governing the constituent parts of the entity—but also "top-down causation"— influences from the larger system of which the entity is a part.

Arthur Peacocke has made an important contribution to the dialogue between theology and science by suggesting that theology be understood as the science at the top of the hierarchy, since it studies the most complex of all systems, the interaction between God and the entire universe. This model assumes that theology is a science (or at least very much like a science).[2]

Peacocke's work provides an important point of departure for the present volume. In making this proposal he has offered a model for the relation of theology and science that does justice to the differences between theology and the sciences but also suggests that theology must bear a relationship to the sciences that is analogous to the relations among the sciences themselves.

---

1. Roy Wood Sellars was one of the first to develop the concept of the hierarchy of the sciences, in connection with his argument for "non-reductive physicalism." He too proposed that ethics should be included in the hierarchy above the social sciences. See *Critical Realism: A Study of the Nature and Conditions of Knowledge* (New York: Russell and Russell, 1916).

2. Peacocke's most thorough exposition is in *Theology for a Scientific Age: Being and Becoming— Natural, Divine, and Human*, 2nd, enlarged ed. (Minneapolis, Minn.: Fortress Press, 1993).

We know from looking at theories within science proper that there are connections between levels—both upward and downward. Insofar as the levels of the hierarchy are interconnected they are mutually explanatory and mutually supportive. The interconnections among the levels serve to constrain scientific theorizing as well. We usually think of this in terms of the requirement that laws and theories of higher levels conform to (i.e., avoid violation of) lower-level laws. The constraint goes both ways, however, because accounts given by lower-level sciences have to permit (even if they cannot predict) the phenomena described by the levels above. We shall make use of this hierarchical view of reality and a corresponding view of the relation of theology to the sciences.

We believe Peacocke's account needs emendation, however, in two principal ways. First, we believe he moves too quickly from science to the (or a) Christian view of God. Second, his system does not give adequate consideration to the ethical dimension of human life, which we take to be an essential ingredient of any adequate account of reality. This is partly consequent on his analysis not distinguishing sufficiently clearly between the natural sciences and the applied sciences—called "the sciences of the artificial" by Herbert A. Simon.[3]

As regards the first issue, we propose, and in the course of our argument will attempt to support, first, a weaker claim, that *some* metaphysical or theological account of the nature of ultimate reality is needed to "top-off" the hierarchy of the sciences. We shall attempt to show how the sciences at the top of the hierarchy call for a concept of ultimate reality in order to answer questions that cannot be answered from within those sciences themselves. We claim that concepts of ultimate reality can be limited and refined by their relation to both cosmology and ethics. Only after making this case in detail do we make the move to a Christian view of God, as a further step in the argument.

To make the move to include ethics and metaphysics or theology in the hierarchy of the sciences it will be necessary to present an epistemology suitable for describing these broader sorts of knowledge, showing first that it is legitimate to count these other disciplines as knowledge and, second, that they have enough in common with the sciences to suppose logical relations from one sort of discipline to the other. The foundations for this claim have been laid in the discussion of the hypothetico-deductive method above; this discussion will be extended in chapters 6 and 10.

The remainder of this chapter is dedicated to examination of the hierarchical ordering of nature and the consequent ordering of the natural sciences.

3. In *The Sciences of the Artificial*, 2nd ed. (Cambridge, Mass.: MIT Press, 1992).

We shall attempt to define top-down causation more precisely than has been done in previous discussions and also to relate this topic to the problem of human free will.

2 HIERARCHIES OF COMPLEXITY

The fundamental way we understand complex systems is by analyzing their structure hierarchically, each level of representation being a "coarse-graining" of lower-level descriptions in that it ignores many of the details relevant at the lower levels. For example, describing a gas in a box by referring simply to its density, pressure, and temperature ignores all the details of molecular motions and positions; the description does not extend to that level of detail. We have then used a "coarse-grained" (macroscopic) representation, which glosses over the finer details of its microscopic structure. Consequently we can represent the state of the gas with far fewer variables than if we attempt a more detailed description; this makes the description more useful for many practical purposes. Similarly we can describe macroscopic properties of a human body (a hearing problem, for example) without having to consider its cell structure. That finer structure might help us *understand* the macroscopic problem, or it might not; but it is not necessary for its *description*.

Higher-level descriptions then allow introduction of higher semantic and explanatory levels that cannot be accommodated within the lower-level description. For example, the concept *loss of hearing* simply cannot be described in terms of the language of molecular biology; nor can the biological concept *cell wall* be directly described by means of the concepts of fundamental physics, even though a cell wall is indeed constituted through the interaction of quarks, electrons, gluons, and so on, which are the subject of fundamental physics.

In hierarchically structured complex systems we find both emergent order and top-down effects. We address each of these in turn.

2.1 Emergent Order

"Emergent order" refers to the appearance of properties and processes that are only describable by means of irreducible concepts, concepts that are simply inapplicable at the lower levels of order.[4] Thus, different levels of order appear and new levels of description are required. However, one should note here that higher- and lower-level descriptions are descriptions of the same

4. See Peacocke, "God's Interaction with the World: The implications of Deterministic 'Chaos' and Interconnected and Interdependent Complexity," in Robert J. Russell, Nancey Murphy, and Arthur Peacocke, eds., *Chaos and Complexity: Scientific Perspectives on Divine Action* (Vatican City State and Berkeley, Calif.: Vatican Observatory and the Center for Theology and the Natural Sciences, 1995), 263–87.

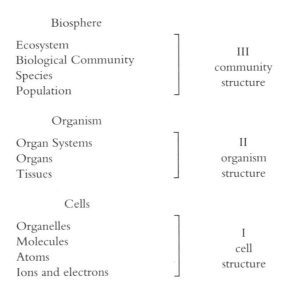

Biosphere

Ecosystem
Biological Community ⎤ III
Species ⎟ community
Population ⎦ structure

Organism

Organ Systems ⎤ II
Organs ⎟ organism
Tissues ⎦ structure

Cells

Organelles ⎤ I
Molecules ⎟ cell
Atoms ⎟ structure
Ions and electrons ⎦

Fig. 2.2. Levels of emergent order in biology.

physical system, applicable at the same time; one can choose at which level to view the nature and action of a single complex system, without in any way changing the nature of the system.

Philosophers have coined the term "supervenience" to refer to the relation between properties of the same system that pertain to different levels of analysis. There are a variety of definitions of supervenience. We use the term as follows: higher-level properties supervene on lower-level properties if they are partially constituted by the lower-level properties but are not directly reducible to them. Thus, for example, mental properties can be said to supervene on properties of the neurological system; moral properties supervene on psychological or sociological properties.[5]

We may note here that all of our descriptions of reality are in fact coarse-grained, as we have not yet determined the ultimate structure of matter; we cannot at present describe the inner structure of a quark or electron. So in all cases we are choosing among different levels of coarse-graining. Certainly our "everyday life" attains much of its apparent nature because it is unavoidably a coarse-grained view of the underlying atomic structure of matter.[6]

In the specific case of biology, we find a hierarchical structure as depicted in Figure 2.2.

5. See sec. 3 below; and N. Murphy, *Anglo-American Postmodernity* (Boulder, Colo.: Westview Press, forthcoming), chap. 10.

6. Arthur Stanley Eddington, *The Nature of the Physical World* (Cambridge: Cambridge University Press, 1928).

According to Neil Campbell:

> With each step upward in the hierarchy of biological order, novel proper-
> ties emerge that were not present at the simpler levels of organization.
> These emergent properties result from interactions between compo-
> nents. . . . Unique properties of organized matter arise from how parts are
> arranged and interact, not from supernatural powers . . . [consequently] we
> cannot fully explain a higher degree of order by breaking it down to its parts.[7]

In a biological system, the two crucial levels of order are those of the cell and
of the individual organism (that is, the whole animal); for at each of these
levels there is a higher degree of autonomy of coherent action than at any of
the other levels. This leads to three major "coarse-grained" levels of structure: the cell structure (I), organism structure (II), and community structure
(III). A biologist regards cells as elementary components of the system, while
(broadly speaking) a microbiologist regards molecules, and a biochemist, ions
and electrons, as the elementary components. (A physicist would continue
down the hierarchical scale, reducing these to quarks, gluons, and electrons.)
Thus, the various sciences that study biological systems naturally occur in a
hierarchy, corresponding to the hierarchy of natural structure.

Not only are such different levels of description permitted, they are required in order to make sense of what is going on. This is true not only of
biological systems: Bernd-Olaf Küppers and Silvan S. Schweber show con-
vincingly that such emergent properties are important even in a simple physical system such as a gas.[8]

2.2 Top-Down Causation

The foregoing description of hierarchical structure allows us to define "top-
down causation." Briefly stated, interactions at the lower levels cannot be
predicted by looking at the structure at those levels alone. Higher-level variables, which cannot be reduced to lower-level properties or processes, have
genuine causal impact (e.g., moving the walls of a container of gas changes
the motion of the gas molecules within it). So the concept of top-down
causation implies that the lower-level laws by themselves do not allow for the
prediction of the outcome.

We will distinguish within the broad category of top-down causation between top-down effects, such as that mentioned above, and top-down action.
Top-down *effects* occur where the macroscopic evolution of a hierarchical
system is completely determined by microscopic laws and states that lead to

7. Neil A. Campbell, *Biology,* 2nd ed. (Redwood City, Calif.: Benjamin Cummings, 1990), 2–3.
    8. Bernd-Olaf Küppers, "Understanding Complexity," in Russell et al., *Chaos and Complexity;*
Silvan S. Schweber, "Physics, Community and the Crisis in Physical Theory," *Physics Today* (November 1993): 34–40.

well-determined microscopic patterns of evolution but conditions described at the higher semantic levels (such as macroscopic boundary conditions) determine the detailed evolution of the system. Top-down *action* occurs when human volition is involved. We discuss the former here, and consider the latter in section 3.

2.3 A Determinate Example: Digital Computers

A particularly clear example of a hierarchically organized system exhibiting top-down *effects* is a modern digital computer, which operates through hierarchies of software. The computer, if considered in abstraction from its operator, is a thoroughly determined system. Nonetheless, it exhibits the emergence of higher levels of order and semantics that cannot be reduced to lower levels.

From the bottom up there are machine language (expressed in binary digits), assembly language (expressed in hexadecimal), operating system and programming language (expressed in ASCII), and application package (e.g., word processor) levels of software. At every level there is a completely deterministic type of behavior described by algorithms applicable at that level. All of this is realized in terms of the motion of electrons flowing in the computer's integrated circuits, as determined by the laws of physics. This is where the real action takes place, but it does so according to orders from the higher semantic levels and thereby effects actions that are meaningful only at the higher levels.[9]

The connections among the different levels in the computer and also among the resulting machine languages at each level, are tightly controlled by the machine hardware and software. In particular, given the machine, the program loaded into particular memory locations, and the data resident in memory, each high-level instruction will result in a unique series of actions at the digital (hardware) level, which in turn will result in a unique series of consequences at each of the higher levels. Consequently, the machine language at each level also has a tight "logical" structure with a very precise set of operations resulting from each statement in that language. By itself, however, this does not determine what actually happens at each level; what happens is determined by the data input to the computer in the language of its top logical level—expressing concepts that are irreducible to lower levels of the structure. The fact that particular data represent a three-dimensional plan of a house, for example, cannot be described in terms of concepts available at the machine-language level.

In biological systems, with hierarchical levels as indicated above, the same

---

9. For a clear exposition of the hierarchical structuring in modern digital computer systems, see S. Tannenbaum, *Structured Computer Organization* (Englewood Cliffs, N.J.: Prentice Hall, 1990).

kind of hierarchical relationships hold. The "languages" at each of the higher levels, however, are much less tightly structured than in the case of the computer; and the links between different levels are correspondingly less rigid.

2.4 Hierarchies of Entities in Their Environments

The environment influences the entity, and these environmental factors cannot be reduced to factors at the same level as the entity. Two examples are an ecological system, where the environment influences the organism, and a computer and its programmer. The programmer, within the limits set by the physics relevant to the circuits themselves, brings higher levels of reality (e.g., mathematical and logical, social, ecological relations) to bear on the operation of the computer.

The level that considers the interaction between an organism and its environment is a higher level of analysis than that of studying the organism in abstraction. Indeed this is a special case of a hierarchy of increasing complexity, since the entity within its environment is necessarily a more complex system than the entity alone. Interactions between any specific entity and its environment will be more loosely coupled than those operating within the entity (for it is precisely the tight nature of its internal coupling that leads us to identify it as an entity of a particular kind). Consequently, only some of the variables in an environment will affect an entity in that environment, and they will usually affect the internal variables of the entity in an imprecise way.

Thus, it is always necessary in characterizing hierarchical systems to define clearly the boundary of each entity, the nature of the environment in which it exists, and the interactions that take place across that boundary—thereby defining the larger system consisting of the entity and its environment. We are always at liberty to consider this system (the entity and its environment) as the system of interest, rather than just the entity with which we began. This progression, too, will happen in a hierarchical fashion: each environment is itself contained in a larger environment (an ecosystem is contained in the biosphere, which is contained in the solar system, and so on), until we reach that environment which consists of the entire universe (the subject of cosmology).

2.5 The Physical Mediation of Top-Down Effects

The argument in this section establishes the following:[10] In any physical system, given the structural equations at some level of description, describing both the physical structuring (e.g., the circuit wiring in a radio) along with equations of state, the physical response laws of the components in the struc-

---

10. Readers who wish to skip over this section can pick up the argument in sec. 2.6.

ture at that level (e.g., the way a resistor responds to voltage changes), it will be the *boundary conditions* at that level of description that determine what happens locally. Furthermore, hierarchical or coarse-graining relations relate what happens at the different levels to each other (e.g., a current flow at a macroscopic level corresponds to motions of electrons at a microscopic level). It is such hierarchical structuring that relates the different levels of description of matter (physical, chemical, macromolecular) and hence underlies the hierarchy of the sciences (e.g., physics, chemistry, material sciences), with each higher-level study being based on but not reducible to that of the level below.

Consider, now, how the hierarchically structured effects occur, in physical terms. We can represent this as follows: for a structured hierarchical physical system S, made up of physical particles interacting only through physical forces, top-down and bottom-up effects are related as follows: The boundary B separates the system S from its environment E. Interaction with the outside world (the environment) takes place by flow of information, energy, or matter in or out through the boundary, and is determined by the boundary conditions at B (for example, the position of a boundary wall and the rate of energy flow in or out across that wall). The structure of the system is determined by its structural conditions, which can be expressed as constitutive relations between the parts (e.g., the wiring diagram of a radio or the equation of state of a gas). We distinguish here the structural conditions, fixed by the initial state of the physical system and remaining constant in a stable physical system—indeed characterizing its physical nature—and "boundary conditions" as usually understood in physics, which may vary continually as conditions in the environment vary.

We consider here classical physical systems such as the atmosphere, and engineering systems such as an aircraft or a digital computer. In each of these systems, the action is strictly deterministic. This is ensured in the engineered systems in order to obtain reliability; any quantum uncertainties are damped out by design. These types of systems are not necessarily predictable, however, both because of deterministic chaos (sensitivity to initial conditions, as in the case of the weather) and sheer complexity (if the computer output were predictable we would not need to run the computer program to determine the output). How do such hierarchical systems function? The bottom level expresses the basic causal relations underlying the system. The components at that level act on each other by regular physical laws, the resulting final state at the bottom level then determining conditions at the higher levels, because they define conditions at the higher levels, through their aggregation (or "coarse-graining") properties. This is what is meant by bottom-up causation.

We run into the paradox here that although the later microscopic state may well be unpredictable (both because of quantum uncertainties and because of sensitive dependence on initial conditions in molecular collisions, as in the classic billiard-ball problem) in many cases a later macroscopic level-state is fully predictable (e.g., as in the standard gas laws). This—the triumph of statistical physics—is because of an essential feature of coarse-graining, that many different microscopic states may correspond to the same macroscopic state.[11] At an even higher level the macroscopic situation may again be unpredictable over long enough time spans, although predictable in the short term (e.g., the case of weather) but this is not the present concern.

The coordination of action occurs through the structural arrangement and interconnection of lower-level entities so as to form higher-level entities. Because the semantics of the higher level are intrinsic to its nature, the language (vocabulary and syntax) at each level cannot be reduced to that at a lower level, even though what happens at each higher level is uniquely determined by the coordinated action taking place at the lower levels, where it is fully described in terms of the lower level language. Thus, the whole shows emergence of new properties not reducible to those of the constituent parts. An example is a computer reading out a text file and printing it on the screen. While this is realized by electrons impinging on the screen the information on the screen cannot be expressed in terms pertaining only to electrons.

Now, the overall macroscopic structure affects what happens microscopically. For example, the position of the boundary of a container of gas (say, a piston in a car engine) determines the nature of the local molecular state of motion because it controls the pressure of the gas. If I alter the position of the wall (I move the piston), then I alter the pressure and so change the local motion of molecules in the gas, resulting in a change in the microstate—molecules move faster—which in turn is expressed also in a resulting change in the macro-state (the temperature goes up). This is a case of a top-down effect, for the concept of a boundary wall is a macroscopic concept, which does not make sense at a microscopic level; while its existence is implicit in any complete description at the microlevel, describing the location and motion of each molecule and electron, the very act of naming it a "boundary wall" invokes macroconcepts that are not part of the microvocabulary. Yet the boundary certainly is crucial in determining what happens at the microlevel.

Given a particular macroscopic set of boundary conditions, realized by a particular set of microscopic conditions (which are not uniquely determined by the macroscopic state—for example, when stating the position of the pis-

---

11. This is the essential feature underlying the concept of entropy. See Roger Penrose, *The Emperor's New Mind: Concerning Computers, Minds, and the Laws of Physics* (Oxford: Oxford University Press, 1989).

ton, I do not need to describe the microstructure of the metal in the surface of the piston), then in principle, barring interference, the later microscopic state is completely determined by the earlier one if the laws are fully deterministic. The degree of certainty of the prediction depends both on the degree of determinism of the microscopic laws and the accuracy with which knowledge of initial conditions determines knowledge of later conditions (sensitivity to initial conditions).

Furthermore, the initial state of the system comprising the gas and the cylinder could not predict this change—it did not know the wall was going to be moved. In this case, when considered macroscopically, new information has been fed into the system that was not implicit in the initial macroscopic state. Indeed, the top-down action in this example is through feeding in new information at the macrolevel, which then alters the microstate through the usual top-down effects as considered in the previous paragraph. This in turn alters the macrostate in response to the top-down action (the altered microstates affecting the macrostates through bottom-up causation, which is described by the hierarchical or coarse-graining relations); in this case, the pressure increases.

Thus, what happens to a given system is controlled by the initial state along with the boundary conditions. The system boundary is either closed (no information enters) or open (information enters; possibly also mass, energy, momentum). In the latter case we have to know what information enters in order to determine the future state of the system.

So, in the case where the microscopic laws are fully determinate, the final state attained at the bottom level is uniquely determined by the prior state at that level (the initial conditions) and the incoming information at that level— that is, by the implications of the "boundary conditions" at that level (assuming a given system structure and given microlaws). This then determines uniquely what happens at the higher levels.

Here we assume that a unique lower-level state determines uniquely the higher-level states through appropriate coarse-graining. When this is not true, the system is either ill-defined (e.g., because our description has omitted some "hidden" variables) or incoherent (it does not really constitute a "system"). Such systems are not our concern in this section; further clarifications are in order in such cases.

> *Note 1:* The above statement does not contradict the idea of top-down causation. Any given macrostate at the top level will correspond to a restricted (perhaps even unique) set of conditions at the basic level. It is through determining a set of microstates as initial conditions at the bottom level, corresponding to the initial macrostate,

that the top-level situation controls the evolution of the system as a whole in the future. How uniquely it does so depends on how uniquely the top-level state determines a state at the bottom (or, equivalently, how much information of the microstates is lost by giving only a top-level description—this information loss defining the entropy of the macroscopic states).[12]

Note 2: At the higher levels the corresponding statement may or may not be true; that is, even when determinate at the microlevel, the system may or may not be causally determinate when regarded as a machine at a higher level. This depends on what microinformation is lost in forming the macrovariables at the higher levels from the microvariables. For example, the final state of a roulette wheel is mechanically determined but unpredictable.

Note 3: Even when the bottom-level system is determinate, prediction of what will happen is in general not possible even at that level, because of the possibility of chaotic behavior (sensitive dependence on initial conditions).

Note 4: Overall guiding properties such as conservation of energy apply at all levels. Apart from such conserved quantities being consistently related at different levels of description, the physical levels of the hierarchy do not interfere with each other, because of the physical nature of matter (specifically, the scaling properties described by the renormalization group).[13] For example, we can consider fluid dynamics or electromagnetic effects without knowing the details of the quark structure of matter or the nature of quantum gravity. The consequence of this discussion is that top-down effects, as distinct from top-down actions, are essentially reduced to the effect of constraints imposed by boundary conditions and initial conditions. This then makes clear that at a deeper level we need a theory of boundary conditions and initial conditions: how are they established, and how do they function to constrain a given system?

Clearly it is this top-down plus bottom-up character of physical interactions, with its hierarchical structuring, that underlies the hierarchical structuring of the physical and biological sciences (Figure 2.1).

2.6 Living Beings as Hierarchical Systems
The issue now is whether the same kind of description applies unaltered to really complex systems: biological and social systems and, in particular, to

12. See Penrose, *The Emperor's New Mind.*
13. See Schweber, "Physics, Community and the Crisis in Physical Theory."

individual human beings (considered as hierarchically structured, physically based entities). The point at issue is how free will can occur in human behavior, when we assume that the human brain is a hierarchically structured system, operating on the physical principles discussed in the previous section.

Our view is that the same level-based analysis of reality is possible in understanding any hierarchical system, including biological systems and the human mind. Indeed, a hierarchical analysis is essential: we cannot understand complex systems without it.[14] Furthermore, true complexity is only possible in a system incorporating a whole series of design principles—hierarchies, abstraction, encapsulation, modularity—which are well understood in the context of computer programs.[15]

At the lower levels the structural laws are embodied in the physical structure of the systems (the design of the computer circuits and hardware, the physical structure of interacting molecules, the shape and materials of an engineering system). In social systems and at the higher levels, however, they are embodied in (a) the psychological structure of the human mind, (b) social structures such as laws, customs, social pressures in society, (c) personal or communal objectives and goals that are set and thereafter guide thought and action, (d) at the highest levels, philosophical thought patterns and understandings (a worldview or *Weltanschauung*) that shape these hierarchical goal structures.[16] The fact that these are not physically realized at their own level does not make them less real; they have a force of their own that shapes what happens at the physical level through top-down action. This will be fundamentally important in what follows: it means that our goals and aims can indeed influence what happens.

Here we are claiming that top-down *action* is always associated with an element of intention. In the example above of a container whose wall was moved, if someone had not intended to move the wall and then carried out the intention, the interior conditions would have remained unchanged. The same is true whenever we use the word "action" in the sense intended here.

One might propose as an alternative that the change arises through some natural phenomenon that does not involve intention, for example, a change in the wind direction. But in that case one can simply enlarge the original system S to obtain a new system S', which includes the old system S along with some of its environment. If one continues such extension of the system, one eventually includes all the quantities that can affect the original system

14. See Robert L. Flood and Ewart R. Carson, *Dealing with Complexity: An Introduction to the Theory and Application of Systems Science* (New York: Plenum Press, 1988); Stafford Beer, *Brain of the Firm*, 2nd ed. (Chichester, U.K.: John Wiley and Sons, 1981).

15. See Grady Booch, *Object Oriented Design with Applications* (Redwood City, Calif.: Benjamin Cummings, 1991).

16. Examples will be given in chaps. 4 and 5.

materially. Thus, the final system can be regarded as an isolated system; no new information or matter enters across its boundaries. One can then carry out the analysis again on this new system (which includes the old one). Then all the natural phenomena that might have affected S are included in S', and we recognize the new information that entered the smaller system as just being due to top-down effects in the larger system. Thus, we might call this "whole-part determinism." Unless intention enters the equation, everything is causally determined (though not necessarily predictable) at each level, as discussed above.

The only way genuinely new information can be internally generated is by processes associated at the macrolevel with free will and conscious thought (indeed this is almost a definition of what we mean by those concepts). For example, I decide to move my arm; that macrolevel decision causes signals to be sent to the muscles that alter microconditions and result in molecular motions which, when aggregated, flex the muscles and bend the arm.

The implication is that given the different levels of semantics associated with the hierarchical structuring of matter, one now has an indeterminism at the microscopic level, in that what happens at that level is not completely determined by the state at that level; it is also influenced by the macrostate (including consciousness) in a way that in some sense was not determined by the existing microstate. If this were not true, the intention would not in fact have any real effect on the action that occurs. So the rigid determinism of top-down causation is a necessary condition for top-down action—that is, for making intentions effective.

3 FREE WILL AND DETERMINISM

In our discussion in the preceding paragraphs we have simply assumed human freedom. If indeed this is the case, then there must exist an adequate physical basis for free actions in the hierarchical structuring of the human brain.[17] This is a profound application of the principle that accounts given at lower levels have to permit, even if they cannot predict, the phenomena described by the levels above.

It is beyond the scope of this book to give an adequate treatment of the issue of free will; indeed, our view is that scholarship is only now at the point where we can begin to make sense of this issue—both as a result of conceptual developments in philosophy (one of which is the development of the concept of top-down causation) and as a consequence of empirical developments in neuropsychology.

17. And we assume throughout that freedom of the will is a necessary condition for morality.

Fig. 2.3. *Two representations of causal relations between mental events and brain events. Arrows represent causal relations; parallel lines represent identity relations.*

Since we have just argued that the term "top-down causation" generally refers to instances of top-down effects, or whole-part determination, we cannot argue straightaway that this development solves the problem of free will and determinism. We do claim, however, that this conceptual development will prove to be essential to the solution in two ways: First, as just mentioned, the concept of top-down effects explains how it is possible for a free decision (if in fact there be such a thing) to be put into effect (at lower levels of the hierarchy) without violating physical laws. Second, the very notion of top-down efficacy defeats the long-held assumption of bottom-up determinism.

Until recently, the problem of free will could be expressed as follows: (1) mental events, such as the decision to raise my arm, must be either identical with or caused by brain events; but (2) brain events are purely physical events and must therefore be determined by the laws of physics. Hence, (3) all mental events must be determined by the laws of physics.

The two "pictures" of the relations between mental and brain events can be represented in Figure 2.3.

In the first case, mental events are supposedly caused by brain events but have no causal efficacy of their own; thus, they are called "epiphenomenal." In the second, they are considered to be identical with brain events but the causal links are assumed to apply to the brain-state descriptions. In neither case is there any way to account for causal efficacy of mental events.

Notice that causal reductionism—bottom-up causation—is simply assumed here. Thus, it is tempting to say that the discovery of top-down causation refutes causal reductionism and thereby solves the problem of free will. Two problems remain, however. One is to show that mental states and brain states do in fact stand in such a relation to one another that it makes sense to suppose that top-down efficacy (from mental event to brain event) is a possibility. Even more important is the question in what sense the mental event itself can be said to reflect free will.

We are assuming here the position called nonreductive physicalism, since it comports well with the hierarchical model of reality developed in this book. That is, a mental state is supervenient on a state of the brain (or of the neurological system more broadly); it is not a state of some nonmaterial entity.

The conditions needed for top-down mental effects are, first, that mental events supervene on brain events. "Supervenience" is variously defined.[18] Our (tentative) understanding is that a mental event supervenes on a brain event if and only if that brain event *constitutes* the mental event, *given some specific context*. To ascribe mental properties to an individual is to describe, at a higher level of complexity, properties that could also be *partially* described (in theory, at least, if not in practice) at the level of neurophysiology. Second, however, the mental properties cannot be simply identical with the brain states. The mental property's greater complexity consists in its relation to environmental variables that cannot themselves be reduced to brain events.

For example, it is well-known that if subjects in an experiment are injected with adrenaline, they will experience the effect either as anger or as fear, depending on the social context. This makes it clear that while a physiological state (arousal) is necessary for the mental perception of fear or anger, the mental state is what it is because of the (nonreducible) social context. This is not to say that the subject's perception of the context as fearful or insulting is not itself realized in some brain state—only that because there can be no one-to-one correlation between fearful contexts and whatever brain state realizes it in this instance, there can be no complete laws at the physical level and hence no causal account at that level alone.

So the mental event (M^1) may supervene on B^1 (arousal) plus B^2 (whatever brain event is the physical realization of the perception of the environment). While it makes sense to attribute B^1 to a purely physical cause, B^2 is clearly caused, at least in part, by the environment.

M^1, then, however it is realized physically, is a possible cause of further states of the body, including physical activity such as fight or flight. So the account of top-down effects presented above provides a helpful model for explaining how the higher-level (mental) properties of the subject can be understood to have causal effects on lower-level (physical) states and actions.

The example we have used here, however, does not establish free will. On the contrary, it is entirely compatible with *environmental determinism* of the subject's reactions.

Free will has been understood in two different ways in the philosophical literature. One approach is to say that a person's action is free if it is self-determined rather than determined by some outside agency. The other approach requires as well that the action be spontaneous and associates it with the lack of all causation.

Free will as self-determination might be understood in terms of the "bal-

---

18. See especially Jaegwon Kim, *Supervenience and Mind: Selected Philosophical Essays* (Cambridge: Cambridge University Press, 1993).

ancing" of the effects of prior mental states. So, for example, I am faced with the choice to continue working on this chapter or not. One train of thought is that I am tired and I know that I do not do my best work when tired. The other train of thought is that I remember that I have promised to finish the project as quickly as possible. Both my desire to do good work and my belief that I must keep my promises are components of my own set of beliefs and goals; whichever I choose will be chosen freely. But there need not be any spontaneity or uncaused choice here at all. My own psychic makeup will actually determine which of the two lines of argument is more persuasive. There may be the appearance of spontaneity, however, because the intersection of chains of thought may be quite complex, and there might also be variables of which I am not consciously aware.

If this is all that free will amounts to, then the understanding of top-down effects, along with the actual relating of that model of causation to mental processes, is all that is needed to establish free will. One might argue, however, that this is not freedom at all, since the reasons, however much they have been internalized, are mainly a product of social conditioning. So this may be an account of disguised social determinism.

What is needed to make this an account of genuine freedom? Consider again the same case: the decision to continue working or not. Suppose that there is in fact no unconscious motive that determines the outcome, and no socially engendered presiding conviction that quantity of work is better than quality, or vice versa. Our phenomenal experience does seem to present us with such cases: opportunities to choose one of several lines of reasoning with no overriding reason to choose one rather than the other. In this case, there is a hierarchy of mental states. There are the mental states that constitute the two lines of reasoning; there is the state of feeling a need to choose; and there is the higher-order, complex state that incorporates all of these, and precedes the final state, the choice to do one or the other. The sense that I am an "I" who chooses seems to amount simply to the fact that I associate myself with the global, transcendent state, rather than with any of its various components.

It may be the case, as Roger Penrose suggests, that quantum indeterminacy is a necessary condition for truly free and spontaneous choice;[19] that is, that the mental state of indecision is, in some sense, supervenient on a (physical) state of quantum indeterminacy. The importance of indeterminacy may be that if the global state of awareness that I associate with myself is to affect, by top-down causation, a delicately balanced neural condition, there must be a

19. See Penrose, *The Emperor's New Mind*; and *idem*, *Shadows of the Mind: A Search for the Missing Science of Consciousness* (Oxford: Oxford University Press, 1994).

looseness in the causal order—slippage at the bottom, so to speak—so that the event is not over-determined causally. This is a promising line of thought, but it is important to state that our arguments in this book depend only on there being freedom of the will; not on how this issue (the role of quantum indeterminacy in consciousness) comes out. It is also necessary to guard against the conclusion that apparent free choice simply reduces to the deterministic effect of a quantum "coin toss"—that some random event at the quantum level actually makes up my mind for me.

Thus, we find it plausible that in some manner yet to be explained, a basic element of free will enters through the openness of quantum uncertainty of microscopic systems.[20] The outcome of a quantum measurement process is uncertain as far as present and foreseeable future physical theory is concerned, but this does not necessarily mean it is ontologically undetermined; it might, for example, be determined by some as yet unmeasured factor associated with consciousness, which may or may not be comprehensible within the domain of physics. This speculation has an element of plausibility in that the quantum measurement process is assumed in many views to be intimately tied in with the existence of consciousness.[21] The main alternative (the many worlds interpretation of quantum mechanics) raises at least as many questions as it answers and is, in addition, a completely unconfirmable theory; it is beyond the danger of any experimental refutation.

So our tentative conclusions are as follows:

1. It is necessary to distinguish between top-down effects (deterministic effects of a larger system on its parts by means of the setting of boundary conditions) and top-down action (effects instigated by a free agent).

2. Recognition of top-down effects defeats the long-held assumption of causal reductionism. One way of putting this issue is to ask if the laws in operation at the higher level can be translated without remainder into the laws of the lower level. If the two sets of laws are not equivalent, then which actually gives an account of the behavior of the system? The reductionist assumption has been that the higher-level laws must be special cases of the lower. Recognition of top-down effects shows that this is not always the case.

---

20. At the present time, physics has not begun to provide an adequate account of the phenomenon of consciousness, despite some claims to the contrary. See, for example, D. C. Dennett, *Consciousness Explained* (London: Penguin, 1991); and the *Journal of Consciousness Studies*.

21. See Penrose, *The Emperor's New Mind;* and idem, *Shadows of the Mind;* Euan Squires, *Conscious Mind in the Physical World* (Bristol, U.K.: Adam Hilger, 1990); and John C. Eccles, *How the Self Controls Its Brain* (Berlin: Springer Verlag, 1994).

3. *If* there is effective freedom of the will, then top-down *action* is possible due to the determinacy of top-down *effects;* I can make things happen at a lower level in the hierarchical system that involves my body only if there are determinate laws linking mental-events-realized-as-brain-events with other physiological processes.
4. While the recognition of top-down efficacy opens the way for the *expression* of free decisions, it does not entail that there are free decisions. We speculate that an account of freedom will involve the supervenience of mental states on indeterminate quantum states.

4 CONFIRMATION AND EXPLANATION IN HIERARCHICAL SYSTEMS

Recognition of the hierarchical structuring of reality, and of the correlative hierarchical ordering of the sciences, has important consequences for understanding the evaluation of theories.

It is an essential feature of science that one can analyze a particular level without knowing anything of lower (or higher) levels.[22] It will in general be true that understanding of the lower and higher levels will enhance understanding of a particular level. But for some purposes this is not necessary for an understanding of the system at that level. For example, we can become motor mechanics without studying the quark nature of matter or the structure of the atom. Thus, we can speak of "local" description and explanation, where "local" means restricted to particular levels of the causal hierarchy. Phenomena at a particular level of the hierarchy of complexity can be described in language proper to that level alone and their behavior examined and understood at that level alone. Hence we can confirm theories of behavior at a particular level, and even attain high levels of certainty in such descriptions (for example, Newton's laws of motion apply to automobiles).

Some ingredients in the understanding provided by a single level in the hierarchy, however, will be merely brute facts when considered from that level alone. For example, the car manufacturer uses measures of the tensile strength of various metals in engineering parts but the variation in tensile strengths can be explained by lower levels of the hierarchy. Similarly, top-down factors such as speed limits affect the design of cars but cannot be explained at the engineering level. So the engineer or mechanic knows all that it is necessary to know in order to build or repair cars without knowing the chemistry and physics that go into metallurgy or the legislative processes

22. See Schweber, "Physics, Community and the Crisis in Physical Theory."

that determine speed limits. Yet the mechanic does not have *complete* under-standing of cars without considering neighboring levels. Facts (observations) at one level are sometimes only explainable by theories at another level.

Since it is the explanatory value of a theory that counts toward its confir-mation, an account of the confirmation of the theories of one level will gen-erally involve an assessment of the theory's explanatory value at neighboring levels, either upward or downward. It may be the case that an explanatory theory at one level becomes a datum to be explained by its neighboring level. Hence we want, where possible, to understand the relation of neighboring levels of the hierarchy, together giving a greater understanding of a particular level than can be attained by concentrating on that level alone.

Thus, a very important issue is the scope of theories, not only the scope of their explanatory power at their own level but also the way they allow us to knit together descriptions and explanations from neighboring levels in the hierarchy. This trans-level explanatory power will be an important consider-ation in evaluating the proposals of the following chapters.

We have seen how environments determine physical causation in hierar-chical systems. We now turn to consider the overall physical environment in which all of this occurs.

Chapter Three

Cosmology

1 OUTLINE OF COSMOLOGY

Scientific cosmology examines the large-scale structure of the universe on the basis of observations made with optical, radio, infrared, ultraviolet, and x-ray telescopes. It analyzes those results on the basis of our understanding of physics, as tested in the laboratory and against data from the solar system.

A plethora of recent books explain the discoveries of modern cosmology, so we will spend relatively little space on this topic.[1] Our overall understanding of physical cosmology can be considered as comprising:

1. a view of nature
2. an understanding of the distribution of matter around us
3. a theory of the evolution of the universe
4. hypotheses on the formation of astronomical structure
5. speculations as to the origin of the universe

In the next sections we look at each of these in turn.

1.1 The Physical Foundation: A View of Nature
The foundation of our understanding of cosmology is our view of nature, understood in terms of matter, whose behavior is determined (or at least

---

1. It is discussed in some detail in George F. R. Ellis, *Before the Beginning* (London: Bowerdean/ Boyars, 1993).

Physical hierarchy	Science
Macroscopic objects	Geology/Engineering/Biology
Materials	Materials science
Molecules	Chemistry
Atoms	Atomic physics
Atomic Nuclei	Nuclear physics
Quarks and electrons	Elementary particle physics

Fig. 3.1. The hierarchical structuring of matter (scales smaller than the Earth; smallest scales at the bottom).

accurately described) by causal laws. Examination of the matter around us shows it is comprised of a hierarchical structure, the bottom level examined thus far comprising identical "elementary" particles, whose behavior is controlled by forces that act on them, these forces being the consequence of the exchange of other kinds of particles. The hierarchical structuring of matter, and consequently of sciences that study each level of that hierarchy, is shown in Figure 3.1.

We model the causal laws at the foundation of the physical world by mathematical equations, which give remarkably successful predictions of the behavior of physical systems. The solutions of these equations depend on boundary conditions, describing the nature of the solution at the boundary of the system (or very far away, if it has no clear-cut boundary), and initial conditions, expressing the initial state of the system. The classic example is Newton's laws of motion, describing how an object will move in an undeviating way at constant speed if no forces act on it, and how its speed and position will change with time if some force acts on it. Other laws describe each of the fundamental forces of nature and their associated properties, such as energy and momentum conservation. It is these physical laws that lead to chemical and biochemical behavior at the higher levels of structure in hierarchical structures; indeed they underlie bottom-up and top-down causation in physical systems, including the hierarchy shown in Figure 3.1; this was essentially taken for granted in the discussion in the previous chapter.

It is important to note that each physical law of which we presently have knowledge is valid within a particular, limited domain of applicability; for example, Newton's laws of motion hold only at low speeds (relative to the speed of light) and in weak gravitational fields (compared to those acting in a black hole). We do not know any physical laws that are valid in all circumstances because we do not at present have a viable theory of quantum gravity (needed to understand the extreme gravitational fields that would have occurred at the origin of the universe). Nevertheless, within their domains of applicability, presently known physical laws can give very accurate predictions for isolated systems. This is the basis of the remarkable success of modern technology.

While different kinds of interactions are described by different physical laws, with complex systems being characterized by structural relations detailing which elements of the system interact with which others and in what way, a set of foundational principles apply in all cases, namely, (a) conservation laws and entropy increase, (b) the relativity principle, (c) quantum behavior in systems of small enough size, (d) broken symmetries. Each has important implications apart from its immediate impact on physics, so we briefly consider them in turn.

a. Conservation laws, particularly those of mass, energy, and momentum, are among the most important factors determining what is and is not possible in daily life, as they underlie the permanence of objects, the predictability of motion, and the material cycles of natural resources. For example, the need to use energy to climb a hill or move an object and the need to conserve scarce resources are based in these conservation laws. Furthermore, energy conservation gives meaning to the binding energies that enable stable patterns of hierarchical structure to emerge. Thus, the stability of the molecular structures that underlie biological life—the DNA molecule, for example—is based on the energy levels associated with the particular ordering of atoms in those molecules: in order to disrupt them one has to apply energy, and the more stable they are, the more energy is needed to break them up.

It is of fundamental importance, however, that although these various quantities are conserved, the usable amount of energy and material always decreases with time. This is because of the global decrease of order associated with an inevitable increase of entropy.[2] Thus, energy is conserved, but usable energy in any isolated system decreases as disorder increases; matter is conserved, but the usable quantity of scarce mineral resources on the Earth decreases (at all times, some fraction is being irreversibly dispersed into the atmosphere, in the seas, or on land). This is one of the major features underlying resource conservation policy.

b. The relativity principle states that we can use any reference frame we wish as the basis for description of a physical system; in particular we can view it from different states of motion without altering the physical laws controlling its behavior. Thus, for example, the laws of physics are the same if we are stationary on the Earth, moving in a train, or traveling in a spacecraft at high speed; none of this alters the way matter behaves. The way we see the system (what we observe or measure), however, will vary with our choice

---

2. Martin Goldstein and Inge F. Goldstein, *The Refrigerator and the Universe: Understanding the Laws of Energy* (Cambridge, Mass.: Harvard University Press, 1993).

of reference frame (particularly our state of motion) and its associated coordinates. This leads to the famous effects of the relativity of space and time measurements, the relativity of mass, and so on; for example, a moving clock "reads slow" relative to a stationary clock. This effect does not mean, however, that what we can observe or experience is totally arbitrary. Indeed, a strict set of rules ("tensor analysis") specifies how a system changes in appearance when we change from one reference frame to another.[3]

Thus, in both special and general relativity theories, there is an underlying invariant physical reality; we obtain different (but strictly related) views of this reality when we observe it using different reference frames. This has obvious—nonrelativistic—implications for understanding other areas of knowledge.

c. Quantum theory governs the behavior of particles on the very smallest scales. This is a highly counter-intuitive theory, leading in particular to wave-particle duality and to the applicability of the uncertainty principle. Thus, under some circumstances light will behave like a particle and under others like a wave, but it is in fact the same entity—it has both wavelike and particle-like properties. We refer to a light particle embodying the minimum allowed energy packet—energy occurs in minimum units called "quanta"—as a "photon." Also, one cannot simultaneously measure accurately the position and velocity of a particle (the measurement process involves energy and momentum exchanges that disturb it and alter its position or velocity). Nor can we predict precisely where a particle or photon will move; when it goes through a slit in a screen, for example, we cannot tell which direction it will move thereafter. Nor can we predict when an unstable atom will decay, although we can predict the average rate of decay with great accuracy.[4] Despite this uncertainty at the foundations of physics, it has a reasonably well-defined deterministic classical limit, leading to the reliability of physical behavior we experience in everyday life. Hence quantum uncertainty is washed out, in general, at large enough scales.

Nevertheless, quantum uncertainty can have profound effects at the macroscopic level in systems where amplifiers of various kinds (e.g., photomultipliers, or the reading of DNA by cell developmental processes) magnify its effects to macroscopic scales. In particular it could possibly underlie the openness of predictability in hierarchical systems that must inevitably be associated with the existence of free will (cf. the discussion in the previous chapter).

3. George F. R. Ellis and R. M. Williams, *Flat and Curved Space-Times* (Oxford: Oxford University Press, 1989).
4. Heinz R. Pagels, *The Cosmic Code* (London: Penguin, 1982); Richard Feynman, *QED: The Strange Theory of Light and Matter* (London: Penguin, 1990).

d. Broken symmetries occur when the physical solution to some set of equations has less symmetry than the equations themselves. An example is when a pencil stands vertically on its tip and then falls over. The laws of physics do not pick out any particular direction around the pencil as preferred, but the pencil falls in one specific direction—which then becomes uniquely marked out, not by the laws governing the motion of the pencil but by the final state of rest of the pencil itself. The equations are symmetric about the initial state, but the physical state that results is not.

Another example occurs in ferromagnetism: above its Curie temperature iron is unmagnetized, but as the temperature decreases through this temperature it spontaneously develops magnetization, which is uniform in regions called domains but different in different domains. Hence the nature of the underlying physical laws is hidden when one observes the solution: it has less symmetry than the underlying laws. In the usual case of spontaneously broken symmetries, it is the ground state, or vacuum solution, which has less symmetry than the full equations (usually represented by a Lagrangian density). This is now known to be a profound principle underlying the nature of interactions between elementary particles. It means that the four fundamental forces of physics could be aspects of a single unified force, although they have very different properties under present physical conditions.

This feature is also of fundamental importance for everyday life. We illustrate this by considering briefly, first, friction and inertia and, second, the arrow of time.

Friction and inertia: One of Newton's great discoveries was his laws of motion, mentioned above. But why did it take so long to discover this law? Why was it not understood much earlier by Greek philosophers, such as Aristotle, or by such great intellects as Galileo, Francis Bacon, or René Descartes? The answer is because the laws are apparently contradicted by virtually all our experience in everyday life. Newton's laws say that the natural tendency of a body is to keep moving forever; but our experience is that moving bodies on Earth always come to a stop, usually very soon, unless we keep pushing them.

The explanation of this paradox (in Newton's terms) is simple: friction acts to prevent the body's doing what its natural tendency dictates. One can regard this as a classic example of a broken symmetry (the conservation of momentum one would see in a freely moving body, associated with the symmetry of the underlying equations, is not what we observe in practice), so its true nature is hidden by the way it actually moves. This is the central reason that even today, teaching Newton's laws to school children—or university students—is not easy: these laws are counter-intuitive because they do not easily conform to our everyday experience.

The point then is that the true (inertial) nature of matter is in fact deeply hidden, despite being right in front of us. To understand this nature, we must focus on the tendency of matter to keep moving (apparent when we throw a solid ball, for example) rather than the tendency for matter to stop moving (apparent when we move objects around or ride a bicycle, for example). Both tendencies are there; we have to discern which is the more fundamental. Before Newton the greatest minds failed to see which was the essential feature.

We shall return to this later as a prime example showing how, in formulating hypotheses, we can and indeed must select, from all the evidence in front of us, some restricted evidence that is the key to understanding the nature of the universe (in this case, the tendency of matter to keep moving), and for the present ignore the counter evidence (here, the tendency for matter to stop). This selection enables us to formulate a general principle based on the restricted evidence (here, Newton's laws of motion) and then to explain apparent counter-evidence—which dominates our everyday experience—in terms of the proposed explanatory hypothesis (Newton's laws), along with some auxiliary hypotheses (here, friction acts and prevents the inherent tendency of bodies to keep in motion from being manifested in their actual behavior). The critical factor is to discern which phenomena point to the hidden nature of reality, for these are not necessarily the obvious features that confront us in our daily lives.

The arrow of time: A similar situation holds with regard to the arrow of time. Our everyday experience strikingly confirms that all physical matter behaves in a time-asymmetric way (hot objects cool down, we all grow older); but physics tells us that the fundamental physical laws are time-symmetric. We could equally have solutions in which the behavior is the opposite (cool bodies spontaneously grow hot, for example). Our experience fundamentally contradicts the claimed time-symmetric nature of fundamental physical laws.

This again is an example of a broken symmetry and still remains something of a puzzle for physics. The explanation has to do with the expansion of the universe, and the different initial and final conditions for physical fields at the beginning and end of the universe.[5] We will not pursue the example further here, except to say, first, that this is profoundly important for everyday life; and, second, that it has the same moral as the previous example: to understand reality you have to select from all the available evidence some specific feature (in this case, time-symmetric behavior) that may occur only seldom in the real world—indeed it may be an ideal that is apparently never attained in

---

5. See Roger Penrose, *The Emperor's New Mind: Concerning Computers, Minds, and the Laws of Physics* (Oxford: Oxford University Press, 1989); and Ellis, *Before the Beginning,* for further discussion.

Physical hierarchy	Science
The universe	Cosmology
Large scale structure	
Clusters of galaxies	Galactic astronomy
Galaxies	
Star clusters	Stellar astronomy
Stars	
Planets	Planetary astronomy

Fig. 3.2. The hierarchical structuring of matter (scales larger than the Earth; smallest scales at the bottom).

practice—and yet is the key to understanding the true nature of reality. One uses this evidence as the basis of an explanatory theory; the task of the resulting synthesis is then to explain the apparent counter-evidence (the dominant apparent behavior) in terms of the new world picture attained by introducing suitable auxiliary hypotheses, which then allow adequate explanation of all the available evidence. The explanatory theory must be confirmed in the hypothetico-deductive manner, that is, by generating predictions that turn out to be correct upon further experiment and observation.

1.2 The Astronomical Universe

1.2.1 The Distribution of Matter around Us

Physical geography investigates the nature and distribution of matter on the Earth; astronomy extends this endeavor beyond the Earth, determining the nature, size, and distribution of the astronomical objects around us and estimating the scale of the entire part of the physical universe that we can observe.

This task is made difficult by the problem of accurate measurement of distances of very distant objects, still not satisfactorily resolved. Nevertheless we know with confidence the broad scales of distribution of matter, which is awe-inspiring. For example, our Sun has a diameter 109 times larger than that of the Earth; a typical galaxy contains about 10^{11} stars, many much larger than the Sun, and is about 50,000 light years in diameter; and we can observe something like 10^{11} galaxies. This implies complete human insignificance, in terms of physical size, relative to the scales of the universe. We find a hierarchical distribution of matter, as sketched in Figure 3.2.

As in the cases discussed above, this is a physical hierarchy with both bottom-up causation and top-down causation. In many cases we do not know which is the dominant effect in terms of determining the nature of the structures we see today.

On the very largest scales that we are able to observe, matter in the universe seems to be uniformly spread out. Thus, the universe is spatially homogeneous on these scales (there is no place we can identify that is the "center of the universe"). The regions we can observe are strictly limited by "horizons," somewhat like the way we cannot see beyond the horizon on Earth. The crucial difference is that on the Earth, we can travel to the horizon and see what lies beyond; in the universe we cannot do this, because the scales involved are too large (it would take billions of years to reach the horizon, even if we were able to travel at the speed of light—which we are unable to do). Therefore, we cannot tell by astronomical observations or by any other observationally based method if the uniformity we observe within the horizon continues beyond the horizon.[6]

1.2.2 A Theory of the Evolution of the Universe

A major discovery of recent times (the last century or so) is the nonstatic nature of everything around us—everything is in flux. In particular the universe itself is evolving: it has expanded from a very hot early stage (the "Hot Big Bang"), when known physical processes led to the formation of the light elements out of elementary particles, and is still expanding today (Edwin Hubble's observations in 1929 determined that the speed of recession of distant galaxies is proportional to their distance from us). The Cosmic Microwave Background Radiation (CBR: highly isotropic black-body radiation with a temperature of 2.75K), which has been extensively studied in recent times, is relic radiation from this hot early state. The heavy elements, necessary both for the formation of the Earth and for the existence of life, formed later in the extremely hot interiors of massive early stars, which formed through gravitational accretion as the universe cooled. These elements were released into space through gigantic explosions as the stars turned into supernovae at the end of their lives.

The evidence for this basic picture of an evolving universe is solid;[7] in particular there is excellent agreement between theories of light element formation and observations of their present abundances. This implies not merely an origin of the elements (in the Big Bang and later in massive stars), but also, classically considered (i.e., for the moment ignoring quantum effects), it implies a beginning of matter, of space-time, even of physics itself, a finite time ago. One is tempted to say, "Before then, there was nothing," but this

6. George F. R. Ellis, "Cosmology and Verifiability," in R. S. Cohen and M. W. Wartofsky, eds., *Physical Sciences and the History of Physics: Boston Studies in the Philosophy of Science* 82 (1984): 93–114.

7. See Joseph Silk, *The Big Bang: The Creation and Evolution of the Universe* (San Francisco: W. H. Freedman, 1980).

is quite inaccurate: as time has a beginning at that point, the very notion of events "before" the beginning of the universe is undefined: there was no "before"! Also "nothing" tends to conjure up in one's mind a picture of empty space, with nothing in it—but space is very much "something," for space has dimension and extension. The nothing physicists have in mind here has none of these features—it is a much more complete nothing than empty space, for it is no space (or time) at all!

Thus, the standard picture envisages a beginning to the universe in a very dramatic sense. Some theorists have found this view troubling, and from time to time alternatives have been proposed. First, we have seen various versions of the steady state universe—a universe that is always unchanging, and so has no beginning. It is unclear, from a philosophical point of view, whether this is a positive move. Further, a series of difficulties arise because the structures we see around us are transient, so their existence in an unchanging, eternal universe would be problematic. In any case these models of the universe are unable to deal with the observed radio source counts and the cosmic background radiation. The other main proposal is the idea of the phoenix universe—that the present state of expansion proceeds from a previous state of contraction, made possible by some kind of quantum effect (for example, physical fields with effective negative energy densities), with the present era being one of an infinite number of cycles of expansion and contraction of the universe. This is a tempting idea, but as yet no firmly accepted physical mechanism for such an evolution is at hand, and it may be ruled out by entropy-density considerations.

1.2.3 Formation of Astronomical Structure

Given the basic (and strongly supported) concept of an expanding and evolving universe, the aim of much current cosmological theory is to explain the origin of large-scale structures (galaxies, clusters of galaxies, and even larger configurations). How could they have spontaneously arisen through physical processes in the expanding universe?

It is accepted that once high-density structures are sufficiently formed, gravitational collapse will rapidly make them grow much more compact; the issue is how they get started in the first place. In recent times, Alan Guth's concept of an inflationary universe—a universe that has an extremely rapid expansion through many, many orders of magnitude at a very early time— has gained wide acceptance because it provides a way to solve a number of problems of classical cosmology, particularly the problem of why the universe is so uniform when looked at on very large scales. It also provides a mechanism for explaining the original seeds that lead to structure formation: they are quantum fluctuations in the very early universe, magnified to a huge size by the inflationary expansion.[8]

This idea is very promising, but the details have yet to be worked out in a way that accords both with the observed distribution of galaxies and with the recently observed anisotropies (i.e., varying temperatures across the sky) in the cosmic background radiation. The particular problem is that we do not know what types of unseen matter may fill the universe—there are strong hints that most of the substance of the universe is unseen, and there are many possible candidates for such "dark matter." The current challenge is to formulate a detailed theory of structure formation, based on a plausible assumption about the matter content of the universe, which is compatible with the (very small) observed background radiation anisotropies.[9]

1.3 Speculations on the Origin of the Universe Itself

Overall, we obtain a compelling description of *what* happened in the universe in the past, together with a solid description of *how* it happened. That is, we know what physical laws suffice to give a causal explanation of what we see, provided the initial conditions at the Big Bang happened to lie in a particular restricted range within the set of all possibilities. This is in many ways a very satisfactory state of affairs—except of course that one would then like an explanation of why the initial conditions were as they were.

Recently bold attempts have been made to tackle this issue of initial conditions. Among interesting proposals is the idea proposed by James Hartle and Stephen Hawking that there could have been a change in the nature of space-time extremely early on (in the era before inflation, when quantum gravity determined the nature of things), so that time no longer existed in the usual sense—there were four spatial dimensions, rather than three spatial dimensions and one time dimension.[10] This allows for a situation in which there is no beginning to the universe itself (this very early geometry is completely smooth), but there is a beginning of time, when the initially completely spatial geometry changes to one with a time dimension.

This concept has led Hartle and Hawking to suggest a "law of initial con-

---

8. Heinz R. Pagels, *Perfect Symmetry* (London: Penguin, 1985).

9. L. Krauss, *The Fifth Essence: The Search for Dark Matter in the Universe* (London: Basic Books, 1989).

10. Described in Stephen Hawking, *A Brief History of Time* (London: Bantam, 1989); see also C. J. Isham, "Quantum Theories of the Creation of the Universe," in Robert J. Russell, Nancey Murphy, and C. J. Isham, eds., *Quantum Cosmology and the Laws of Nature: Scientific Perspectives on Divine Action* (Vatican City State and Berkeley, Calif.: Vatican Observatory and Center for Theology and the Natural Sciences, 1993), 49–89.

ditions" for the universe—a major step forward, if successful, for without something like this the description is nonunique and the universe does not necessarily evolve into what we see. Their proposal does not yield unique solutions, however, as was once hoped. Furthermore, this proposal is untestable in the usual sense, so it is hard to evaluate its scientific status. It is based on assumptions about physics that are major extrapolations from what is presently (or indeed will ever be) testable. New developments in the theory of particle physics or quantum gravity could lead to totally new proposals here, or to confirmation that this is indeed the best proposal we are likely to get. Until this situation is clarified, one should regard them as interesting proposals rather than established theory.

2 THE EXISTENCE OF LIFE

Some of the most intriguing—and controversial—questions about the physical universe are raised by the existence of life, and in particular intelligent (self-conscious) life. How did such highly ordered structures come into being? Is this a major phenomenon to be taken into account by cosmology, or is it an irrelevant sideshow? And *if* it is important in the grand scheme of things, *what* is its significance?

We now know that human beings are insignificant in terms of physical scale; however, they are the most complexly structured functional systems we are aware of in the physical universe, with the extraordinary ability to reflect on the nature and causes of their own existence and even on their own self-consciousness. Apart from our particular interest in our own origins, the fact that we have come to be in a universe where previously there was no life at all raises profound issues about the nature of physical cosmology. Thus, we arrive at the *anthropic question:* why is the universe of a nature that allows intelligent life to exist?[11] We can usefully separate this question into two parts:

1. Why do we exist at this time and place in the universe?
2. Why does the universe permit the evolution and existence of intelligent beings at any time or place?

We look at these issues in turn, after considering the current understanding of how life came to arise in the universe.

11. See J. D. Barrow and F. J. Tipler, *The Anthropic Cosmological Principle* (Oxford: Oxford University Press, 1986); J. Leslie, *Universes* (New York: Routledge, 1989); Y. V. Balashov, "Resource Letter AP–1: The Anthropic Principle," *American Journal of Physics* 59 (1991): 1069–76.

2.1 Origins of Life in the Universe

Given the nature of the physical universe and the specific laws of nature that govern the behavior of matter, we can in broad terms understand the origin of plant and animal life on Earth as taking place by means of the following:

1. self-assembly of basic self-replicating biological molecules, in two stages: first, prebiotic chemical evolution of amino acids and other non-self-replicating molecules necessary for life, followed by the assembly of these molecules into replicating ones—a key transition;

2. development and aggregation of more complex molecules in hospitable environments to form the first living cells—an immensely complex task, involving not only development of molecules such as DNA and RNA but also hundreds of thousands of amino acids that form complex feedback loops in these cells, as well as the cellular structure and machinery—the cell nucleus, cytoplasm, mitochondria, membranes, and so on;

3. a process of Darwinian evolution acting over a very long period of time, leading by natural selection to the development from the first simple life forms of the wide variety of extremely complex plants and animals that exist today.

This evolutionary process is not only a way of comprehending the historical record but also a major organizing principle enabling us to understand many features of present-day biology.

Our understanding of the mechanisms of evolution are supported by a mass of detailed evidence, so even though we cannot follow all the steps in the historical process (in particular, many questions arise as to how the first RNA came into being and how the first living cell could ever have started to function), we can have confidence in the broad picture of evolution that emerges. It undermines the old idea that animals were each specifically and purposefully designed by a Creator, replacing this by the concept of biological mechanisms (random variation of genes leading to a population with varied characteristics, followed by selection in this group taking place through survival of the fittest) that can lead, in a suitable environment over the course of time, to apparent "design," beautifully honed and functional.

This evolution could not take place very early in the universe, when it was too hot, or very late, when it will be too cold (because all the stars will have died out). It cannot have taken place in the depths of interstellar space, where nutrients cannot be found in sufficient quantity, nor too close to the surface of a star, where radiation will destroy incipient life as it forms. Thus, this process of evolution can only take place at particular times and places in the universe, where the environment is right. The surface of the Earth is a place where conditions have been favorable enough that life could form and evolve to high levels of development, particularly because there is so much free water available, an essential facilitating factor for life on Earth.

An unsolved issue is whether these kinds of conditions are highly exceptional in the universe or commonplace. An informed guess suggests the latter because there are so many stars around us and hence, presumably, a huge number of planets; but there are many who believe otherwise. We do not take seriously here those hand-waving arguments that talk at length about probabilities but estimate none;[12] however, some serious estimates of the chain of required probabilities conclude that the overall probability of life is quite small, while others conclude that it is rather large. In any case, the universe is such that there are some places and times suitable for life to evolve—as otherwise, we would not be here. The simplest explanation is that the probability for life to evolve is not vanishingly small, in which case there are likely to be many other planets on which life flourishes.

2.2 Anthropic Principles
The developmental process outlined above is only possible because of the following:

1. the development of favorable environments for life during the evolution of the universe, and
2. the physics at work, specifically, the nature of quantum mechanics (essentially the Schrödinger equation) and of the forces and particles described by physics (essentially the electromagnetic force acting on the proton and the electron, together with the strong force binding the protons and neutrons in the atomic nuclei), which together control the nature of atomic structure and chemistry, and hence of biological activity.

Relatively small changes in either of these features would make all life impossible, and consequently no process at all would take place. For example, if we consider laws of physics different from those we observe but something like them, then we require the existence of heavy elements, sufficient time for evolution of advanced life-forms to take place, regions that are neither too hot nor too cold, restricted values of fundamental constants that control

---

12. See, e.g., Ernst Mayr, *Toward a New Philosophy of Biology: Observations of an Evolutionist* (Cambridge, Mass.: Harvard University Press, 1988), 67–74.

chemistry and local physics, and so on.[13] This emphasizes how only particular laws of physics and particular initial conditions in the universe allow the existence of intelligent life.

Thus, both in terms of the physical processes in operation and initial conditions that determined the development of local physical environments, the universe appears to be "fine-tuned" to allow the existence of life. The anthropic question, then, is why this should be so. There are two scientific approaches to this issue, namely, the weak anthropic principle (W.A.P.), and the strong anthropic principle (S.A.P.). The W.A.P. focuses on the issues raised by the first question, why this time and place? The S.A.P. focuses on those raised by the second, why any intelligent beings at all?

2.2.1 The Weak Anthropic Principle

According to the view labeled the Weak Anthropic Principle, the real scientific question we can ask relates to a selection effect implicit in the following statement: *We can observe the universe only from places and times where intelligent life can exist (and can have evolved).*[14] At first this seems merely a tautology, but it is more than that. Given suitable laws and initial conditions that allow the existence of life, pursuing this line of investigation can in principle help determine from what situations we can observe a universe (we could not exist very early on in the universe, for example). Furthermore, if we consider an ensemble of universes, or a universe where physical constants and initial conditions vary spatially or vary in each of a series of expansion phases, it can help provide new insights into relations in physics and biology by asking: how much variation in laws and initial conditions can there be and still allow intelligent life to exist? Life will occur only in restricted regions in such an ensemble of universes or environments; if we can characterize the necessary conditions to allow life to develop (in terms of both physical laws and initial conditions), we can try to ascertain in which regions life may possibly exist and perhaps estimate the probability of occurrence of such regions.

This viewpoint provides a partial but illuminating answer as to why we are where we are. It gives an indication that too great a deviation from the aged, almost isotropic universe we see around us would preclude the existence of life. But it does not predict accurately that it has to be as isotropic as we see it to be. It indicates that the "constants" of the laws of physics (which could in principle vary in value from place to place or from time to

13. See B. J. Carr and M. J. Rees, "The Anthropic Principle and the Structure of the Physical World," *Nature* 278 (1972): 605–12; Barrow and Tipler, *The Anthropic Cosmological Principle*.

14. Brandon Carter, "The Anthropic Principle: Self-Selection as an Adjunct to Natural Selection," in C. V. Vishveshswara, ed., *Cosmic Perspectives* (Cambridge: Cambridge University Press, 1988).

time) cannot deviate too much from their observed values and still allow life to function but it does not fix their values precisely.

This approach to understanding the development of life, however, does not really answer the second part of the anthropic question: why do conditions occur that allow any life to exist at all? For even if we consider an ensemble of initial conditions that will allow life to develop in some regions and not in others, the questions remain: Why does this ensemble exist? Why does it include any regions at all that are favorable to the existence of life? In many, if not most, universes of which we can conceive, no life at all would be possible.

2.2.2 The Strong Anthropic Principle

The only strictly scientific approach to this question has been phrased in terms of the Strong Anthropic Principle. This is the statement that: *Intelligent life must exist in the universe; it is a necessity.* The strongest scientific basis for the claim is the argument that intelligent life is required for the consistency of quantum mechanics, which in some formulations depends in a crucial sense on the concept of an "observer".[15] A considerable problem arises, however, in showing that this is indeed a requirement, in view of the differing interpretations of quantum theory. It is compounded by a lack of testable consequences so far; thus, the claim is very controversial.

Further, the Strong Anthropic Principle is again an intermediate answer. Suppose we could confirm this hypothesis. Then we can ask: why is this (quantum mechanics) necessary? It takes us back in a chain of regression; it is not obviously necessary that quantum mechanics should be valid, unless we can conclusively argue that physics must include quantum features to be consistent. This argument is difficult, however, because quantum theory itself neither has fully satisfactory foundations nor is fully self-consistent in the sense of avoiding singularities. This quantum-mechanical argument therefore does not command a large following, and so there is no widely accepted scientific justification for the S.A.P.

3 ULTIMATE CAUSATION

The failure of the S.A.P., scientifically considered, means that if we take seriously the issue of why life exists, the purely scientific approach fails to give a satisfactory answer. We end up without a resolution of the issue, essentially

---

15. Barrow and Tipler, *The Anthropic Cosmological Principle*; C. J. Isham, "Quantum Gravity," in M. A. H. MacCallum, ed., *GR11: General Relativity and Gravitation* (Cambridge: Cambridge University Press, 1987), 99–129.

because science attains reasonable certainty by limiting its considerations to restricted aspects of reality. Even if it occasionally strays into the area in rash moments, science is not designed to deal with questions of ultimate causation. But that is where we have to look if we wish to make progress on the anthropic issue. Indeed, it must be part of any attempt to understand the more fundamental aspects of cosmology, whether we link them to anthropic issues or not.

3.1 Alternative Viewpoints

There appear to be five basic approaches to ultimate causation in cosmology, regarding it as essentially based in:

1. random chance
2. high probability
3. necessity
4. universality
5. design[16]

We briefly consider these in turn, noting also that multiple causation may be a possibility; that is, several such causes may be in operation simultaneously.

3.1.1 Pure Chance

One proposed explanation is that conditions in the universe occurred initially by pure chance and led to things being the way they are now. Probability does not apply. There is no further level of relevant explanation.

This is certainly logically possible but not satisfying as an explanation except to a total reductionist; we obtain no unification of ideas or predictive power from this approach. Nevertheless, some scientists implicitly or explicitly hold this view. There is no way to test its validity.

3.1.2 High Probability

The "high probability" approach argues, that while the structure of the universe appears very improbable, for various physical reasons it is in fact highly probable. Such is the idea underlying the "chaotic cosmology" program, which tries to show that any initial conditions whatever will lead to a universe like the one we see around us. Hence the very improbable state shown to us by astronomical measurements (the universe seems very homogeneous and isotropic on the largest scales, which a priori is very unlikely) in fact is not

---

16. For a more thorough discussion of these options, see George F. R. Ellis, "Major Themes in the Relation between Philosophy and Cosmology," *Memoirs of the Italian Astronomical Society* 62 (1991): 553–605.

unlikely because physical forces will lead to this result, whatever the initial state of the universe.

These arguments are only partially successful even in their own terms, for they run into problems if we consider the full space of possibilities (many discussions implicitly or explicitly restrict the allowed set of possibilities a priori); and we do not have a proper measure to apply to the phase space (i.e., the "logical space" of possibilities), enabling us to assess these probabilities. Furthermore, application of probability arguments to the universe itself is dubious because the universe is unique. Nonetheless, this approach has considerable support in the scientific community.

One could, in principle, give evidence supporting this view if one could show that models we previously believed were improbable are in fact probable (indeed, this is essentially the move made by the inflationary universe argument). To do this properly, however, requires, first, determining in an unambiguous way a plausible measure of probability in the space of possible cosmologies and, second, showing that the existing universe is in fact probable within the set of all possible initial conditions. Neither step has so far been completed satisfactorily (the best measures proposed so far diverge; and the concept of the inflationary universe only works in a subset of models, as did its predecessor, the mechanism of chaotic cosmology proposed by Charles Misner). If one could complete these steps, it would still not show that probabilities apply to the universe. That is untestable.

3.1.3 Necessity

On the "necessity" approach, things have to be the way they are; there is no option. This can be taken in a strong or weak form. The strong form is the claim that the features we see and the laws underlying them are demanded by the unity of the universe (coherence and consistency require that things must be the way they are; the apparent alternatives are illusory). Thus, this is the claim that only one kind of physics is self-consistent; all logically possible universes must obey the same physics. The weak form is that only one kind of physics is consistent with the sort of world we actually see around us.

Proof of this view would be a powerful argument, potentially leading to a self-consistent and complete scientific view; but we can imagine alternative universes! Why are they excluded? Furthermore, we run into the problem that neither quantum physics nor mathematics is on solid, consistent foundations. Until these issues are resolved, this line cannot be pursued to a successful conclusion; any argument that purports to prove it can be countered by querying if its boundaries are broad enough (does it allow sufficient flexibility and imagination?).

If we could succeed in providing an argument of this type, then testing it would be highly problematic: we would have to show there is no other possible logically consistent physics. Support of this claim would require that we understand fully not only the physics we have, but also all other logical possibilities—where we must allow all types of logic (consider the logical problems involved in understanding quantum mechanics). Given our inability to ground either mathematics or quantum mechanics in a satisfactory and logically sound way, this is clearly beyond our abilities in the foreseeable future. Even supposing that we had a watertight theory of this kind, we could not confirm it experimentally.

3.1.4 Universality

"Universality" is the view that "all that is possible, happens"; an ensemble of universes is realized in reality.[17] Three variations on this view have been pursued:

1. It may be that variation occurs in space through random initial conditions as in chaotic inflation[18] or across time in the infinite set of expansions of a Phoenix Universe. While this view provides a legitimate framework for application of probability, from the viewpoint of ultimate explanation it does not really succeed, for there is still one unique universe whose (random) initial conditions need explanation.

2. An alternative explanation is the Everett-Wheeler "many worlds" interpretation of quantum cosmology, where all possibilities occur through quantum branching; the history we experience is one particular set of such branchings.[19] This view is controversial; it is accepted by some but not all quantum theorists. If we hold to it, we then have to explain the properties of the particular history we observe (why does our macroscopic universe develop to have high symmetries when almost all these branchings will not?).

3. Finally all possibilities could occur as completely disconnected universes as a sort of ultimate logical extension of the Feynman approach to Quantum Field Theory; there really is an ensemble of universes, in

17. John Leslie, *Universes*; D. W. Sciama, "The Anthropic Principle and the Non-Uniqueness of the Universe," in F. Bertola and V. Curi, eds., *The Anthropic Principle* (Cambridge: Cambridge University Press, 1989), 109–112.

18. See George F. R. Ellis, "The Homogeneity of the Universe," *General Relativity and Gravitation* 11 (1979): 281–289; Andrei Linde, "The Self-Reproducing Inflationary Universe," *Scientific American* (November 1994):32–39.

19. See, e.g., J. J. Halliwell, "Introductory Lectures on Quantum Cosmology," in S. Coleman, J. B. Hartle, T. Piran, and S. Weinberg, eds., *Quantum Cosmology and Baby Universes* (Singapore: World Scientific, 1991), 159–244; R. Penrose, *The Emperor's New Mind*.

which all that is possible occurs.[20] It is somewhat difficult seeing what is intended here, for there is then the problem of what determines what is possible. What about the laws of mathematics or of logic? Are these laws inviolable in considering all possibilities, or can we let our fancy run completely free?[21] Again, in this case we have to explain the properties of the particular history we observe.

In all three approaches, in order to explain our actual observations, one has of necessity to introduce an (anthropic) selection element, for most of the universe(s) will not look like an isotropic model. Why do we live in a region that does? Furthermore, all of these explanations violate Occam's razor: they are all very uneconomical in their mode of explanation.[22] Finally, none of these proposals is testable.

3.1.5 Design

The symmetries and delicate balances we observe in the universe require an extraordinary coherence of conditions and cooperation of laws and effects, suggesting that in some sense they have been purposefully designed. That is, they give evidence of intention, realized both in the setting of the laws of physics and in the choice of boundary conditions for the universe.[23] This is the basic theological view. To make sense of it, one must accept the idea of transcendence: that the designer exists in a totally different order of reality or being, not restrained within the bounds of the universe itself.[24] The ultimate ground of the existence of this higher reality and of the designer remains unanswered in this view. The ultimate questions of existence, however, remain unanswered in all approaches.

The concept of design invoked here is more complex than one might at first suppose, on two counts. First, as will be discussed later, the kind of design envisaged includes leaving large areas of reality "free from definite design," so that we (humans) might freely respond by adding or determining those free sectors through our own "designing" activity. Second, a simple idea of design does not apply, because for every species now in existence, thousands of species are extinct, representing evolutionary experiments and blind alleys

---

20. D. W. Sciama, "The Anthropic Principle and the Non-Uniqueness of the Universe."

21. Leslie, *Universes*, 97–98.

22. P. C. W. Davies, *The Mind of God* (New York: Simon and Schuster, 1992).

23. Barrow and Tipler, *The Anthropic Cosmological Principle*; cf. G. Gale, "A Revised Design: Teleology and Big Questions in Contemporary Cosmology," *Biology and Philosophy* 2 (1987): 475–91.

24. See Ernan McMullin, "Natural Science and Belief in a Creator: Historical Notes," in Robert J. Russell, William R. Stoeger, S.J., and George V. Coyne, S.J., eds., *Physics, Philosophy, and Theology: A Common Quest for Understanding* (Vatican City State: Vatican Observatory, 1988), 49–79.

leading "nowhere."[25] Thus, natural selection gives no support for supposing a direct process of design.

What we have to do, then, is to reconcile a lack of design at these levels with the "meta-design" that allows and even favors our existence in the long term. The laws of physics and chemistry are such as to allow the functioning of living cells, individuals, and ecosystems of incredible complexity and variety, and it is this meta-design that has made evolution possible. What requires explanation is why the laws of physics are such as to allow this complex functioning to take place. According to this view, it is precisely in the designer's choice and institution of particular physical laws, allowing evolutionary development, that the profound creative activity takes place.

The problem is that this "design" theory leads to no scientifically testable predictions (we have no way of deducing, say, the particular nature of the chemical elements, or features such as the density of matter in the universe, from the thesis of the existence of God). Hence, a problem of scientific confirmation arises; and much effort is aimed at using the other approaches to avoid this option. It should be noted, however, that untestability is one of the major features of the roots of cosmology; it seems unavoidable in all approaches to fundamental causation (as is clear in the discussion above). Second, other forms of data can be taken to provide evidence supporting this view, coming from moral, aesthetic, and religious worldviews and experience, as will be discussed later. Furthermore, these data can be used to provide *novel* confirmation, in Imre Lakatos's terms (see the last section of this chapter).

3.1.6 Multiple Causation

In approaching these topics it is important to note that multiple layers of explanation and interpretation can apply to any particular situation.[26] Realizing the existence of multiple levels of explanation and organization, and the way in which many intersecting causal chains lead to particular outcomes, we can avoid the mistake of assuming that the various categories of explanation are mutually exclusive. For example, a designer might equally well work through several of the other specific mechanisms. That is, God might have chosen to produce all possible worlds with the intention that by chance one or more would turn out to be anthropic. The same applies to pure chance; it could also be involved in several of these other mechanisms. So it is possible that more than one of the lines characterized above as "fundamental approaches" could apply to the real universe.

25. Mayr, *Toward a New Philosophy of Biology*.

26. P. C. W. Davies, *The Cosmic Blueprint* (London: Heinemann, 1987); Ian Barbour, "Ways of Relating Science and Theology," in Russell et al., *Physics, Philosophy, and Theology*, 21–48; Ellis, *Before the Beginning*.

3.2 A Tentative Assessment

If one takes the anthropic question seriously, "pure chance" is difficult to sustain as an account of ultimate causation in cosmology, despite its logical unassailability. It seems a totally inadequate explanation of the complexity we see (it must be emphasized that the order of complexity in life is totally different from that in, say, a crystal structure, a mountain range, or a fire). We cannot at present satisfactorily complete the argument of "necessity"; this seems destined to remain an unfulfilled dream. Some form of "high probability" or "universality" is possible as an ultimate account, although these accounts are very uneconomical and suffer from severe problems of confirmation. And in the end each is really just a more sophisticated version of pure chance, dressed up to appear more palatable.

Comparing the different possibilities, it is difficult to avoid the conclusion that the design concept is one of the most satisfactory overall approaches, necessarily taking us outside the strictly scientific arena.[27] This larger framework is inevitable when looking at ultimate causation, for the universe is unique and therefore cannot be accounted for in terms of confirmable scientific laws.

In summary, the essential possibilities that arise in tackling the anthropic issue are: (1) it can be interpreted in terms of a selection principle, but then there must be an ensemble of universe states from which to select; one needs to account for the existence of this ensemble of universes and give some hint of how the proposal could be confirmed. No ultimate explanation is provided by this viewpoint in itself. Given that an argument from necessity is likely to remain unattainable, the approaches that do tackle this issue with some success are (2) pure chance, or (3) purposeful design. In the former case we have a complete but unsatisfying explanation. If one proposes the latter, science by itself can neither prove nor disprove this supposition. From the purely scientific viewpoint, life will have occurred by chance, for science itself does not have room for a designer. However, this is a narrow view of the possible explanatory framework and evidence. We shall argue that a broader framework is appropriate.

4 THE NEED FOR A LARGER VIEW

The position that has just been taken is that life, the ground of consciousness, is such a unique feature of the universe that its existence seems to require special explanation.[28] Even if life is insignificant in terms of physical scales, the question of its origin is basic for cosmology. As we have seen, science by

---

27. See, e.g., W. Norris Clarke, "Is a Natural Theology Still Possible Today?" in Russell et al., *Physics, Philosophy, and Theology*, 103–23; Murphy, "Evidence of Design in the Fine-Tuning of the Universe," in Russell et al., *Quantum Cosmology*, 407–36.

28. P. C. W. Davies, *The Mind of God*.

itself cannot provide a satisfactory answer; one has to probe further, to the domain of fundamental explanation, to make any progress. This is what we shall do in the remainder of this book—indeed, even extending the scope of the anthropic investigation to the further domain of ethics, which is not usually taken into account.

Not all cosmologists, however, take the anthropic issue seriously. We argue further that even without considering this question—which we ourselves believe to be of fundamental importance—in the end, physical cosmology by itself cannot achieve all we hope for in terms of understanding the universe. It has substantial internal limitations and, in addition, major restrictions on what it can achieve because of the scope of what it considers as its subject matter. Consequently, even apart from the anthropic question, issues of major importance in cosmology lie outside the domain of strictly scientific exploration. A larger view is required.

4.1 Limitations of Cosmology Based on Science

Physical cosmology is limited in what it can achieve both because of limits *on* its own proper domain and *within* its own domain.

First, limitations in cosmology in scientific terms are due to difficulties of confirmation and also, fundamentally, to the uniqueness of the universe. This uniqueness limits the application of the usual scientific method (e.g., use of probability calculus) in studying the whole.

These issues[29] are of considerable interest in their own right but not essential to what follows. We shall not pursue them further except to say that they come particularly to the fore in considering the question of origins and initial conditions of the universe. Although its resolution is one of the main reasons we are interested in studying the universe, physical cosmology cannot by itself supply a satisfactory doctrine of creation. The proposed theories of the quantum creation of the universe are at best partial answers; however, the fact that they have been developed and pursued with vigor confirms that this is an area of major importance to cosmology.

Second, we must recognize the incompleteness of physical science apart from a metaphysical superstructure. In fact, it is in considering cosmology that this incompleteness becomes a fundamental issue. In the rest of science we can take the existence both of the universe and of the laws of nature for granted, and, while we spend a great deal of time and energy in determining the nature of these laws, we do not have to consider why they have the form they do. Cosmology, however, in the end calls for an explanation of these issues:

---

29. Considered in Ellis, *Before the Beginning*.

1. Why is there a universe at all?
2. Why are there any regularities in nature at all (enabling us to comprehend it in terms of physical laws)?
3. Why do those regularities and physical laws take the particular form
   they do? (This last question includes in particular the fine-tuning question raised in the anthropic argument of the previous sections.)

Hence, we note the fundamental major metaphysical issues that purely
scientific cosmology by itself cannot tackle—the problems of existence (what
is the ultimate origin of physical reality?) and the origin and determination
of the specific nature of physical laws—for these all lie outside the domain
of scientific investigation. The basic reason is that there is no way that any of
these issues can be addressed experimentally. The experimental method can
be used to test existent physical laws but not to examine why those laws are in
existence. One can investigate these issues using the hypothetico-deductive
method (indeed that is the aim of the present book), but one cannot then
conduct physical, chemical, or biological experiments or observations that
will confirm or disconfirm the proposed hypotheses.

Indeed, these issues are all taken for granted as the starting point from
which ordinary scientific investigation proceeds, underlying its endeavors,
and so cannot be investigated in terms of its own methods. The foundations
on which science rests cannot themselves be the subject of purely scientific
investigation (if they could, we would have an unsupported self-referential
system). Thus, the hierarchy of natural sciences is incomplete; it needs further
layers for its completion, layers of a metaphysical nature.[30]

Furthermore, these additional layers can either be considered to have a
narrower or wider scope. In the former case, they will try to answer only the
metaphysical issues just stated, without encompassing all the broader aspects
of meaning and purpose in human life. In the latter case, it will be regarded
as a legitimate part of the enterprise of Cosmology (with a capital C)[31] to
relate to these higher issues of purpose. Indeed, in the following pages we
argue that any viewpoint that leaves out these aspects will, by that fact, doom
itself to be narrow and insubstantial in the broader scheme of things (even if
it attains a great deal of understanding in terms of purely scientific explanation). Thus, we conclude that from the broader view of human interests and
values, physical cosmology is clearly incomplete, even apart from questions
of origin and determination, as it does not provide a doctrine of human nature or an account of the source of morality.

---

30. Cf. the discussion of the previous section.
31. See chap. 1 above; and Ellis, *Before the Beginning*.

In response, one might say that these further issues are not the concern of science and therefore should not be the concern of serious thinkers. But *scientism* of that dogmatic form is responsible for rejection of science in many quarters.[32]

The alternative is to look for a broader and more comprehensive view, as attempted in this book, encompassing the results of science but going beyond them to address these further issues. To undertake this task we need to look at a broader class of evidence and adopt approaches that can lead to a more comprehensive understanding than is possible with a purely scientific approach. In doing so, we will find that the hierarchy of human sciences is incomplete; it needs further layers of an ethical nature, and these in turn need higher layers of a metaphysical (or theological) nature for their completion.

4.2 Cosmology and Theories of Ultimate Reality

A corollary of what has been discussed in the previous section is that only limited help can be given by cosmology in formulating a theory of ultimate reality. It constrains higher explanatory layers in some ways, but certainly does not determine their form—for if it did, they would not be needed as extra layers in order to attain satisfactory explanation! This point would not be worth making were it not that people repeatedly try to extend the conclusions of physical cosmology to areas it cannot handle—despite several hundred years of failure. An extreme example is Frank Tipler's recent work,[33] which pushes (supposed) science to the borders of absurdity.[34]

More plausible misconceptions have also repeatedly clouded the discussion. These are the use of the Big Bang theory in Christian apologetics, and the corollaries of this argument: the idea that either the Steady State theory or the Hartle-Hawking no-boundary proposal leave no role for God. These arise from confusion of the scientific idea of a beginning with the concept of ultimate causation.

The response in each case is that particular models of the nature of the physical universe (a Big-Bang origin, a Steady State universe without temporal origin, a universe originating according to the Hartle-Hawking no-boundary theory, an eternal Chaotic Inflationary or Phoenix Universe) do not necessarily affect the issue of ultimate causation. A priori, any of the

32. Cf. Bryan Appleyard, *Understanding the Present: Science and the Soul of Modern Man* (London: Pan Books, 1992).

33. *The Physics of Immortality: Modern Cosmology, God and the Resurrection of the Dead* (New York: Doubleday, 1994).

34. See George F. R. Ellis, "Piety in the Sky," *Nature* 371 (September 1994): 115; and W. Stoeger and George F. R. Ellis: "A Response to Tipler's Omega-Point Theory." In *Science and Christian Belief*, vol. 7, no. 2, pp. 163–72 (1995) for a brief outline of some of the problems with the argument of Tipler's book.

possible ultimate causes could be compatible with any of these modes of realization of a physical universe.[35] In essence, this truth has been known since the time of St. Augustine, even if this knowledge has not diffused into parts of the modern scientific community.

This qualification does not mean, however, that in terms of ultimate causation or metaphysics nothing can be gained from cosmological studies. Some metaphysical views will be compatible with the physical world as we know it; others will not. Of those compatible, some metaphysics will be fully in tune with the nature of physical and human reality; others will be only awkwardly suited to it.

In particular, we have argued elsewhere that the fine-tuning of the cosmos can add important evidence to some theories of ultimate reality. In the most general terms, we claim that the relation between fine-tuning and the theory of design is hypothetico-deductive: *if* there is a designer, this fact explains the fine-tuning and is thereby confirmed. More specifically, our claim is that, given a theological research program that includes the theory that the universe was created (designed) by a God whose aim was personal relations with sentient beings, the fine-tuning of the universe can be seen to provide *novel* confirmation, in Imre Lakatos's terms.[36] The fact that none of the other hypotheses offered to account for the fine-tuning is part of an ongoing research program, with prior confirmation, means that none can be confirmed by the fine-tuning in this more dramatic way. That is, the fine-tuning cannot provide *independent* confirmation for those other theories.

It is important to note, however, that fine-tuning alone does not provide a great deal of support for any particular designer hypothesis, because there are many such hypotheses, all of which are equally well supported. It requires extra evidence—of the kind we elaborate in following chapters—to give weight to one particular hypothesis rather than another. Thus, we need to acknowledge the failure of any attempts based purely on science to produce an overarching worldview of adequate scope, even if it goes so far as to include the anthropic issue as usually conceived. The scope of evidence utilized in such an approach is not broad enough (for example, the moral domain is not included in the data considered). Consequently the method of argumentation used, and conclusions reached, are too restricted.

We begin to investigate this in the following chapter by considering the role of ethics in the human and applied sciences.

35. See Ian Barbour, *Religion in an Age of Science* (San Francisco: Harper and Row, 1990); Arthur Peacocke, *Creation and the World of Science* (Oxford: Clarendon Press, 1979); and Willem B. Drees, *Beyond the Big Bang* (La Salle: Open Court, 1990).

36. See Murphy, "Evidence of Design in the Fine-Tuning of the Universe," in Russell et al., *Quantum Cosmology.*

Chapter Four

Revision of the Hierarchy

1 THE BRANCHING HIERARCHY OF SCIENCES

The hierarchy of the sciences is a model or idealization, and it cannot be used to give a flawless account of all the sciences and their interrelations. It has no specific place for the historical sciences, and fails to represent disciplines that cut across levels, such as genetics. Most importantly, it is necessarily ambiguous as to whether higher levels pertain to more encompassing wholes (such as ecology, as the scientific study of organisms in relation to one another within their natural environment) or to more complex systems. These two criteria usually overlap, but not in every case. If the hierarchy is taken to be based on more encompassing wholes, then cosmology is the highest possible science in the hierarchy. If the hierarchy of the sciences is based on increasing complexity of the systems studied, however, then the question arises whether a social system is or is not more complex than the abstract account of the cosmos as a whole provided by cosmologists.

Our judgment is that social systems are the more complex; but this is a controversial opinion and will not be agreed upon by all scientists (one of the problems being that it is not easy to define precisely what one means by complexity). It is helpful to sidestep the issue and simultaneously emphasize the differing nature of natural and social systems by representing the relations among the sciences by a branching hierarchy, with the human sciences forming one branch and the natural sciences above biology forming the other, as

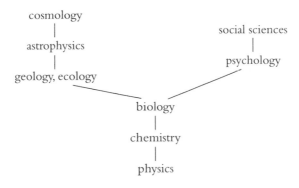

Fig. 4.1 Branching hierarchy of the sciences.

indicated in Figure 4.1. We will see later that there are also good functional reasons for such a split.

Of course, debate is ongoing regarding the status of the so-called social or human sciences—are they in fact scientific? To make the case for considering them an essential component of the hierarchy of the sciences, it will be useful to survey the variety within the natural sciences, there is as much variation within the natural sciences as there is between the natural and social sciences. Furthermore, important connections exist between the social sciences and some of the natural sciences: in brief, the "pure" natural sciences are incomplete without the applied sciences, and the applied sciences are incomplete without the social sciences.

2 THE VARIETY OF SCIENCES

In this section we distinguish different kinds of scientific disciplines according to the different forms of testing or confirmation they employ.

2.1 *The Analytic and Integrative Sciences*

The natural sciences may conveniently be thought of as comprised of two types: The analytic (or reductive) sciences (e.g., physics, chemistry) function by reducing the object of study to its constituent parts, which are then studied in isolation and in simple interaction with each other. The integrative (or synthetic) sciences (e.g., physiology) emphasize not the behavior of the parts of a system, but rather the behavior of an entire complex system made up of many interacting parts.

The analytic method allows us to isolate dependable, repetitive behavior because of the underlying regularities of nature. We are able to determine well-defined and reliable laws of behavior for the component parts of systems (e.g., electrons, protons, atoms, molecules) by varying initial data so as to determine the response of an isolated element to altered conditions. We can do this at different levels of a hierarchical system. For example, we can determine dependable laws of behavior for resistors, capacitors, and transistors, regarded as elements of an electric circuit or for complex integrated circuits such as a computer central processing unit, regarded as a "black box."

Clearly the integrative sciences build on the analytic sciences: as we attain a better understanding of the behavior of the components of a complex system, we are in a better position to comprehend the whole. They cannot be reduced to the analytic sciences, however; it is precisely the relations between the parts of a human body that enable the whole to function, and this cannot be understood by examining the parts in isolation (indeed, this was a central theme in the discussion of hierarchical systems in the previous chapter). That is why physiology is of necessity an integrative science. Similar considerations apply, for example, to ecology, and to any attempts to understand the functioning of a hierarchical structure in itself (that is, how it functions as a hierarchy).

Furthermore, one should note that while the objects of study in the reductive sciences can be identical to each other (each proton is identical to every other proton; similarly for electrons and neutrinos), in the case of the integrative sciences, despite similarities, there will always be some differences (each human body is different from each other one; each ecosystem has its own individuality). This means that once we leave the level of simplicity of elementary components we can never test and compare behavior of identical systems; we can only compare very similar ones. The systems may, in some cases, be essentially equivalent at higher levels of description while quite different at the more detailed lower levels (e.g., gases in two "identical" containers). However, for the most interesting cases there will of necessity be genuine differences at all hierarchical levels between the most similar complex systems we are able to study. Thus, a crucial question in determining "laws of behavior" for such systems is, what are the common features that lead us to regard the objects considered as being essentially of the same kind?

2.2 Historical and Geographical Sciences

We distinguish from the analytic and integrative sciences the historical and geographical sciences, such as geology and astronomy, where we examine the nature, history, and origin of unique natural systems (the Rocky Mountains, the Earth, the Local Cluster of galaxies, and so on). Here there is only one object or history to study. Major examples are the investigation of the creation of the solar system, of the structure of our galaxy, of the history of continental drift on Earth, and of the evolution of life on Earth.

In these cases, we cannot set initial conditions so as to repeat the situation that occurred in the past; experimental tests in the usual sense are not possible, because we are concerned with specific events that have only happened once in the universe. We can, however, look at properties of similar systems or events, hoping they will help us to understand this particular one (the issue being how similar or different the other examples are). And we can make observations that indirectly investigate the specific historical event concerned by examining features that are necessary consequences if our theory is correct (e.g., we can search for similarities in the DNA patterns of animals we believe to be closely related through evolution, or we can compare by measurements of radioactive decay the ages of different fossils we believe are related).

Thus, on the basis of our current best theories about the specific historical event in question, we can try to predict the results of observations that have not yet been made (e.g., we may predict that various rocks must be similar in South America and South Africa if continental drift indeed occurred) and then investigate whether or not these predictions are borne out. We may also be able to measure present behavior that tends to confirm our ideas about the past because it is due to the same process occurring at the present time (we can, for example, measure the present rate of change of distances between the continents, and observe mutations presently occurring in populations.

All of this provides corroborative evidence that may be convincing, but it is still not the same as observing the unique course of events that took place in the past, detailing the effect of altering initial conditions at that time, or carrying out experiments that repeat the same course of events. The historical sciences build on the analytic and integrative sciences in that the latter provide guidelines as to the kinds of behavior to expect and put strict limits on the kinds of things that could have happened in the past—assuming that the fundamental laws were the same then as now, a basic assumption to a certain extent susceptible to test.

2.3 Applied Science (Technology)

The applied sciences, such as engineering and computer science, are integrative disciplines, with both technical and social aspects. The social aspects will be discussed in the following sections.

In many cases, remarkable technical success has been achieved; for example, we can now use computer simulations to predict the behavior of aircraft before they have been manufactured, on the basis of Newtonian dynamics and the theory of fluid flow. As in the analytic sciences, these understandings of how complex systems function are open to experimental test, based on predicting the result of what will happen after we prepare the system in a precisely defined way (and provided we can isolate it adequately from outside interference).

One of the main differences between simple and complex systems is that usually we cannot test all possible types of initial configurations of a complex system. We can only check its behavior under a representative sample of initial conditions and hope that this gives us sufficient insight into its behavior in the face of all the conditions that will be encountered in reality (e.g., we test the computers that control aircraft in a way we believe will adequately reflect the whole range of conditions they will encounter in practice, although we cannot test all conditions that might occur). In some cases (e.g., the management and medical spheres) an inevitable human element enters the system, so the "laws" governing its behavior will often be rather loosely defined. Thus, as in the natural sciences, different applied sciences have differing status in terms of possible testing and confirmation.

2.4 The Human Sciences

A major objection to the claims of the social sciences is the apparent variability and lack of lawlikeness in social phenomena. In the social sciences, we study aspects of human behavior and interaction where consciousness, emotions, and intelligence play a part. Each event is unique and involves complex interactions. Furthermore, human behavior is very much culture-dependent.

There is no possibility here of obtaining solid predictive power, as in the physical sciences, or even "retrodiction"—a precise after-the-fact account— as in many instances in biology, because of the tremendous variability of human behavior. We may nonetheless obtain good understanding of general behavioral patterns and trends. We can still test theories by comparing predictions with observations, but far less agreement obtains on the shape of the theories—the underlying assumptions and modes of analysis—than in the "hard" sciences. Indeed, it can be asked if these subjects are cumulative in the same sense as the other sciences, establishing well-tested areas that provide an agreed basis for new explorations; in may cases even the approach to be taken is still in dispute. Nevertheless, the same *broad* principles of testing apply in these areas as in the "hard" sciences, and sophisticated statistical methods make up in some degree for the impossibility of isolating systems (as in laboratory experimentation).

Furthermore, to conclude that social phenomena are not subject to scientific analysis does not adequately take account of the comparable difficulties encountered in the natural sciences themselves. We emphasized in chapter 3 the hidden character of the reality that natural sciences uncover. We contend that the task of the social sciences differs from that of the natural sciences only in degree. Recognition of underlying regularities in the natural sciences is accomplished by means of brilliant insights combined with methods of study that artificially simplify and isolate systems. In the social sciences, underlying patterns should be expected to be more difficult to discover due to the added complexity of the systems involved and also to the fact that experimentation is often impossible. So the current state of the human sciences (psychology and the social sciences) can be described as a mixture of (sometimes) brilliant speculation and a developing skill in experimental design. However, these two types of advance are not yet often coordinated; that is, a growing body of data from controlled experimentation has not yet connected with the bolder speculations in the field.

It is important, also, to recognize the vast diversity within the natural sciences themselves. When we take into account the differences between the analytic sciences and the historical sciences, in terms of their ability to study repeatable phenomena versus individual events, we see no greater difference between the natural and the social sciences in terms of their ability to assign causes to observed phenomena. The important issue in the latter case is the question of cultural dependence of both behavior and analysis; we turn to this in later sections.

2.5 Sciences and Confirmation

Putting together the foregoing accounts of the natural and social sciences, and including the purely logical disciplines (which are not subject to experimental testing), we obtain the table in Figure 4.2 showing the range of disciplines that one can loosely place under the label of "science." This categorization is illustrated by a representative sample of subjects that fall under each heading (a full listing would be far longer).

Scientific Discipline

Logical	Natural Science		Historical	Human
	Analytical	Synthetic		
Logic	Physics	Ecology	Geology	Sociology
Mathematics	Chemistry	Astrophysics	Evolution	Economics
Statistics	Molecular Biology	Physiology	Astronomy	Psychology

		Applied Science	
Technology	Production	Medical	Social/Management
Engineering	Agriculture	Medicine	Human Resources
Energy	Mining	Surgery	Finance Information
Manufacturing		Psychiatry	Planning

Fig. 4.2. A classification of the different kinds of sciences, with examples of each kind listed.

The layout of this table is designed to reflect the susceptibility of each type of theory to testing and confirmation (we use the latter term advisedly; it is not possible to verify any empirical theory in the sense of proving that it is correct, but one can confirm it by providing more and better evidence). In both sections of the table, the difficulty of confirmation increases considerably as one moves from the types of subject listed on the left side to those listed toward the right.

The main point of the table, then, can be stated as follows: Many discussions of confirmation of scientific theories examine those theories labeled above as analytic, in which the basic process is relatively straightforward, rather than the integrative sciences. Even in the analytic case, of course, considerable difficulties arise as one approaches the boundaries of the known, where theories predict phenomena at or beyond the limit of modern experimental and detection techniques. The situation is considerably more complex for the other "hard" sciences (e.g., those labeled as historical), as well as for the social or human sciences. This will be important for us later, when we look at the broader spectrum of human disciplines that do not belong to the "scientific" categories above (ethics and theology). The problem one has to address is what kind of approach to confirmation is usable across a range of topics as wide as those shown above and capable as well of extension to these "nonscientific" topics. In chapter 1 we have provided abstract accounts of the "logic" of confirmation and of acceptability criteria, which abstract from the particularities of the various sciences. In later chapters we shall address the application of these criteria to nonscientific disciplines.

Note that while this table is of considerable interest in comparing the different sciences with respect to confirmation, it does not help us with further understanding of the hierarchical classification of the sciences. We now turn to that question, proceeding first by examining further the nature of the applied sciences, and then using the insights so gained to offer a hierarchical classification of the social sciences. As a preliminary we consider the relation between pure and applied sciences and between the applied and social sciences.

3 PURE SCIENCE AND APPLIED SCIENCES

Bruno Latour argues that whereas modern thinkers have pretended to be able to distinguish between the natural world on the one hand and power and human policies on the other, any cursory glance at a newspaper will show that reality does not divide so neatly.[1] Hybrid articles that "sketch out imbro-

---

1. *We Have Never Been Modern,* trans. Catherine Porter (Cambridge, Mass.: Harvard University Press, 1993), 2.

glios of science, politics, economy, law, religion, technology, fiction" are multiplying.

In a similar vein, we argue that the natural sciences provide imperfect understanding without the applied sciences. This is for a number of reasons, not least of which is the fact that the "pure" sciences depend on the products of technology for their success; much of the modern progress in scientific understanding is very largely dependent on improved measurement techniques and instruments that technology has made available. A much stronger case can be made, however, stemming partly from the role of science and scientists in society: Why does society support and pay for scientific research? What role should scientists play, as responsible citizens of their own society? But ultimately our argument is based on the overall worldview sketched in the whole of this volume, which places an obligation on all people, including scientists, to strive in appropriate ways for the betterment of others. This view does not prescribe the way individual scientists should act, but it does place an obligation on the scientific enterprise as a whole to take seriously the issue of application and implies that applied scientific work providing positive benefits is of considerable value. Thus, science itself is unintelligible if stripped of its social context, and the consequence is that the understanding it provides of reality is shallow—we do not know what *kind* of understanding it is providing us.

This argument goes against the tendency in many academic circles to regard the applied sciences as of lower status than so-called pure sciences and hence to view them in a somewhat disparaging way. In our view they should not be regarded as inferior either in terms of their intrinsic value or in terms of the intellectual challenges they offer. Indeed, for reasons that will be made clear below, applied sciences are in some ways more demanding than "pure" studies; not least because their predictions are put to the test over and over again—and the outcome matters in that it affects people's lives (e.g., consider the case of a computer programmer whose work is used to control the flight of a passenger aircraft).

Our view will be the same in the case of the human sciences: they too are incomplete without incorporating an "applied" element. This will be discussed further in section 6.1.

4 APPLIED SCIENCE AND THE SOCIAL SCIENCES

All applied sciences (technologies) involve social-science elements: they cannot be properly carried out without involving decisions of an economic, social, political, and legal nature, whether this is acknowledged explicitly or not. Because the applied sciences also involve psychological and cognitive elements, they are incomplete without the social sciences. One of Latour's examples:

> On page four of my daily newspaper, I learn that the measurements taken above the Antarctic are not good this year: the hole in the ozone layer is growing ominously larger. Reading on, I turn from upper-atmosphere chemists to Chief Executive Officers of Atochem and Monsanto, companies that are modifying their assembly lines in order to replace the innocent chlorofluorocarbons, accused of crimes against the ecosphere. A few paragraphs later, I come across heads of state of major industrialized countries who are getting involved with chemistry, refrigerators, aerosols and inert gases. But at the end of the article, I discover that the meteorologists don't agree with the chemists; they're talking about cyclical fluctuations unrelated to human activity. So now the industrialists don't know what to do. The heads of state are also holding back. Should we wait? Is it already too late? Towards the bottom of the page, Third World countries and ecologists add their grain of salt and talk about international treaties, moratoriums, the rights of future generations, and the right to development.
>
> The same article mixes together chemical reactions and political reactions. A single thread links the most esoteric sciences and the most sordid politics, the most distant sky and some factory in the Lyon suburbs, dangers on a global scale and the impending local elections or the next board meeting. The horizons, the stakes, the time frames, the actors—none of these is commensurable, yet there they are, caught up in the same story.[2]

This is but one example of the relations between ecology and environmental science. And we could make the same point by considering many other sciences; this one happens to be topical at present. As we construe these terms, ecology focuses on interacting natural systems in themselves. It gives limited information on management policies; that is, it discusses scientific (ecological) aspects of management but without relating this in any detail to costs and social aspects. In contrast to this, environmental studies leads on to full management and policy aspects and so integrates information from ecology with subjects such as economics and law, and has political dimensions, without which it would be incomplete.

To pursue the example in more detail, the factors that come into consideration in making environmental planning decisions are:

1. Scientific/ecological: what is scientifically possible? It is here that a sound analysis based on ecology, including applied natural sciences (environmental physics, geophysics, chemistry, and geochemistry), is a necessary component of any decision.

2. Ibid., 1.

2. Environmental economics: what can be afforded and what gives best value? This is where economic data are needed (prices, interest rates, subsidies, loan conditions, etc.) and where the assumptions of welfare economics enter, as well as criteria for what is an improved situation.

3. Environmental psychology and sociology: personal and societal preferences affect one's choice of these criteria.

4. Environmental philosophy and ethics: one's worldview determines the frame from which one approaches the decision.[3]

5. Environmental politics: political programs and power groups have influence over environmental policy.

6. Land and property law, water law: property ownership and property rights affect what can be done.

7. Implementability of the decision: finally one must consider how policies will be implemented and whether they will in fact succeed.

All of these elements are inevitably involved; thus one cannot adequately deal with environmental issues without becoming to some extent involved in the human sciences. It is important to recognize and make explicit the role played by these other disciplines in environmental management. Conversely, it is important to separate out those aspects—studied by botany, zoology, meteorology, environmental physics, chemistry, geology, and in particular ecology—that are independent of the economic, social, political, and ethical foundations chosen for policy and management.

The same kinds of considerations necessarily apply in engineering, information technology, energy technology, medicine—indeed in all the applied sciences. This situation is true regardless of how those disciplines conceive of themselves; whether or not they make these elements explicit in their own deliberations and training programs, there is a need for specific study of applied social sciences in order to manage technology properly. This contingency is one of the reasons they are more difficult than "pure" subjects.

5 THE SCIENCES OF THE ARTIFICIAL

The discussion so far has not made clear the essential element that distinguishes the applied sciences from the pure ones. This has been analyzed in depth in Herbert A. Simon's illuminating work.[4] Simon's point is that all applied sciences involve an attempt to create a situation that does not presently exist and so is not natural; it has not come into existence spontaneously

---

3. See, e.g., Ian Barbour, *Ethics in an Age of Technology: The Gifford Lectures, Volume Two* (San Francisco, Calif.: HarperSanFrancisco, 1993), chap. 3.

4. *The Sciences of the Artificial*, 2nd ed. (Cambridge, Mass.: MIT Press, 1992).

through natural processes, for if it had there would be no need for the application of science to create the desired situation. These sciences thus involve comparison of some image of what might be with what actually exists, and then the manipulation of reality to attempt to achieve this envisioned state of affairs. The image of the desired state may be very precise, or may be rather ill-defined; it may be a specific state, or just an impression of a general direction that is desired. Nevertheless, it represents a goal toward which to strive. Thus, the applied sciences are driven by goals, which are images of desired states, and these goals are chosen by some agent. To analyze this further, it is helpful to consider the nature of goal-seeking in general. We can then consider those cases in which something similar happens in the natural sciences.

5.1 Goals and Feedback-Control Systems
Goals are reliably attained only in systems that are goal-seeking, as opposed to those that run on the basis of some preprogrammed set of rules. The difference can be seen by comparing the V2 rocket used by the German army in World War II with its modern equivalents. The V2 was aimed at a target and then fired; thereafter it traveled on its preprogrammed course, irrespective of what happened later (e.g., winds that blew it off course).

By contrast, in modern rockets the target coordinates are programmed in. They keep track of their course after being fired, and if necessary make corrections in their flight paths to keep themselves on target. Thus, in both cases they are aimed at a goal, in the sense of being fired at a specific target. But the first method proceeds by stipulating that the projectile should follow a preplanned path: an initial plan is implemented and then followed automatically, irrespective of the present state of the system. The second method is actively goal-seeking: it monitors what is happening and corrects for errors as they occur.

Goal-seeking processes work by means of feedback control: Large or small things will go wrong, outside influences will interfere with one's plans, or one's initial ideas or actions may be slightly inaccurate in their aims or implementation. Therefore, continual corrective action is needed to keep the activity on course. This requires determining what is happening, comparing it with what should be happening, and then taking whatever action is necessary

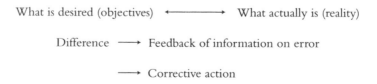

What is desired (objectives)   ←——————→   What actually is (reality)

Difference ——→ Feedback of information on error

——→ Corrective action

Fig. 4.3. The process underlying feedback control.

Fig. 4.4. Information flow in feedback control. The goals convey information on the desired system state. Comparison with the actual system state generates an error message. This is sent to the controller, which acts to alter the state of the system in the direction needed to correct the error.

to make reality coincide with the previously chosen plan or goals. More formally, what is desired is compared with actuality, the difference generates an error massage, and that error message is sent ("fed back") to a controlling element of some kind that corrects for the error (see Figure 4.3).

Such is the fundamental principle of feedback control.[5] It is helpful to picture this process in terms of the information flow that occurs in a feedback-control system (see Figure 4.4). Simple examples include controlling the temperature of a shower or driving an automobile along a chosen course. The principle is of much wider applicability than suggested by these simple examples, however; it underlies the way that all engineering control systems and all living organisms function. Indeed, all purposive activity that reliably attains its goal works this way. Engineering systems are the simplest and clearest cases, where the design can easily be seen and understood (e.g., a thermostat controlling the temperature of water, a governor controlling the speed of an engine, or an automatic pilot in an aircraft). Such systems have been thoroughly analyzed and are well understood.[6]

Biological systems also involve feedback mechanisms. Immensely complex feedback-control systems are embedded in plant and animal physiology, resulting in goal seeking (apparently purposeful activity) at all levels of the biological hierarchy[7]. For example, the processes in each living cell are controlled by hundreds of thousands of feedback-control loops associated with the activities of enzymes; the temperature of the human body is maintained extremely accurately through physiological control loops at the macroscopic scale; heartbeats are automatically regulated with high consistency; and so on.

Thus, plants and living beings embody hierarchically-structured feedback control, with some of the lower-level control loops operating autonomously, while others are controlled by top-down effects in the hierarchical structure.

5. See Stafford Beer, *Decision and Control* (London: Wiley, 1966).
6. See, e.g., D. Graham and D. McCruer, *Analysis of Non-Linear Control Systems* (New York: Dover, 1961).
7. See H. Milsum, *Biological Control Systems Analysis* (New York: McGraw-Hill, 1966).

The most complex such hierarchical control systems are those associated with the human brain and control of the body by the brain.[8]

The principle of feedback control also applies in public service, business, education, involuntary organizations, and indeed all properly conducted purposeful organizational activity. It is the foundation of successful social organization.[9] One should note here that society itself is a social organization of sorts, albeit a rather loosely linked one. To a considerable degree, its success in providing for the needs of its members depends on how efficiently it succeeds in functioning as a goal-directed feedback-control system.[10]

5.2 Hierarchies of Goals

All purposefully conducted human activity is directed by a hierarchy of goals. Those goals at the top level give general guidance as to aims, while those at the bottom level state the next practical step to take toward attaining the general goals. Thus, each more specific goal specifies a task to be completed in order to achieve the next goal up the hierarchy. Together, the aims and goals of an organization provide its members with agreed visions of the future they wish to attain, the aims being broad and more visionary, the goals being detailed and specific, so that in due course the members of the organization can check if they have in fact been achieved.

It is convenient to distinguish between different levels of choice. The overall aims and high-level goals of an organization determine where it is going and the broad strategy to be used to get there. They may be formalized in a mission statement (e.g., "We aim to assist the unemployed materially and in terms of human dignity by helping them create their own businesses"). These lead to the organizational strategic goals that govern its long-range activities (e.g., "We aim to double the number of people assisted this year"). The organizational decisions that specify how this will be done, embodying the tactics to be used to attain the higher-level goals by guiding actions on a shorter time scale, lead to tactical goals (e.g., "We aim to run a training program for 120 people").

The lower-level, specific goals, which are needed to direct daily operations of the enterprise and are the product of frequent consideration, will be called operational goals (e.g., "We'll plan the training program today"), and the minute-by-minute goals are the working goals (e.g., "I'll telephone Fred to see if he can teach"). These are routinely handled by the people actually doing the work. The managers of the organization, who are not actually

---

8. See Stafford Beer, *Brain of the Firm,* 2nd ed. (Chichester, U.K.: John Wiley and Sons, 1981).

9. Stafford Beer, *Platform for Change* (London: Wiley, 1978).

10. See George F. R. Ellis, "Dimensions of Poverty," *Social Indicators Research* 15 (1984): 229–53.

carrying them out, need only be concerned with them if they are going wrong.

A similar principle holds in all hierarchically structured control systems (e.g., plant or animal physiology, an aircraft automatic pilot): hierarchical structuring of a control system implies hierarchical structuring of its goals. The higher-level goals determine the broad aims of the system as a whole and are phrased in terms of higher levels of description encoded at these levels of the hierarchy.[11] Lower-level goals deal with more local and detailed issues, with a correspondingly lower level of description; their range of influence and concern is more limited. Explanation of system function will be incomplete without linking the levels of goals in a consistent way.

5.3 Goals and Values

Given the hierarchical structuring of goals in an organization, the highest-level goals are described in terms of "values" and "meaning." Effective fulfillment of organizational or social roles depends on the belief that what is being done is meaningful and of value—that is, participants need to believe that the activities of the organization have intrinsic worth or significance. This is seen most clearly in settings such as the church, army, or political organizations, but it is true generally. Successful leaders emphasize the value and worth of the organizational aims and roles wherever possible and appropriate: "The role of the leader is one of orchestrator and labeler: taking what can be gotten in the way of action and shaping it into lasting commitment to a new strategic direction. In short, he makes meaning."[12] The meaning perceived will entail a set of values applicable to specific areas of action. Robert Nozick comments:

> Values involve something being integrated within its own boundaries, while meaning involves its having some connection beyond those boundaries. The problem of meaning is raised by the presence of limits. . . . To seek to give life meaning is to transcend the limits of one's individual life.[13]

Meaning will be found in an overall worldview; values are embodied in the vision put forward for any particular organization, including society as a whole, providing its highest-level goals. These goals may be based on an implicit or explicit credo; their selection and embodiment in the organizational vision give direction to all its activities. When successfully communicated to the members and employees, this process leads to an organizational

---

11. Cf. chap. 2.
12. Thomas J. Peters and Robert H. Waterman, Jr., *In Search of Excellence* (New York: Warner Books, 1982), 75.
13. *The Examined Life: Philosophical Meditations* (New York: Touchstone Books, 1990), 160.

culture based on the values and vision, which creates a sense of common purpose in the organization. It may be strengthened and renewed through use of ritual, ceremony, or sacraments, and also possibly through uniforms, robes, costumes, decorations, and architecture that convey the same message. In addition to their general influence through the organizational culture, the vision and values are incorporated into its activity through specific structures, roles, and procedures designed to further those aims.

In this description so far, the goals have been implicitly taken as given. They themselves are not immutable, however, and can therefore be improved with experience. Thus, the feedback process can also be applied to the goals themselves, including the guiding values; we can have goal-seeking systems that search for the best goals, forming another hierarchical layer in the feed-back control system.[14] Clearly this is a critically important activity, for setting the goals—and particularly those at the highest levels—determines the shape of everything else that follows. It is therefore important to add two observations about this search for the highest-level goals:

First, these higher goals lay down principles about what are or are not acceptable lower-level goals for the system in question.

Second, a goal-seeking system that searches for the highest goals must itself be guided by something other than these goals. Thus, this search must always be conducted in terms of some higher goals that are outside or above the system doing the seeking. There is always a meta-layer that, from the view-point of the system, has to be taken as given. We cannot "boot-strap" to create the ultimate values from within the system itself; for whatever goals may be within the system itself, they themselves are subject to testing and improvement. That search, however, requires other goals to give direction to the improvement. Here we see the relevance of Nozick's concept of meaning as a relation of the system to something outside itself.

Thus, analysis of the functioning of a social organization, with its hierarchy of goals, leads to considerations belonging to ethics. The organization will presuppose certain judgments about worthy goals, but those presuppositions are themselves open to question and can only be justified in light of a theory of ethics—an account of the ultimate good for human life. We return to this theme in the following chapter.

6 THE SOCIAL SCIENCES

Given the above understanding of hierarchical control systems, we can return to the question of the nature of the social sciences. As already mentioned, we

---

14. Cf. Alasdair MacIntyre on social practices, and his specification that healthy practices aim, among other things, at the systematic extension of conceptions of the ends and goods involved. See his *After Virtue*, 2nd ed. (Notre Dame, Ind.: University of Notre Dame Press, 1984), 175.

run into considerable problems in determining any behavioral regularities resembling those described by the "laws" of the natural sciences. Further, more interpretation enters the formulation of those understandings that we do attain because human behavior is culturally defined, and even within a single culture a large range of variation occurs in individual behavior. So some have asked if the social sciences can be anything more than descriptive.[15]

Our position is that while vast differences from one social structure to the next make the task of finding an underlying regularity appear daunting, there is nevertheless a great deal of uniformity in much of social behavior and practice, so long as one moves to a level of description that is abstract enough. One can, for example, show that the functioning of societies is made possible by (formal or informal) allocation of different roles to the different members of society; that there will be some kinds of mechanisms for allocation of resources among the members of the society; and that there will be some kind of sanctions supporting compliance with specific expected standards of behavior. The details will vary widely from society to society, but these abstract principles will operate in all.[16]

In addition, we share not only a common physical nature but also common economic, social, and psychological needs, which are met in a variety of culture-dependent ways.[17] One can, of course, focus on either the similarities or the differences, and each is a fascinating study in its own right. Those who find the similarities uninteresting and focus on the differences are defining their fields of study in a legitimate way; however, focus on the common underlying features is equally legitimate.

6.1 Pure and Applied Social Sciences

As in the natural sciences, we can distinguish between pure and applied social sciences. We argue that the pure social sciences are incomplete insofar as they ignore both the issue of ultimate values (ethics) and the need to use the results of social science research in order to manage society.

The form of academic snobbery expressed in the insistence that applied studies are not "academic" is paradoxical in that it defines academics as people who are unable to make a useful contribution to the running of society. Another paradox is the development of supposedly applied studies (e.g., education and psychiatry) that have developed "theoretical" approaches that are not in fact interested in applications and that avoid the tools that might enable them to be properly applied (for example, evaluation indices).

---

15. See Daniel Little, *Varieties of Social Explanation* (Boulder, Colo.: Westview Press, 1991).

16. See D. F. Aberle et al., "The Functional Pre-requisites of a Society," *Ethics* 60 (1950): 100–111.

17. See Jerome H. Barkow, Leda Cosmides, and John Tooby, eds., *The Adapted Mind: Evolutionary Psychology and the Generation of Culture* (Oxford: Oxford University Press, 1992) for consideration of how this could have come about.

By contrast, all policy making and management are based explicitly or implicitly on theories and valuations from the applied social sciences, which in turn depend on a set of value assumptions. One can turn away from these areas, retreating to "pure" studies, in view of the difficulties involved in evaluation and in particular in the choice of a defensible set of values. Or one can acknowledge that, despite the difficulties, these issues are essential to applications of social science, which in turn are required both to complete the "pure" social sciences and the applied hard sciences (engineering and technology). We take the latter route. Our view is that the "pure" social sciences are ultimately a legitimate and interesting field of study only if they are completed by applied studies.

6.2 Hierarchizing the Social Sciences

Our contention regarding the natural sciences is that while they often study what is in one sense a single reality, they focus on that reality from a variety of perspectives. Each level of analysis requires its own set of concepts appropriate to that level. The same is true for the variety of social sciences. Sociology (or anthropology), economics, political science, and jurisprudence all study a single social reality: human beings interacting with one another and with the natural world.

A natural hierarchical ordering of these social sciences can be constructed by examining the interaction of factors influencing quality of life. We argue that the various social sciences pertain to different causal levels that determine the well-being or poverty of a group of people; these levels are interconnected by means of feedback loops. We use the term "poverty" here to refer to a broader condition than economic poverty. Thus, the converse of poverty, "well-being," must also be understood more broadly. At a minimum, each of them has social, economic, political, and legal dimensions.[18]

Well-being in this broad sense is dependent on the availability of resources, also defined in a broad sense (money is a resource, as are education, time, and peace and quiet; so are infrastructure, mineral resources, and wilderness areas). Indeed, by definition, "resource" will be used here to mean anything that can be deployed to give an individual or group an increased quality of life or well-being.

Causal levels determine the welfare of a group in terms of its ability to deploy resources as it wishes; the welfare status at each level is determined by factors at the preceding levels in this causal hierarchy. The basic level of welfare of a specific group is that of its *state of welfare;* we call this Level 0 (see Figure 4.5). It can be considered as having two major components, one con-

18. See Ellis, "Dimensions of Poverty."

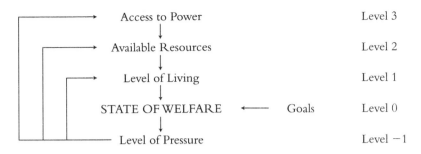

Fig. 4.5. The basic welfare feedback system.

cerned with material well-being and one with nonmaterial aspects (psychological and sociocultural).

The next level above is the first level of control, the *level of living* (Level 1). This is concerned with deployment of the flow of available resources and amenities that make possible the maintenance and improvement of the state of welfare—for example, the expenditure of available income on food and medical services, on rental or other payments to maintain shelter, and so on. Given the broad concept of resources and use here described, however, it would also include "use" of clean air and quiet, unspoiled countryside, sonnets and symphonies. The four main categories of such resource use are: for physical welfare and safety; for future security; for "higher" needs;[19] and for organizational purposes.

What can be achieved by choices at this level is determined by the total flow of resources available to the group. The second level of control is therefore that specifying the quantity and nature of *resources available* to the group (Level 2). We can consider these resources to be divided into the categories of natural resources, human resources, economic resources, technological resources, and enabling resources. Resources may be convertible from one category to another at some "exchange rate" or "terms of trade" (e.g., by a manufacturing process or by trading). Because of their ease of convertibility, financial resources are clearly important.

The resources available to the group are in turn determined by the group's access to power structures in the society. Thus, the third level of control is

19. We place "higher" in quotation marks here because there will be great variation regarding what counts as higher needs—more variation than in determining basic needs. Not only are there vast cultural differences—Abraham Maslow's "self-actualization" is very Western. But, in addition, this is a point at which the social sciences intersect with ethics, since the choice among, say, aesthetic, interpersonal, and spiritual goods will depend first on ethical judgments and, ultimately, on theological or metaphysical accounts of reality. Charles Taylor argues that the social sciences cannot be value-free if they are to be able to understand the judgments of worth that comprise much of their subject-matter. See chap. 5, sec. 2.2 and references there.

that of *access to power* (Level 3). By definition, "power" here refers to those features of the social system that can lead to allocation of new resources to the group's benefit or that shape the conditions under which resource allocation takes place. Such power can be exerted by virtue of coercion, trust, standing or authority in the community, or other essentially political mechanisms. Access to power need not be direct as long as it is effective. Institutional forms and controlling regulations are particularly important in modern society, so the ability to control these features is an important aspect of power.

The three higher levels so far discussed each control the level below, and so collectively determine the zero-level (the state of welfare). The final level in the main set lies below the state of welfare, and will be called the *level of pressure* (Level −1). This is the level manifesting the results of either a good state of welfare or the lack of it. The two main kinds of pressure are what we might call consequential pressure (automatic results of the state of welfare, e.g., a high death rate following a poor health situation) and societal pressure, which may act through institutional channels or in other ways (e.g., protests may be sent to officials; complaints may be made through "the proper channels"; public protest meetings may be held; or general discontent be attested in opinion polls and manifested in high crime rates and general disorder).

The final element in the main set of levels is what will be called the *goals* of the group, acting as a reference signal determining the direction in which the group wishes to influence events; they are themselves hierarchically structured (cf. the previous section). Comparing this desired state with the actual state results in control signals (evidenced in the "level of pressure") that flow through three major feedback loops to the top three levels of control, thereby attempting to influence the group's future in the desired direction.

Thus, this model views the welfare of a group in society as determined by a standard feedback-control system (cf. Figure 4.4) but hierarchically structured in that there are three levels of controlling factors, one above the other (Figure 4.5; note that we have not shown a separate comparator mechanism here, as in Figure 4.4, for in the case of human society the processes of determining welfare and comparing the goals with the true situation are not readily distinguishable). The group's welfare is determined by how effectively this feedback control system responds to its needs and desires (within the overall societal context that determines what is feasible and what is not).

Although this is not necessarily the way it will happen in practice, it is convenient to think of the three main feedback loops operating sequentially. One tries to attain one's goal by readjusting the use of the available flow of resources; that is, activating feedback to level 1 (e.g., by switching expenditure from entertainment to education). If this does not work, one converts some of one's available resources into new forms so that the flow of resources is altered; that is, by feedback to level 2 (e.g., by selling off some belongings). Finally, if that does not work, one tries to increase the resource base allocated to one; that is, by feedback to level 3 (e.g., by asking the boss for a raise). In general, the first level of feedback is of a social nature, the second is economic in nature, and the third is political. Note here the generality of the description: it can be applied to small or large groups, to individuals, or to a whole society; and it applies irrespective of the ideology or cultural beliefs of the people involved (although the detailed way it works will be highly dependent on these features).

To complete the overall picture of the feedback system, three further significant features must be included (Figure 4.6). First, an important mode of resource consumption is the use of a resource flow to build up further resources; that is, investment. This covers a broad range of activity where a resource flow is not used for immediate improvement of the state of welfare, but rather to build up resources at the second level and so increase the capability of later increasing welfare, or to build up a power base at the third level that will later result in increased resource accrual to the group. Thus, we include here economic and political investment in all their manifold forms.

Second, when obvious malfunctioning occurs in any of the three major feedback loops, action may be taken to correct the situation through specific error-correction mechanisms in society. These operate through review boards, appeal procedures, and so on; they are broadly of a legal nature, and form the highest level of control in the system (Level 4) because in principle they can correct any of the lower levels (even the head of state is usually, in principle, subject to scrutiny by judges). Thus, we call this control level legal access.

Third, the goals of the group concerned, whether consciously chosen or relatively unreflective, are influenced by a variety of factors: they depend partly on the group's overall welfare situation and psychological state but also reflect ethical, ideological, and other features related to how the group views its situation. All such influences have been classed under the label of ideology.

Inclusion of the element of ideology reminds us that the functioning of the system—and the perceived levels of welfare—can be altered by changing the features that determine the goals chosen (e.g., through propaganda or an advertising campaign). One can analyze the steps by which goals are chosen, both individually as is done by psychologists studying human moral development and within social groups. We will not pursue this analysis here, however, except to remark that some of these factors have an ethical character and that one cannot obtain a complete understanding of social reality without the capacity to evaluate these ethical ingredients—a claim we pursue in the next chapter. The links between ethical judgments and the philosophical or

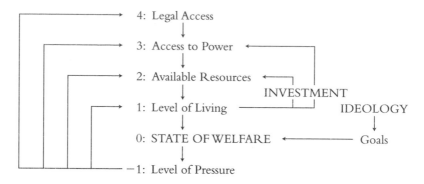

Fig. 4.6. The completed welfare feedback system.

SOCIAL SCIENCES

Jurisprudence	Level 4
Political Studies	Level 3
Economics	Level 2
Social Studies	Level 1 (Sociology, Anthropology)

Fig. 4.7. The hierarchy of social sciences.

ideological factors that govern them have been omitted from Figure 4.6 for simplicity. This does not mean they are unimportant.

Overall what we have here is a richly structured model of the functioning of goal-oriented action by a coherent social group in the attempt to attain a desired situation. We claim that this is the process that underlies the achievement of good quality of life by human beings in society.[20]

There immediately results from this a classification of the social sciences, shown in Figure 4.7, in which the different sciences are shown at a level corresponding to their domain of application in the welfare feedback system.

One should note here that this organization of the social sciences is based not on a hierarchy of complexity, as in Figure 4.1, but on causal levels, each of approximately the same degree of complexity. There are thus two separate hierarchical principles in operation here. The social sciences just discussed are of the same level of complexity but focused on different quality-of-life causa-

---

20. For a development of this scheme in detail, more nuanced than is possible in the brief presentation here, see these works by George F. R. Ellis: "The Quality of Life Concept: An Overall Framework for Assessment Schemes," South African Labor and Development Research Unit (SALDRU), University of Cape Town Working Paper no. 30 (July 1980); "A Quality of Life and Basic Needs Measurement System with Application to Elsies River," SALDRU Working Paper no. 56 (1983); "An Overall Framework for Quality of Life Evaluation Schemes, with Application to the Ciskei (South Africa)," in J. G. M. Hilhorst and M. Klatter, eds., *Social Development in the Third World* (London: Croom Helm, 1985), 63–90; and Ellis, "Dimensions of Poverty."

Subject of concern:	Discipline:
Ideology	Metaphysics, Ethics
Aims and Goals	Motivational Studies
Social Activity	Human and Applied Sciences

Fig. 4.8. The higher levels of the human-science branch of the hierarchy of sciences.

tion levels. Hence all of Figures 4.5 and 4.7 should be thought of as at the same complexity level. In Figure 4.6, the elements that are not at the same level of complexity (or generality) as the rest are those of goals and of ideology, which each represent higher levels of generality and implication.

Thus, we can identify the higher levels of the hierarchy of complexity: those of motivation, dealing with intentions (aims and goals), which shape the form of social action; and meaning and morality (labeled ideology), which shape the framework within which intentions are formed. These levels and the corresponding studies are illustrated in Figure 4.8.

Now, the causal hierarchy, as presented in our analysis above, in fact operates in the same way at many levels in the overall hierarchy of complexity and generality. For example, one can claim that a system similar to that presented in Figure 4.4 operates at the cellular level in plants and animals, and at the level of individuals, as well as at the level of groups in society or of societies as a whole. We also can examine the corresponding classification of the higher levels of the hierarchy of complexity (Figure 4.8). We obtain a classification of ideological factors and one of motivational factors (the two right-hand columns of Figure 4.9), showing the fine structure of the hierarchy of complexity.

To put this together, the different columns shown in Figure 4.9 should be imagined each cut out and placed above the other (that on the right placed on top, that on the left placed underneath). This shows how we have two different but interrelated hierarchies at work. Together they establish a hierarchy of causal levels at each level of the hierarchy of complexity.

HUMAN SCIENCES: **Social Activity**	**MOTIVATION:** **Aims and Goals**	**IDEOLOGY:** **Meaning, Morality**
Legal Access	Legal Goals	Legal Ethics
Power	Political Goals	Political Ethics
Resources	Economic Goals	Economic Ethics
Level of Living	Social Goals	Social Ethics

Fig. 4.9. The different aspects of the higher levels of the hierarchy of human sciences. The three columns can be thought of as lying one above the other (the one on the right on top).

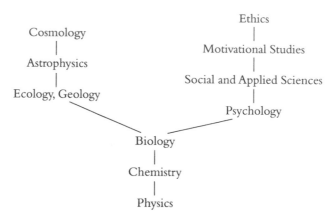

Fig. 4.10. *Branching hierarchy of the sciences.*

7 THE BRANCHING HIERARCHY REVISITED

We have now determined all that is needed to elaborate the hierarchy of sciences (see Figure 4.10, which amalgamates Figures 4.1 and 4.8, but without the fine detail of Figure 4.9). Given the above discussion, the distinction between the two branches of the hierarchy is very clear: that on the right is the branch of "the sciences of the artificial"—the human sciences and applied natural sciences—while that on the left is the branch of the natural sciences. Those on the right depend on or examine the effects of goal structures associated with human intentionality; those on the left concern only natural processes. This involvement of evaluative judgments and interpretation is the factor traditionally cited in arguments for the distinction between the natural and human sciences.

7.1 Ethics and the Hierarchy of Goals

The discussion above makes clear that the applied and social sciences are incomplete without ethics. The "pure" social sciences are incomplete apart from the applied sciences, which very explicitly require ethical judgments. Indeed, in examining the social sciences we run up against the fact that the social sciences do not provide full understanding of their subject matter unless one introduces concepts of goals, values, and, finally, of ultimate worth.

The requisite ethical concepts and judgments are not, however, themselves amenable to scientific examination or testing, as ordinarily understood (see our argument in sec. 5.3). Social sciences can only operate in terms of *presupposed* goals and values. Thus, there is a higher dimension—one beyond the scope of examination by the traditional sciences—that has to be introduced to attain a satisfactory *understanding and application* of the social sciences. This provides the top level of the hierarchy of goals, which in turn comprise the higher levels of social meaning studied by the human sciences.

We conclude, therefore, that the hierarchy of the human sciences calls for a top layer, as did the top level of the physical sciences. That is, to complete the task of the social sciences, it is necessary to have an answer to the question of the ultimate meaning of human life, or to use a less ambiguous term, of the final purpose or *telos* of human life. This has traditionally been understood as the province of ethics. The burden of the next chapter will be to argue that ethics itself can be understood as one of the hierarchy of the human sciences, and further chapters will argue that what underlies satisfactory value and meaning is that the understandings expressed in them are true reflections of the nature of ultimate reality. In other words, we reject the subjective concepts that see value and meaning as dependent merely upon human choice.

Chapter Five

Ethics, Theology, and the Social Sciences

1 OVERVIEW OF THE ARGUMENT

This chapter gives further consideration to the human-science branch of the hierarchy of sciences. We argue here for a deeper involvement of ethics in the social sciences than we argued in chapter 4, in that the theories and methods of the social sciences are themselves imbued with ethical judgments. If these judgments are to be amenable to rational adjudication, then the hierarchy of the social and applied sciences requires a "science" of ethics at its top. Furthermore, theology (or metaphysics) is needed above ethics in order to provide objective grounding for this latter discipline.

We argued in chapter 4 that it is useful to conceive of the human sciences as forming a causal hierarchy, positioned within the total hierarchy of increasing complexity, with ethics and motivational studies lying at higher levels in that hierarchy (see Figure 5.1). Our goal in this chapter is to examine further the reasons for counting ethics as the topmost member of the social-science hierarchy. We then argue that although ethics cannot be based in the "hard" sciences, nevertheless it has been a peculiar and unfortunate feature of modern (Enlightenment) thought to place it in an entirely different *category* than science. Indeed, ethics itself can be reconceived as a science; we argue that ethics can take the form of a scientific research program and that empirical studies of suitable means for embodying ethical ideals and norms then become an important ingredient in any ethical system.

Ethics
Motivational Studies
Social Sciences: jurisprudence political science economics sociology/anthropology
Psychology

Fig. 5.1. The causal hierarchy of the social sciences, embedded in the hierarchy of complexity and generality.

We shall also claim (following Alasdair MacIntyre) that just as social science needs ethics, so too, ethics needs social science. We do not consider here the specific content of ethics; that will be discussed in the following chapter.

Finally, we shall argue that Figure 5.1 is still incomplete: ethics in turn needs completion by a metaphysical layer of some sort; in many cases this layer will be of a theological kind. One consequence of this view is that theology will be constrained to a considerable degree by the requirement that it be relevant to the hierarchy of social and applied sciences. Chapter 8 will consider the appropriate content of that theological layer, such that it be consistent with and supportive of the ethical vision advanced in chapter 6. Chapter 9 will look at the relation of this theological position to the natural-science side of the hierarchy. We will argue that the same theology that best completes the human-sciences-and-ethics side also provides suitable completion for the hierarchy of the natural sciences and is confirmed by the coherence it creates between these two branches of knowledge.

2 SOCIAL SCIENCE AND THE NEED FOR ETHICS

Auguste Comte (1798–1857), who coined the name "sociology," understood that discipline as the science of the improvement of society. Hence, a concept of what is good for society was an essential ingredient of the new science.[1] Max Weber (1864–1920) is often cited as originator of the opposing view that the social sciences can and must be value-free. Weber believed that blurring the distinction between fact and value led to unwarranted prejudices:

---

1. See "Plan des travaux scientifiques nécessaires par organiser la societe," in *Opuscules de philosophie sociale 1819–1828* (Paris, 1883).

Empirical scientific investigation could lead to the discovery of the ultimate motives of human behavior, which would serve as a preliminary to an adequate causal explanation of historical events; it could show otherwise unsuspected by-products of alternative policies. Philosophical analysis could lay bare the conceptual structure of various evaluative systems, place them with respect to other possible ultimate values, and delimit their respective spheres of validity. But such studies could not show that any particular answers to evaluative questions were correct.[2]

Decisions about how to employ the "objective" results of social scientific research are the job of practical politics, according to Weber; and politics, in turn, depends on the choice of ethical and cultural values. Unlike many of his contemporary counterparts, however, Weber believed that ethical conflicts could be settled rationally.

Arguments regarding the role of values in the social sciences proliferated in the heyday of the neo-positivists, and by the 1970s the proponents of value-free social science, at least in the English-speaking world, seemed to be winning the day. They claimed that if the social sciences were to be scientific at all, they needed to strive for objectivity, meaning that scientists' own values must be prevented from obscuring their view of the facts. This was then taken to imply, further, that there is no objective way of supporting or evaluating value judgments—a quite different proposition.

There seems, however, to have been a shift between the 1970s and the 1990s, involving both a correction of the neo-positivists' over-simplified account of the nature of science itself as well as general doubt that the sharp distinction between fact and value is supportable. Thus, Alexander Rosenberg, a contemporary philosopher of the social sciences, can say that the twentieth-century trend, evinced in economics and other disciplines, to divest the social sciences of a moral voice, has never met with general agreement, and through the vicissitudes of the century, the plea for value neutrality has sometimes been reduced to the opinion of a small minority.[3] Rosenberg sees the present arguments as overwhelmingly favoring the rejection of both the possibility and the desirability of value-free social science.

We have argued in the previous chapter that if the social sciences were value-free, then values would need to be supplied in order to apply the findings of sciences (of both the natural and the social variety). There we said nothing that was not already recognized by Weber. A further implication is that the "pure" social sciences themselves must change in character so as to

2. Peter Winch, "Max Weber," in Paul Edwards, ed., *Encyclopedia of Philosophy* (New York: Macmillan, 1967), 8:280.

3. Rosenberg, *Philosophy of Social Science* (Boulder, Colo.: Westview Press, 1988), 204.

take values adequately into account—or rather, we would say, to make their ethical presuppositions explicit. In this chapter we argue that ethical positions are in fact already incorporated into the social sciences, both in the theories they propound and in the methodological choices they make. These assumptions, of course, need not only to be made explicit but also to be evaluated. This evaluation is the job of ethics. Hence, we claim that the social sciences raise boundary questions that can only be answered by means of results from (the science of) ethics.

2.1 Ethical Assumptions within the Social Sciences

We intend now to show that in fact the "pure" social sciences regularly employ ethically loaded conceptions of human nature, such as assumptions about the intrinsic egoism of individuals, conceptions of human dignity, or more broadly, conceptions of human good or human flourishing. In this section, we briefly survey some of the ethical viewpoints embedded in commonly held social-scientific theories; in the next section, we examine how ethical assumptions affect the very methods of the social sciences.

We shall look at the content of only three of the social sciences: economics, social or political theory, and jurisprudence. We choose economics because one still encounters frequent arguments there for the value-free character of the science. We take up issues in sociology and political theory because the standard account here will provide background for the development of our own ethical theory in chapters 6 and 7. Finally, we turn to the field of legal theory because we believe that our conception of law as the body of knowledge located directly below ethics but above the other social sciences in their causal hierarchy throws light on an important issue in philosophy of law: the debate over "legal realism." We claim that our ability to provide a fresh interpretation of this debate adds support to our thesis about the role and position of ethics in the hierarchy of the sciences.

2.1.1 Ethics in Economics

To explore the ethical content of economics, let us begin with some of the science's simplest explanatory devices: rational-choice theory and game theory. Rational-choice theory states that actions are a product of the agent's beliefs and values. Spelled out at greater length:

For any agent x, if:

1. x wants d
2. x believes that doing a is a means to bring about d, under the circumstances

3. there is no action believed by x to be a way of bringing about d that under the circumstances is more preferred by x
4. x has no wants that override d
5. x knows how to do a
6. x is able to do a, then
7. x does a.[4]

This "thin" description of human behavior is held to apply across cultures, and in fact is often taken as a definition of rational behavior. It is called a thin description because it is neutral regarding the actual values of those being studied.

Economists tend, however, to add one substantive assumption regarding human values: egoism. They assume that each economic agent is solely or largely concerned with maximizing his or her own private interests.[5] This theory, economists claim, along with the assumption of egoism, serves to explain or predict a great deal of economic behavior.

Another important tool used by economists is game theory. Game theory is a means for investigating how rational individuals choose strategies for maximizing utility in the face of other individuals with competing aims. A classic example is the use of the "prisoner's dilemma" to model social and economic behavior. Here is Rosenberg's version:

> Suppose you and I set out to rob a bank by night. However, we are caught with our safe-cracking tools even before we can break into the bank. In one another's presence we are . . . offered the following "deal." If neither of us confesses, we shall be charged with possession of safe-cracking tools and imprisoned for two years each. If we both confess to attempted bank robbery, a more serious crime, we will each receive a five-year sentence. If, however, only one confesses and the other remains silent, the confessor will receive a one-year sentence in return for his confession, and the other will receive a ten-year sentence. . . . Before we have any opportunity to communicate with one another, we are separated for further investigation. The question each of us faces is whether to confess or not.
>
> Let's go through my reasoning process. As a rational agent I want to minimize my time in jail. So, if I think you're going to confess, then to minimize my prison sentence, I had better confess too. Otherwise I'll end up with ten years and you'll get just one. But come to think about it, if I confess and you don't, then I'll get the one-year sentence. Now it begins to dawn on me that whatever you do, I had better confess. If you keep

4. Rosenberg, *Philosophy of Social Science*, 26.
5. Daniel Little, *Varieties of Social Explanation: An Introduction to the Philosophy of Social Science* (Boulder, Colo.: Westview Press, 1991).

quiet, I'll get the shortest jail sentence possible. If you confess, then I'd be crazy not to confess as well, because otherwise I'd get the worst possible outcome, ten years. So, I conclude that the only rational thing for me to do is to confess.

Now, how about your reasoning process? Well, it's exactly the same as mine. . . .

The result is that we both confess and both get five years in the slammer. . . .

[So] rationality, maximizing our utility, led us to a "suboptimal" outcome, one less desirable than another that was "attainable."[6]

The moral of this little story is that one person's behavior will be influenced by predictions about the other person's behavior. If I believe the other will cooperate, it is to my benefit to cooperate; if the other is expected to act egoistically, then I must do likewise to avoid the worst possible outcome for myself.

Game theory and rational-choice theory appear to be ethically neutral. But one of the features of the social sciences is that they are reflexive. That is, results of the studies affect those who are studied whenever they affect the subjects' beliefs. Game theory deals with the effects on my behavior of beliefs I hold about others' intentions and motives. Let us put together the rather innocuous assumptions of the two theories and see where they lead:

1. To be rational is to maximize my utility. (Note that this is not entirely neutral: "rational" is in fact a positively valued term.)
2. Economic exchange can be modeled by competitive games.
3. I must choose my moves on the basis of expectations of how my opponent will play.
4. I expect all (other) rational agents to act to maximize their own utility.
5. Therefore, I must always adopt the most egoistic strategy rather than the cooperative strategy.

Thus, insofar as economists propose egoism as a theory about human motivation, it easily becomes part of a *justification* for egoism when combined with other assumptions of game theory and rational choice theory.

Consider another example of the way apparently value-neutral theses can be combined to produce powerful social imperatives. Recently a booklet titled *Reader on Economics and Religion*[7] was mailed to seminary professors in

6. Rosenberg, *Philosophy of Social Science*, 149–50.
7. Published by the Public Policy Education Fund in Grove City, Pa. Page numbers in text refer to this publication.

the U.S. The purpose of the mailing, according to the editor, John Sparks, was to educate seminarians on economic issues.

In the booklet Ronald Nash devotes most of the first essay, "The Economic Way of Thinking—Subjective Value," to explaining the shift in economics from the nineteenth-century conception of economic value as objective to the current view that economic value is entirely subjective; it is determined wholly by what someone is willing to pay for an item. Nash then distinguishes between two senses of the word "value": that which people do in fact value, and that which people ought to value:

> Telling people that certain values ought to be ranked higher in their preference scales is the proper task of the pastor, moralist, theologian, or spiritual counselor. The economist simply deals with how people do in fact make their choices with regard to the allocation of scarce resources (3).

This essay nicely reflects the supposed value-neutrality of social science. It is not the economist's job to tell people what ought to be valued; economics ought only to study the empirical facts of what is valued by whom and the laws according to which those values vary.

The present chapter was being written on the tenth anniversary of the Bhopal chemical plant disaster. One striking economic fact is that the level of compensation paid per death in that setting was much lower than could have been expected were the victims U.S. citizens. We could, perhaps, explain the discrepancies by reference to other economic facts: a villager in Bhopal could be expected to earn much less than a typical American over the rest of his or her life span. So the economic loss to the family is less, and so on.

So economic theory leads us to conclude that a Bhopalese life is worth less than an American life. This might sound like an ethical claim (a rather shocking one), but Nash would remind us that we are mistaken to think in this way. It is to confuse two senses of the word "value"—its economic sense of what people actually value with the moral sense of what people should value.

The next essay, "Prices—the Cornerstone of a Free Economy," is by Hans F. Sennholz. Sennholz also explains the concept of ascribed value but goes on to argue for a free-market economy based on the fact that price controls produce shortages and surpluses. He concludes that "freely allowing the valuations of men and women to determine prices is the wisest 'policy' that limited constitutional governments have generally followed and which they ought to continue to advocate for the well-being of all (7)."

In the third essay, John C. Moorhouse moves the argument from one of prudence or means-ends reasoning to a full-blown moral claim (in "Markets,

Specialization and the Economic Order"). While Sennholz could be read as making the modest means-ends claim that *if* your goal is to avoid economic shortages and surpluses, *then* the prudent policy is to advocate a market economy, Moorhouse begins with the prudential argument, but then adds:

> it is worth stressing that a market economy in which individuals are free to engage in economic activities of their own choosing is the only economic system compatible with liberty. . . . Americans have long recognized that freedom of choice and acceptance of responsibility for making choices are necessary to human dignity and the essence of liberty. We value our rights to free speech, publication, association and worship. However, no less important are outcroppings of liberty in the economic realm: free markets, freedom to produce what we want, freedom to work for whom and at what we want. . . . Thus, the free market economy is the natural result of our ideal of liberty being carried out in the economic dimension of life (10).

Let us go back now to Nash's neat separation between the role of the economist to study the facts of human economic valuation and the role of the pastor to tell us what we ought to value. The fact is that Bhopalese villagers are valued less than Americans. If that is morally wrong, the economists have nothing to do with it.

Unless of course we broaden our perspective and ask what free-market economics might have to do with the price of labor, the price of insurance coverage, safety regulations, and a host of other factors that have contributed to the differentials between the economic facts in Bhopal and those in the U.S. The next question, then, is: why is the free-market system preferable to others? By the time we reach the third essay, the answer is clearly a moral one: because the market system is the only one compatible with liberty, and liberty is necessary to human dignity. But where does this judgment about the relation between liberty and the essence of human dignity come from?

Moorehouse's move is just the sort of thing that Weber's call for value-free economics was intended to rule out. Thus, one might say that pure economics must be restricted to the sorts of claims made in the first two essays. It is not so easy, however, to make a distinction between Sennholz's "prudential" argument and Moorehouse's ethical claim. For supposing that it is the case that a free-market system will result in some human lives being attributed less value than others, we are faced with an ethical decision. Is the "well-being of all" (7) best served by a system that avoids surpluses and shortages and at the same time produces an unequal valuation of human life, or might it be better served by a system that results in equal valuation of individuals at the cost of a less efficient economy?

Again we find that a social-science judgment taken by itself appears ethically innocuous—who would cavil with the claim that it is good for society to avoid shortages?—but when combined with other facts and assumptions, it turns out to raise ethical issues of the most serious sort. The truly moral issues are unavoidable when prudential goals need to be balanced against one another. Similar points have been made by "maverick" economist Kenneth Boulding. Leonard Silk says of him:

> He does not believe that economists can rest neutrally with the question "How do people get what they want?" He contends that it is not even ethically neutral to help people get what they want. Rather, as social science develops, Boulding sees the critique of ends as becoming more and more important. The question, "Do I (or does anybody) want the right things?" becomes inescapable. But it is precisely the critique of ends, says Boulding, "which is the great moral task of religion."[8]

Boulding would probably have approved of the present project, since he had a life-long interest in relating economics to other social sciences, and also to ethics and religion. "Economic problems have no sharp edges; they shade off imperceptibly into politics, sociology, and ethics."[9]

2.1.2 Ethics, Sociology, and Political Theory

For another example of the role of ethical assumptions in social theory, consider modern positions on the necessity for violent coercion in society. This assumption can be traced to Thomas Hobbes' claim that the state of nature, prior to the social contract, is the war of each against all. Most social theorists since then have claimed that coercion is necessary to maintain society and that violence is merely the ultimate form of coercion. Max Weber's classic statement on the relation between politics and violence is found in "Politics as Vocation": "Ultimately, one can define the modern state sociologically only in terms of the specific *means* peculiar to it, as to every political association, namely, the use of physical force . . . the state is a relation of men dominating men, a relation supported by means of legitimate . . . violence.[10]

Reinhold Niebuhr has affected a generation of policymakers with the thesis he developed in *Moral Man and Immoral Society:* the needs of an institution for its very survival require the people involved in it to do things they would not do (and would not be morally justified in doing) as individuals. Niebuhr's thesis has been dubbed with the congratulatory title of "Christian realism":

---

8. Leonard Silk, *The Economists* (New York: Avon, 1976), 176.
9. Boulding, *The Economics of Peace* (1945), 252; quoted by Silk, *The Economists*, 191.
10. *Politics as a Vocation* (Philadelphia: Fortress Press, 1965), 1.

The thesis to be elaborated in these pages is that a sharp distinction must be drawn between the moral and social behavior of individuals and of social groups, national, racial, and economic; and that this distinction justifies and necessitates political policies which a purely individualistic ethic must always find embarrassing. . . . In every human group there is less reason to guide and check impulse, less capacity for self-transcendence, less ability to comprehend the needs of others and therefore more unrestrained egoism than the individuals, who compose the group, reveal in their personal relationships. . . . When collective power, whether in the form of imperialism or class domination, exploits weakness, it can never be dislodged unless power is raised against it.[11]

More recently, Peter Berger has concurred that there is inevitably an element of coercion required in order that society not be destroyed by the disruptive forces within it. "Violence is the ultimate foundation of any political order."[12]

Now in what sense is this an ethical assumption? Is it not, rather, simply a statement of empirical fact, a law of human behavior? The very fact that one of the theorists quoted here, Niebuhr, is known primarily as a Christian ethicist might at least make us suspicious that we are not dealing with pure social fact.

Niebuhr's views on the possibility of noncoercive, nonviolent social structures is dependent on a prior ethical judgment, a judgment regarding the highest good for humankind. This view of the human good is in turn the consequence of a particular theological doctrine. Niebuhr writes:

Justice rather than unselfishness [is society's] highest moral ideal. . . . [T]his realistic social ethic needs to be contrasted with the ethics of religious idealism. . . . Society must strive for justice even if it is forced to use means, such as self-assertion, resistance, coercion and perhaps resentment, which cannot gain the moral sanction of the most sensitive moral spirit. . . .[13]

Niebuhr's judgment that justice is the highest good that can reasonably be expected to be attained in human history is in turn based on his eschatology, that is, his theological understanding of the end of time. Salvation, the kingdom of God, the eschaton, are essentially *beyond* history. The reason Niebuhr takes this stand on eschatology, in contrast to a view of the kingdom as realizable within history, is that he has set up the question in terms of the problem of the temporal and the eternal. Since it is not possible to conceive of the eternal being realized in the temporal, he concludes that the kingdom of God

---

11. *Moral Man and Immoral Society* (New York: Charles Scribner's Sons, 1932), xi–xii.
12. *Invitation to Sociology: A Humanistic Perspective* (New York: Doubleday, 1963), 69.
13. *Moral Man*, 257–58.

is beyond history; and this, in turn, means that guilt and moral ambiguity must be permanent features of the interim.

Weber's justification is also overtly ethical: it is based on a distinction between an "ethic of ultimate ends" and an "ethic of responsibility." The ethic of ultimate ends is concerned with pure intent and pure means. The ethic of responsibility is concerned with the politically foreseeable results of one's actions in a political order where imperfection and evil are presupposed. The political realist is committed to achieving ends even at the expense of morally dubious means. And as already noted, the decisive means for politics is violence.[14]

So, contrary to claims for the value-free character of the social sciences, it takes but a little scratching to find ethical judgments under the surface. These judgments may be taken for granted within the mainstream of the intellectual world: for instance, who could doubt that liberty is a good thing or that justice is the highest good at which governments aim?

But these assumptions are questionable; there are alternative points of view,[15] and we need to know whether and how such judgments are justifiable. Thus, we have another example to support our claim that the social sciences raise questions that they alone are not competent to answer—boundary questions—and that these questions are only answerable by turning to ethics.

2.1.3 Ethics and Law

We do not look here at particular examples of the inclusion of ethical judgments but rather report on arguments regarding the general relation between ethics and law. Whether ethical positions are (partially) constitutive of law is a hotly debated issue. We hope to show that our scheme for relating jurisprudence to both ethics (above) and to the social sciences (below) is useful for interpreting these debates in the philosophy of law. We end with the note that the more firmly one rules ethics out of the legal sphere the more necessary it is to make the extralegal judgment as to whether the legal system itself is just or moral. That is, the more clearly one distinguishes questions of legality (e.g., of an apartheid law) from questions of morality, the greater need there is to ask whether the legal system *itself* is moral.

If our location of law within the hierarchy of the sciences is reasonable, we should expect to find arguments in jurisprudence that parallel arguments regarding the (other) social sciences: can propositions of law be *reduced* to a

---

14. Account found in James W. Douglass, *The Non-Violent Cross: A Theology of Revolution and Peace* (Toronto: Macmillan, 1966), 262–63.

15. In chap. 8 we present an alternative theological account of social structures employing the Pauline doctrine of the "principalities and powers." Here social structures are God's creatures, not mere human inventions; they are "fallen," yet they are redeemable.

lower level in the hierarchy (e.g., to social realities); or do propositions of law need to be subsumed under higher-order concepts (e.g., ethical principles, metaphysics); or, finally, is law an autonomous discipline, with its own irreducible concepts and styles of reasoning? To shift from the formal (linguistic) mode of speech to the material: are there legal realities in addition to social, economic, and political realities?

These questions do in fact find application in contemporary debates in jurisprudence. An important issue is the debate over legal realism. Legal realists claim that a proposition of law is made true by its correspondence to some extralegal reality. We find it interesting that among legal realists, some seek this reality in domains below law in our hierarchy, others above.

H. L. A. Hart argues for a form of legal positivism according to which the truth of a proposition of law depends on its origin or *social* pedigree, such as its having been enacted by a specific legislative body, or its customary practice, or its relation to judicial decisions.[16] The claim that propositions of law are made true by social or political practices or processes is a bottom-up account of legal realities. The stronger claim can also be made that this is a reductionist account of law, since it denies the autonomy of legal characterizations of reality; they are reducible to sociopolitical descriptions.

Michael Moore is another legal realist. Central to his position is the argument that the truth of a legal proposition depends, at least in part, on a true *moral* proposition.[17] That is, there are facts of the matter independent of our reasoning or knowledge, which make legal propositions true or false. These facts—existence of moral turpitude, or justice, or kindness—are moral facts. Legal interpretations and decisions are merely provisional theories about these moral realities. Thus, we have a second sort of legal realism, which also denies the reality of the legal sphere, but (we have no established vocabulary here) "subsumes" it under higher-level categories rather than reducing it to lower-level categories.

Philip Bobbitt intends to produce a nonreductive account of legality in the sense that he denies that truth in law is dependent on correspondence of its propositions to extralegal realities. He claims, instead, that it is forms of argument intrinsic to the practice of law (six modalities of legal argument) that result in propositions being true or false. However, Bobbitt's account of the law seems not to imply that it is entirely insulated from disciplines above and below, since one of the modalities is ethical argumentation and another is the structural, involving political and social factors.

Bobbitt, however, does not do a thorough job of maintaining the auton-

16. This account is found in Dennis Patterson, *Law and Truth* (Oxford: Oxford University Press, 1996), 59–62.

17. Ibid., 44.

omy of the legal when he answers the question of what a jurist is to do if the various modes of reasoning result in conflicting claims. His answer is that the jurist must resort to individual conscience; in fact, it is this feature of legal practice, says Bobbitt, that ensures the justice of the system.

Dennis Paterson rejects Bobbitt's resort to private conscience and argues for the complete autonomy of legal reality: propositions of law are true solely in virtue of forms of reasoning within the legal sphere. In rejecting the role of conscience as a guarantee that the legal system produces just outcomes, however, Patterson recognizes that this position pushes the question of justice to that of the legal system itself.[18]

We do not venture to take sides on these issues except to suggest that the very existence of these arguments confirms the wisdom of our placement of jurisprudence in the hierarchy between ethics and the social sciences. Furthermore, if arguments for the autonomy of law are sound, it confirms our general anti-reductionist (and "anti-subsumptionist") stance with regard to the sciences—especially if Bobbitt's and Patterson's modalities of argument provide for the possibility of both top-down and bottom-up factors conditioning (but not replacing) the legal sphere.

Finally, we claim that the argument over the role of ethics *in* law or as judge *over* the law, however it comes out, confirms our general claim for the incompleteness of the social sciences apart from an account of the ethical.

2.2 Ethical Determinants of Social-Science Methods

The preceding cases can only serve as a sort of inductive argument for the implication of ethics in the social sciences. The reader may object that, as in the case of any inductive argument, these instances may be rare exceptions to the norm. A more thoroughgoing argument for the role of ethical judgments in the social sciences, and hence for the need for systematic study of such judgments, comes from recognition that the very methods of social-scientific research involve ethical judgments.

Rosenberg argues that "taking sides on questions of scientific method may commit us to taking sides in fundamental matters of moral philosophy."[19] Consider, for example, the question of whether informed consent ought to be required for experimentation on human subjects. Deontological ethics is based on the categorical imperative, one of whose formulations is that others must always be treated as ends in themselves, never as mere means. Thus, no one can be used for research purposes without consent. But for utilitarians the moral criterion is the greatest good for the greatest number. Thus, it is conceivable that, so long as an experiment does little or no harm to the

18. Ibid., chap. 7.
19. Rosenberg, *Philosophy of Social Science*, 177.

subjects and brings about great good for society as a whole, subjects *ought* to be used without informed consent if informing them would ruin the experiment. So ethical differences contribute to significant differences in experimental design.

In fact, the relations between ethical systems and social science methodology go even deeper. Rosenberg argues for a special affinity between utilitarianism in ethics and naturalism in social science, on the one hand, and between deontological ethics and anti-naturalism on the other. Naturalism is the view that the social sciences can and should emulate the methods of the natural sciences; this is possible because there is no significant difference between humans and the natural world that would prevent human behavior from being understood by means of observation and formation of causal laws. This approach can be said to emphasize bottom-up causation at the human levels of the hierarchy of the sciences. "Anti-naturalism" refers mainly to the hermeneutic approach to social science. On this view, human behavior cannot be understood or predicted without understanding the meaning humans attach to their actions. This intentional character of human behavior rules out any causal analysis that ignores the issue of meanings. In our terms, this approach emphasizes top-down analyses.

Rosenberg argues that utilitarian ethics needs naturalistic social science because its recommendations for social policy require that it make predictions about the causal effects of various policy options. Naturalism, in turn, needs the utilitarian's argument that it is in fact morally justifiable to treat other human beings as objects (rather than persons).

There is a similar congruence between the hermeneutic approach and the deontologists' emphasis on the necessity of respect for persons. Rosenberg makes the point as follows:

> According to Kant one of the features of an ethics that makes rights and duties paramount and subordinates consequences is that moral assessment must focus on *motives* for actions. . . . And according to Kant, the relation among our beliefs about our duties, or desires to fulfill them, and the actions they explain, could not be understood causally without robbing human action of its moral dimension altogether. . . . It is pretty clear how much this moral theory leans on a social science that takes human action and intentionality seriously.[20]

So what we see is that different methodological orientations in the social sciences depend essentially on different conceptions of the nature of the human person. These conceptions are the very stuff of philosophical ethics.

Charles Taylor has probably argued this thesis most carefully and thor-

20. Ibid., 181–82.

oughly, arguing against the understanding of human life and action implicit in naturalist approaches to the human sciences. The problem with naturalism is that it fails to recognize a crucial feature of human agency, namely, the involvement of distinctions of worth. Consequently, the naturalistic approach is doomed to fail: a self who can only be understood against the background of distinctions of worth cannot be captured by a scientific language that essentially aspires to neutrality.

But, says Taylor, if he is correct in holding that agents act on the basis of value-laden motives, then he ought to be able to explain why naturalistic social scientists value the value-neutral conception of their sciences. The reason, he suggests, is that naturalists hold to a particular ideal of selfhood: "I am saying that it is the hold of a particular set of background distinctions of worth, those of the disengaged identity, which leads people to espouse what are ultimately rather implausible epistemological doctrines."[21] As he elaborates:

> The ideal of disengagement defines a certain—typically modern—notion of freedom, as the ability to act on one's own, without outside interference or subordination to outside authority. It defines its own peculiar notion of human dignity, closely connected to freedom. And these in turn are linked to ideals of efficacy, power, unperturbability, which for all their links with earlier ideals are original with modern culture.
>
> The great attraction of these ideals, all the more powerful in that this understanding of the agent is woven into a host of modern practices—economic, scientific, technological, psychotherapeutic, and so on—lends great weight and credence to the disengaged images of the self. The liberation through objectification wrought by the cosmological revolution of the seventeenth century has become for many the model of the agent's relation to the world, and hence sets the very definition of what is to be an agent.[22]

Taylor concludes as follows:

> If, as I said above, the ultimate basis of naturalism turns out to be a certain definition of agency and the background of worth, does the critique terminate with the proof that this is so (supposing I finally bring it off), or is there a way we can go on and rationally assess this and other definitions of worth? This is, in fact, a particular way of putting the general question: what are the capacities of practical reason? Is it quite helpless before such basic differences in spiritual outlook, like that between the disengaged identity and its opponents? Or is there, at least in principle, a way in which

---

21. Charles Taylor, *Philosophy and the Human Sciences: Philosophical Papers*, 2 vols. (Cambridge: Cambridge University Press, 1985), 2:6.

22. Ibid., 2:5.

this kind of question can be rationally arbitrated? I am fiercely committed to the latter view, and I recognize that the onus is on me to come up with a good argument. I am working on it, and I hope at not too remote a date to be able to publish something convincing (at least to some) on this.[23]

Let us see if we can translate Taylor's project, both conclusions and aspirations, into the language of this book. Taylor's point about the failure of naturalistic social science can be stated as follows: human behavior needs to be understood from the perspective of a hierarchy of social sciences. It cannot be understood solely in terms of bottom-up causation. It can only be fully understood by recognizing the role that interpretations play in determining human action—that is, in terms of concepts at home in the higher levels of the human-science hierarchy.

Now, if ethics is counted as the science at the top of the hierarchy of the human sciences, then Taylor's concern that social science not neglect agents' attributions of worth (including moral worth) shows up as a natural corollary to the hermeneutic view of social-science methodology. That is, top-down explanation involving moral concepts will be as much a regular aspect of social science as top-down explanations employing legal, political, or economic concepts.

In addition, counting ethics as the topmost social science, we believe, provides important guidance for the task to which Taylor aspires: the rational arbitration between "basic differences in spiritual outlook."

It is worth noting that Taylor here describes these as spiritual rather than moral differences. Before proceeding (in chaps. 6 and 7) to propose a scientifically supportable ethic, we shall turn first to the proposition that ethics is indeed a science, and then (in sec. 5) to the question of whether there are, in addition to ethical assumptions, theological concepts or judgments embedded in the social sciences.

3 THE NATURE OF ETHICS

We have just completed our arguments for the claim that ethical judgments are involved intrinsically in the human and applied sciences. Given a widely accepted view of the nature of ethics, this can only be bad news—for moral judgments, the substance of ethics, are essentially contestable. The most extreme view is that "values" are merely personal (or cultural) choices.[24] We mentioned in chapter 1 that the predominance of this view makes us hesitant

---

23. Ibid., 2:12.
24. See, for instance, Hunter Lewis, *A Question of Values: Six Ways We Make the Personal Choices That Shape Our Lives* (San Francisco: HarperSanFrancisco, 1991).

to use the term "value." Less extreme views see moral reasoning as reducible to one of several systems (e.g., Kantian, utilitarian), which yield different results on some moral issues, and concede that there is no rational means for choosing one system over the others.

Obviously, we must hope (with Charles Taylor) that there *is* a way to resolve the issue of moral relativism. Otherwise recognition of the intrinsic role of ethics in science will simply spread the intellectual rot to these disciplines—just what the proponents of value-free science hoped to prevent.

It will be helpful, in defeating moral relativism, to understand its history. We noted in chapter 1 that prior to modernity, Westerners tended to embrace worldviews that related humankind both to the natural world and to ultimate reality.[25] Moral questions could then be answered with reference to the nature of things, or to the purposes of God, or both.

Jeffrey Stout describes the development of modern thought as "the flight from authority."[26] That is, in the attempt to evade the divisive influences of warring religious authorities, Enlightenment ethicists set out to sever moral thought from religious traditions and to base it solely on the deliverances of human reason. This strategy, however, was doomed to failure, argues Alasdair MacIntyre. Modern philosophical ethicists were surprisingly traditional in their views of the content of morality (although they took predominantly Christian morality to be universal human morality), but what they gave up in rejecting the authority of the Christian tradition was a concept of the human person that was necessary for justifying those traditional moral precepts. Medieval Christianity (as well as its two sources, the Hebraic tradition and Greek philosophy) provided answers to the question, what is a human being for? Or, in MacIntyre's words, what is the end or purpose of human life (the Greek word *telos* captures both ideas)? Without the traditional answer(s) to this question, traditional accounts of morality proved not to be justifiable. This failure, however, has not been seen by moderns as their own particular historical predicament but rather as a universal feature of morality itself.[27]

A second sense in which moral reasoning has become autonomous is its isolation from science. The claim that ethics ("practical reason") is intrinsically distinct from science ("pure reason") goes back to Immanuel Kant and his attempt to preserve the realm of human freedom and responsibility from the determinism of Newtonian physics. This strategy has borne bitter fruit in the fact-value distinction.

25. See Stephen E. Toulmin, *Cosmopolis: The Hidden Agenda of Modernity* (N.Y.: Free Press, 1990).

26. See The *Flight from Authority: Religion, Morality, and the Quest for Autonomy* (Notre Dame, Ind.: University of Notre Dame Press, 1981).

27. See *After Virtue*, 2nd ed. (Notre Dame, Ind.: University of Notre Dame Press, 1984).

The consequence of these two moves, isolating ethics first from theology and then from science, has been the conclusion that moral disputes are inherently unresolvable. That is, when we clear away misunderstandings, we trace different moral judgments back to different sets of values. But values, by definition, cannot be confirmed by the facts; they must be based on pure personal choice. So, paradoxically, the Enlightenment attempt to ground morality in universal human reason led to a view of ethics as intrinsically a-rational. And there is always the threat of pure subjectivism.

3.1 The Science of Ethics

To understand better what ethics used to be—and to see why we are prepared to argue that ethics can be and ought to be a science—consider the following: Despite the current tendency to equate values with personal or group preferences, there are many cases wherein value judgments are as straightforward and objective as factual judgments. For example, information provided by sources such as *Consumer Reports* enables us to make judgments regarding consumer products. If we agree on the purpose of, say, a vacuum cleaner, then a short list of facts about suction power, durability, weight, and so forth enables us to make an unambiguous judgment that product *x* is the best on the market, or at least that some brands are better than others.

By parity of reasoning, if we had an answer to the question what is the *telos* of human life, we would be able to judge among life stories and conclude that certain characteristics, practices, achievements, constitute a good life, or at least that some ways of life or characteristics are better than others. That is, given any decent answer to the question, what is the ultimate purpose of human life? it is possible to ascertain by means of experience and reflection, what social institutions and practices, what patterns of living and acquired characteristics (virtues) contribute to attainment of that end. This possibility is what leads MacIntyre to claim that it is a historical aberration to think that ethical disputes are immune to rational adjudication and that ethics is intrinsically isolated from factual knowledge.

These considerations lead us to claim that ethics itself could become a scientific discipline. To appreciate the possibilities for a science of ethics, it is necessary to recall the logical structure of science outlined in chapter 1. There we drew heavily on Imre Lakatos's concept of a research program: a metaphysical hard core is defined and supported by its protective belt of auxiliary hypotheses—lower-level theories that apply the central idea of the program in a variety of cases and thus, when successful, allow for its empirical confirmation.

The notion of a metaphysical core is especially useful in thinking about ethics. The hard core of a research program here, we suggest, would be a claim about the ultimate purpose or goal of human life. The auxiliary hypotheses, then, would be statements of the form: "If you are to achieve your *telos* in circumstance *c,* then perform action *a* (create institution *i;* follow rule *r;* cultivate virtue *v*)." Thus, for the most part, an ethical research program will be comprised of *information* about how to achieve set goals—information based in part on experience.

We can now see, from the ethics side, the sense in which ethics and the human sciences are mutually dependent. The social and applied sciences provide a wealth of information on means-ends relationships: if you are to achieve *x,* then do *a.* The incompleteness of the human sciences results from the fact that these sciences alone are incapable of answering the question whether one *ought* to aim at achieving *x.* Partial answers can be provided by developing a hierarchy of goals (motivational studies), but judgments about ultimately worthy goals are the province of ethics.

Thus, ethics completes the social sciences by providing the top layer of their hierarchies of goals—or perhaps one ought better to say that ethics provides the final criterion for hierarchizing lesser goals. The social sciences, in turn, provide the material for ethical research programs by answering theoretical and empirical questions about how it is possible to achieve the goals dictated by the ethical research program's hard core. We therefore endorse MacIntyre's conclusion:

> A moral philosophy . . . characteristically presupposes a sociology. For every moral philosophy offers explicitly or implicitly at least a partial conceptual analysis of the relationship of an agent to his or her reasons, motives, intentions and actions, and in so doing generally presupposes some claim that these concepts are embodied or at least can be in the real social world. . . . Thus it would generally be a decisive refutation of a moral philosophy to show that moral agency on its own account of the matter could never be socially embodied; and it also follows that we have not yet fully understood the claims of any moral philosophy until we have spelled out what its social embodiment would be. Some moral philosophers in the past, perhaps most, have understood this spelling out as one part of the task of moral philosophy.[28]

In the following chapter we present a preliminary sketch of what we believe to be the most promising socioethical program. Presenting it in sufficient detail to show that there is a viable core, a heuristic, auxiliary hypotheses, and ways to compare its conclusions with data will establish the claim that ethics can be viewed as a science (in the sense defined by Lakatos). Posi-

---

28. *After Virtue,* 23.

tive evidence in favor of this particular program, some of which will be discussed later in this book, then gives it a degree of confirmation. In the process, we shall provide ample illustration of the mutual dependence of ethics and the social sciences.

4 ETHICS AND THEOLOGY

Restoring the bonds between moral knowledge and the human sciences is an important step in defeating moral relativism. If we stopped here, however, we would still find a variety of ethical research programs, each with its core theory, each with its confirmatory social analyses and data. These programs then raise the further question, which account of human purposes is correct? Answers to this question have traditionally been provided by religious or metaphysical systems.

Several philosophical ethicists have recently called into question the Enlightenment's quest for ethics without religion—its "flight from [religious] authority." For this reason it is no overstatement to claim that a revolution has taken place in ethics within the past half generation. In the 1970s the most talked-about and written-about book in philosophical ethics was John Rawls's *A Theory of Justice*,[29] a brilliant synthesis of themes from the three most significant attempts to found ethics on pure reason: Kant's deontological program, utilitarianism, and social contract theory.

In 1981, however, Alasdair MacIntyre published *After Virtue*, in which he argued, as we have just seen, that the Enlightenment project of basing morals on pure reason was a costly mistake; an ethical system that was not based on a tradition (such as the Christian tradition) was bound to fail. It has been estimated that *After Virtue* is now the most widely read American book on philosophical ethics.[30]

Less well-known is a thin volume by Bernard Williams with the modest title *Morality*. Williams provides a devastating critique of both subjectivism and moral relativism, and then goes on to survey the major positive approaches to ethics from antiquity to the present. He finds most of them defective in that they are not capable of answering the question, why be moral (at all)? There is also, however a sort of theory

> that . . . seeks to provide, in terms of the transcendental framework, something that man is for: if he understands properly his role in the basic scheme of things, he will see that there are some particular sorts of ends which are properly his and which he ought to realize. One archetypal form of such

29. Cambridge, Mass.: Harvard University Press, 1971.
30. "What Is Virtue?" in *Newsweek* (June 13, 1994), 38–39.

a view is the belief that man was created by a God who also has certain expectations of him.[31]

Williams says that it has been practically a philosopher's platitude that even if a God did exist, this would make no difference to the situation of morality. But Williams believes this platitude to be based on mistaken reasoning: "If God existed, there might well be special, and acceptable, reasons for subscribing to morality."[32] Unfortunately, concludes Williams the atheist, the very concept of God is incoherent; religion itself is incurably unintelligible.

It is interesting to note that MacIntyre's own career as a philosophical atheist came to an end at about the same time that he recognized the need for some tradition in order to make sense of morality and published a book in which he argued that the synthesis of the Aristotelian tradition of the virtues with Augustinian Christianity in the work of Thomas Aquinas is the most intellectually compelling of all available options.[33]

4.1 The Metaphysical Basis of Ethics

Our conclusion, then, is that the science of ethics raises its own boundary question: *which* concept of the human good? This question must be answered by turning to yet another discipline in the hierarchy of the sciences—to a discipline that answers questions about ultimate reality. Some metaphysical systems provide atheistic accounts of ultimate reality; the more familiar examples are religious.

To illustrate the dependence of ethics on such systems, we turn to a recent article by Stanley Hauerwas.[34] Hauerwas compares his own work in Christian ethics with that of novelist and philosopher Iris Murdoch. Murdoch claims explicitly that her ethical system follows from a metaphysical theory. Hauerwas examines the contrasting metaphysic implicit in the Christian doctrine of creation and uses these metaphysical differences to explain differences in their ethical conclusions, despite close agreement on methods of moral reasoning.

Murdoch is an atheist; for her, the modern technological age has demythologized religion and made traditional theological claims unintelligible. The ontological argument proves the *impossibility* of God's existence. Her

---

31. *Morality*, 9th ed. (Cambridge: Cambridge University Press, 1993), 63.

32. Ibid., 72.

33. In *Whose Justice? Which Rationality?* (Notre Dame, Ind.: University of Notre Dame Press, 1988); and again in *idem, Three Rival Versions of Moral Enquiry: Encyclopaedia, Genealogy, and Tradition* (Notre Dame, Ind.: University of Notre Dame Press, 1989).

34. "Murdochian Muddles: Can We Get Through Them If God Does Not Exist?" in Maria Antonaccio and Bill Schweiker, eds., *Picturing the Human: Metaphysics, Morality, and Religion in the Thought of Iris Murdoch* (Chicago: University of Chicago Press, forthcoming).

alternative to traditional religion is a Christianity "without a personal God or a risen Christ, without beliefs in supernatural places and happenings, such as heaven and life after death, but retaining the mystical figure of Christ occupying a place analogous to that of Buddha: a Christ who can console and save, but who is to be found as a living force within each human soul and not in some supernatural elsewhere." The mystic Christ is an image of the Good. As absolute, above all the virtues, this *idea* or *concept* of the Good is a pure source, "the principle which creatively relates the virtues to each other in our moral lives."[35]

Despite her denial of the existence of a personal God, Murdoch takes prayer to be an essential exercise. But here prayer is meditation: "A withdrawal, through some disciplined quietness, into the great chamber of the soul."[36] More specifically, prayer is attention to the Good, which allows us to escape self-deception and egocentric attachments. (She uses an argument parallel to the ontological argument to show the necessity of the Good.)

We venture to state the core theory of Murdoch's (Platonic-Kantian) ethical system as follows: There is no end, no reward for human life. While it is necessary to pursue the Good, it is ultimately unattainable. Thus, morality has no point beyond itself. The goal of life, therefore, must be to recognize and accept this fact, along with the facts of the frailty and unreality of the ego and the emptiness of worldly desires. Or, more briefly, to be moral is to recognize full well that morality, though necessary, has no point.

The resignation, the *dis-illusionment*, the bowing to necessity that characterize the good life for Murdoch are in sharp contrast to the virtues given place in Hauerwas's system. Hauerwas connects his account of the Christian moral life to Christian theology by means of the metaphysical doctrine of creation *ex nihilo* (out of nothing). The Christian teaching of the *ex nihilo* character of the divine creative act was intended to underscore God's freedom in creating—God acted out of love rather than necessity—and hence the contingent character of all created being.

From the perspective of creation *ex nihilo*, Murdoch's account of necessity and contingency is reversed. The task is not to see the particular as necessary, but to see the contingent as just that—contingent—or, more accurately, in Christian language, as created. The task is not to see purposelessness in the sheer existence of the contingent, but rather to see the contingent as "gift" whose purpose is to praise the creator. Respect of and care for all of God's creatures is the primary means of doxological acknowledgment of God the creator in creation.

---

35. *Metaphysics as a Guide to Morals* (London: Penguin Books, 1992), 419, 507.
36. Ibid., 73.

In contrast to Murdoch's account of the absolute pointlessness of existence, Hauerwas claims, Christians believe that God means for all creation to worship God. Further:

> Christians . . . believe our lives are at once more captured by sin and yet sustained by a hope than Dame Murdoch can account. The Christian account of sin and hope is, moreover, correlative to an account of creation that sustains a teleological account of the world and our place in it. Accordingly Christians must ask more of ourselves and the world in which we find ourselves than, I think, Dame Murdoch can believe is warranted. . . . [We] are creatures with purposes we did not create.[37]

Along with Murdoch, Hauerwas argues for the importance of pursuing clear moral vision, but, in line with his own core theory, he believes such knowledge comes from being part of a community with its exercises in communal prayer, reconciliation, and care for others—communal practices that form characters that reflect the recognition that life is a gift.

How is one to choose between these two starkly different attitudes or approaches to life: Murdoch's purposeless dedication to morality versus Hauerwas's emphasis on hope? Hauerwas himself expresses puzzlement:

> I wish I knew better how to engage her in argument. There are surely metaphysical issues that would be worth pursuing. Yet how that is to be or should be done has been made difficult by Murdoch because she rightly, I think, refuses to separate metaphysics and morality. So it is finally not a question of how to characterize "what is" but how "what is" reflects as well as is determined by what we are or should be.[38]

We concur with Hauerwas, that the metaphysics and moral systems cannot be characterized or evaluated in isolation from one another. Our larger claim is that these two components must be seen as of a piece with the sciences, both natural and human, as well. We save the issue of evaluation of these grand systems for chapter 10.

5 THEOLOGY IN THE SOCIAL SCIENCES

We have argued above that the social sciences involve concepts of the person whose natural home is ethics. We also argued, however, that ethics is dependent in turn upon metaphysical or theological answers to the question: what is the *telos* of human life; what is its final good? We looked briefly at answers provided by Hauerwas, a Christian theologian, and Murdoch, a philosophical

---

37. Hauerwas, "Murdochian Muddles," ms. 4–5.
38. Ibid., ms. 22.

atheist. If both of our claims are correct, we should not be surprised to find theological or metaphysical conceptions of the nature and purpose of life embedded in the social sciences.

In this section we look at the work of John Milbank, who argues that the social sciences are imbued with theological concepts of the human person and of nature that are "heretical" from a Christian standpoint. Thus, the social sciences are not non-theological but anti-theological.

5.1 John Milbank on Social-Scientific Heresies

Thomas Hobbes's political theory has had a pervasive influence on modern ethics and social theory. Here is how one author, describing Hobbes's influence in modern economics, relates his view of the "state of nature" and the formation of the "social contract":

> In nature, man "finds no stop in doing what he has the will, desire or inclination to do." To Hobbes the "Natural Right" of every individual in this Edenic state is "the liberty each man has to use his own power for the preservation of his own nature, that is to say his own life . . . and consequently of doing anything which in his own judgment and reason he shall conceive to be the aptest means thereunto." Here, particularly in the concluding phrase, we see a statement of a modern notion of liberty. But in the next breath Hobbes gives it all away! Unhappily, he says, in this free and natural state the condition of life is "solitary, poor, nasty, brutish and short" because there is a perpetual "war . . . of every man against every man." Hence, to procure security, and the progress of civilization, humans reluctantly surrender the liberty of nature, entering into a "social contract to live under the rule of law."[39]

It is revealing that O'Toole uses the phrase "Edenic state" to describe the state of nature, for what we have in social contract theory is a new myth of origins at variance with the account in Genesis. In fact, Hobbes's myth is the antithesis of the biblical story. At least as we receive it through Augustine's interpretation, life for the original inhabitants in the biblical Eden is cooperative, not a state of war; bountiful, not poor; idyllic, not nasty; angelic, not brutish; and everlasting. It represents an aberration, a Fall, when the earth-creatures assert their will (against God, not one another) to take that for which they have a desire and inclination.

These two myths of origin reveal antithetical theories of the nature of the person, two antithetical theologies. It is the "counter-biblical" theology of

39. James O'Toole, *The Executive's Compass: Business and the Good Society* (New York: Oxford University Press, 1993), 35–36.

the modern social sciences that John Milbank sets out to uncover in his work. Milbank addresses both theologians and social theorists:

> To social theorists I shall attempt to disclose the possibility of a sceptical demolition of modern, secular social theory from a perspective with which it is at variance: in this case, that of Christianity. I will try to demonstrate that all the most important governing assumptions of such theory are bound up with the modification or the rejection of orthodox Christian positions. These fundamental intellectual shifts are, I shall argue, no more rationally "justifiable" than the Christian positions themselves. . . . "Scientific" social theories are themselves theologies or anti-theologies in disguise.[40]

We shall only be able to examine a small fraction of Milbank's argument and thus will concentrate on one step in the argument that will be most relevant to our own constructive work in the following chapters. In this step Milbank sets out to show that scientific politics and political economy are "complicit with an 'ontology of violence,' a reading of the world which assumes the priority of force and tells how this force is best managed and confined by counter-force."[41] Orthodox Christianity, in contrast, recognizes no original violence. It construes the infinite not as chaos but as harmonic peace.

Milbank's method is genealogical; that is, he calls secular social theory into question by uncovering the intellectual turns that shaped it and showing that these were unreasoned changes. In brief, his argument is the following: Whereas the typical assumption of the social sciences is that the secular is the natural and religion is an intrusion or usurpation, it is more accurate to say that the secular realm had to be invented; it was created first by inventing the category of the natural over against the theological or religious.[42] Thus, Grotius, Hobbes, and Spinoza created a degree of autonomy for political theory over against theology. For moderns, the natural becomes a sealed-off totality, operating on the basis of invariable rules. Furthermore, these are rules precisely of power and passion.

A second step in the creation of the secular was to associate culture with human creation, Milbank claims. This "sphere of the artificial," marked out by moderns as the space of secularity, forms the "dominium" granted to Adam in the Garden:[43]

40. John Milbank, Theology and Social Theory (Cambridge: Basil Blackwell, 1990), 1, 3.
41. Ibid., 4.
42. For a complementary view, see the account of the development of the modern sense of nature in Louis Dupré, *Passage to Modernity* (New Haven, Conn.: Yale University Press, 1993).
43. For a critique of the association of culture with the artificial, over against the natural, see Bruno Latour, *We Have Never Been Modern*, trans. Catherine Porter (Cambridge, Mass.: Harvard University Press, 1993).

Both insofar as it was deemed natural and insofar as it was deemed artificial, the new autonomous object of political science was not, therefore, simply "uncovered." The space of the secular had to be invented as the space of "pure power." This invention was itself a . . . theological achievement.[44]

Milbank traces the development of a politics of pure power from ancient Greece, where *dominium* most commonly meant dominion over oneself by virtue of which one could manage others and property. For Aquinas, dominion was subjected to the good of society in general. It is only in the modern period that we find a concept of pure power to do as one likes with one's person and one's property. This concept recognizes no providential purpose in the hands of God and, with its individualistic account of the will, has difficulty understanding any genuinely social process. "To keep notions of the state free from any suggestion of a collective essence or generally recognized *telos,* it must be constructed on the individualist model of *dominium.*"[45]

These concepts, of unrestricted dominion over private property and of individual will restrainable only by means of absolute sovereignty (Hobbes), were given legitimacy by means of *theological* arguments. Human *dominium* as pure power could only come to be seen as the essence of the human because it was promoted as a reflection of the divine essence—an outworking of medieval voluntarist conceptions of God. "The later middle ages," Milbank writes, "retrieved in a new and more drastic guise the antique connection between monotheism and monarchic unity which was affirmed in Christian tradition by the semi-Arian Eusebius and then became part of both imperial and papal ideology."[46] This is in contrast to concepts of the trinity that emphasize relationship over will.

Milbank hopes that by showing the extent to which these and other secular social-scientific presuppositions are based on (unwarranted) theological positions, he will be able to call them into question, making room for the restoration of theology to its rightful position as metadiscourse for Western culture. He aims to pick up hints of a "counter-modern" position that is theologically realist and orthodox. In such a position social knowledge will be:

the continuation of ecclesial practice, the imagination in action of a peaceful, reconciled social order. . . . It is this lived narrative which itself both projects and "represents" the triune God, who is transcendental peace through differential relation. And the same narrative is also a continuous reading and positioning of other social realities. If truth is social, it can only

44. Milbank, *Theology and Social Theory,* 12.
45. Ibid., 13.
46. Ibid., 14.

be through a claim to offer the ultimate "social science" that theology can establish itself and give any content to the notion of "God." And in practice, providing such a content means making a historical difference in the world.[47]

We cannot give a representative survey of Milbank's obscure tome here, let alone evaluate his arguments. Suffice it to say that insofar as his arguments are sound, his work provides striking confirmation for a variety of theses advanced here. His claim that there is no such thing as truly secular social science—that all so-called secular social theory is in fact imbued with theological positions—confirms our argument that the social sciences are inherently incomplete and that they can only be completed, finally, by means of some theological position or other. We shall argue in the following chapter against the predominant view of the nature of social order as dependent on violence for its maintenance. In chapter 8 we shall present our own account of the transcendent God of peace.

6 CONCLUSION

We have presented an argument for the necessity of embedding the social sciences in a scheme with greater scope of understanding than can be attained by means of the sciences alone—for a worldview with more layers of structure than pure science can offer. This entails completion of the social-science side of the hierarchy of sciences by placing metaphysics or theology (or "anti-theology") as the top level, above the ethical. Such a view then offers the possibility of increased coherence of understanding by providing the missing metaphysical layer essential to a full understanding of cosmology, to which we return in chapter 9.

47. Ibid., 6.

Chapter Six

The Ethical Core

1 OVERVIEW

We claimed in chapter 5 that ethics can be organized and pursued scientifically. That is, ethical theories can be organized around a central, unifying vision of the good for humankind. This "hard core" will ordinarily be derived from metaphysical or theological presuppositions (in chap. 8 we explore these connections). The "auxiliary hypotheses"—the specific claims about good actions, good human characteristics, good social organizations—will be derived from the hard core, along with empirical information, and will have the form (implicitly, at least): "If you are to achieve your *telos,* then do (or be) *x.*"

In this chapter we state the core of an ethical theory, which we hope to support, and examine some of its consequences for both individual and social practices. It will soon become apparent that there is no sharp line between ethics, at least as we conceive it, and the social sciences. In fact, as noted above, an ethic can only be understood and evaluated when it is embodied in a sociology. In the words of Alasdair MacIntyre:

> A moral philosophy . . . characteristically presupposes a sociology. For every moral philosophy offers explicitly or implicitly at least a partial conceptual analysis of the relationship of an agent to his or her reasons, motives, intentions and actions, and in so doing generally presupposes some claim that these concepts are embodied or at least can be in the real social

world. . . . Thus it would generally be a decisive refutation of a moral philosophy to show that moral agency on its own account of the matter could never be socially embodied; and it also follows that we have not yet fully understood the claims of any moral philosophy until we have spelled out what its social embodiment would be. Some moral philosophers in the past, perhaps most, have understood this spelling out as itself one part of the task of moral philosophy.[1]

Thus, while it will be the business of this chapter to describe an ethical theory and of the next chapter to treat its empirical consequences, we shall find the attention to the empirical aspects an important aid in getting clear about the actual content of the ethics.

It has been common in recent intellectual history to distinguish between personal and social ethics. In our view, it is not possible or helpful to make such a distinction; individual behavior and individual characteristics can only be understood, developed, and evaluated within a social context. We are indebted (again) to MacIntyre for the form our analysis will take—a form in which the good for individual life is intrinsically related to social practices and institutions.

1.1 The Structure of Ethics

According to MacIntyre, the focus of ethics for the individual is not in the first instance behavior, but character traits—*virtues*. What will count as a virtue rather than a vice or a morally indifferent characteristic, however, is determined by the needs of social *practices* and by the location of those characteristics within the whole of a *life story*. Practices and life stories, in turn, are evaluated morally in relation to the *telos* of human life. MacIntyre has made an important contribution to ethics by defining the concept of a practice— a social activity aimed at the achievement of some good. In his words, a practice is:

> any coherent and complex form of socially established cooperative human activity through which goods internal to that form of activity are realized in the course of trying to achieve those standards of excellence which are appropriate to, and partially definitive of, that form of activity, with the result that human powers to achieve excellence, and human conceptions of the ends and goods involved, are systematically extended.[2]

Medicine and architecture are examples of practices. Goods internal to a practice are those that the practice aims at intrinsically, such as the goal of

---

1. Alasdair MacIntyre, *After Virtue,* 2nd ed. (Notre Dame, Ind.: University of Notre Dame Press, 1984), 23.
2. Ibid., 187.

health for the practice of medicine, of usable space and beauty for architecture. These are to be contrasted with external goods, such as the money one earns as a result of practicing medicine.

The definition of a practice is an important contribution to ethics not only because it helps individualistic Westerners to perceive a level of social reality that might otherwise be missed—a level of complexity above less structured interpersonal relationships and below institutions and societies—but also because the concept of a practice serves a critical function in defining virtues. A virtue can be defined in a preliminary way as "an acquired human quality, the possession and exercise of which tends to enable us to achieve those goods which are internal to practices and the lack of which effectively prevents us from achieving any such goods."[3] Thus, reliability, carefulness, and technical ability in medicine or architecture are examples of virtues. This is not yet a complete definition, however, for practices themselves, and the characteristics that allow them to flourish, must be evaluated within the context of the whole of a human life story, and ultimately against the *telos* provided by a tradition. These are needed to complete the definition of what is indeed good.

Social practices are generally located within institutions. For example, the practice of medicine is housed within clinics, hospitals, and medical schools. Theological education is generally housed in seminaries. Institutions can either promote the development of practices or deform them.

So the relations between social ethics and "individual" or "personal" ethics can be conceived of hierarchically on the basis of successively broader contexts (see Figure 6.1).

Since the ultimate context is the purpose of human life as a whole, which is a theological concept, we might represent the relations as follows: Theology has consequences for judgments of social entities, and these in turn for

SOCIAL CONTEXT	institutions
COOPERATIVE ACTIVITY	practices
INDIVIDUAL QUALITIES	virtues

Fig. 6.1. The hierarchical relation between social and individual ethical concepts. Here virtues are individual qualities whose moral desirability is a consequence of their role in achieving goods internal to practices, and institutions provide the social context for practices.

3. Ibid., 191.

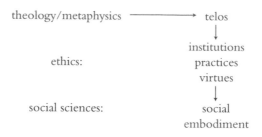

Fig. 6.2. The hierarchical structuring of ethics, above the social sciences but below theology/metaphysics.

judgments of individual characteristics. These ethical judgments have consequences in turn for the social sciences. Ethics mediates a concept of ultimate reality to these lower levels (see Figure 6.2).

Given this general structuring, the actual content of the ethic depends on the *telos* or purpose derived from the theology or metaphysics at the topmost level. Thus, to understand an ethical position one must relate it to the corresponding view of ultimate reality.

2 THE HARD CORE: SELF-RENUNCIATION

Although we will explore its theological sources in chapter 8, we state the core of our ethical theory here as follows:

Self-renunciation for the sake of the other is humankind's highest good.

A variety of authors have contributed to a theory of ethics as renunciation. John Hick sees the change from self-centeredness to other-centeredness as the primary goal of all major religious systems of ethics. In fact, he equates this change with salvation:

The function of religion in each case is to provide contexts for salvation/ liberation, which consists in various forms of transformation of human existence from self-centeredness to Reality-centeredness. . . . and the salvific transformation is most readily observed by its moral fruits, which can be identified by means of the ethical ideal, common to all the great traditions, of *agape/karuna* (love/compassion).[4]

Similarly, Robert N. Bellah writes:

the deepest truth I have discovered is that if one accepts the loss, if one gives up clinging to what is irretrievably gone, then the nothing which is left is not barren but is enormously fruitful. Everything that one has lost

4. *An Interpretation of Religion* (New Haven, Conn.: Yale University Press, 1989), 14.

comes flooding back again out of the darkness, and one's relation to it is new—free and unclinging. But the richness of the nothing contains more, it is the all-possible, it is the spring of freedom.[5]

It is easy for statements about personal self-sacrifice, renunciation, other-centeredness to sound platitudinous in a culture widely affected by Christianity. The writings of Simone Weil,[6] however, expand on the theme of self-renunciation in a way that makes the claims of such an ethic stand out starkly. She expresses the connection between the ethical principle of renunciation and its theological grounding as follows:

> Renunciation. Imitation of God's renunciation in creation. In a sense God renounces being everything. . . . He emptied himself of his divinity . . . (12). We should renounce being something. That is our only good (29).

In chapter 8, we pick up the theme of God's renunciation, often referred to by the Greek term, *kenosis;* thus, we call our related ethic "kenotic." For the present, the issue is what this principle of renunication or kenosis entails in terms of ethics. It is extremely wide ranging in its implications at both the personal and the social level. Renunciation is:

> To forgive debts. To accept the past without asking for future compensation. To stop time at the present instant. This is also the acceptance of death. . . (12). To empty ourselves of the world. To take the form of a slave. To reduce ourselves to the point we occupy in space and time. . . (12). To strip ourselves of the imaginary royalty of the world. Absolute solitude. Then we possess the truth of the world (12).

Some of the consequences or exemplifications of this ethic, with articulations by Weil, follow:

1. *Renunciation involves detachment from material possessions:*
   Two ways of renouncing material possessions: To give them up with a view to some spiritual advantage. To conceive of them and feel them as conducive to spiritual well-being (for example: hunger, fatigue and humiliation cloud the mind and hinder meditation) and yet to renounce them. Only the second kind of renunciation means nakedness of spirit (12).

   To detach our desire from all good things and to wait. Experience proves that this waiting is satisfied. It is then we touch the absolute good (13).

---

5. *Beyond Belief: Essays on Religion in a Post-Traditional World* (New York: Harper and Row, 1970), xx-xxi.

6. *Gravity and Grace* (London: Routledge, 1992; first published in English in 1952). Parenthetical page references are to the 1992 edition.

2. *It is to renounce our rights to rewards:*

   The necessity for a reward, the need to receive the equivalent of what
   we give. But if, doing violence to this necessity, we leave a vacuum, as
   it were a suction of air is produced and a supernatural reward results. It
   does not come if we receive other wages: it is this vacuum that makes
   it come (10).

3. *Renunciation entails choosing not to harm another person when we have been
   harmed:*

   To harm a person is to receive something from him. What? What have
   we gained (and what will have to be repaid) when we have done harm?
   We have gained in importance. We have expanded. We have filled an
   emptiness in ourselves by creating one in somebody else (6).

4. *Renunciation calls for nonviolence:*

   We should strive to become such that we are able to be non-violent.
   This depends also on the adversary . . . (77). The cause of wars: there is
   in every man and in every group of men a feeling that they have a just
   and legitimate claim to be masters of the universe—to possess it (77).

   Whoever takes up the sword shall perish by the sword. And whoever
   does not take up the sword (or lets it go) shall perish on the cross (79).

5. *Renunciation calls for acceptance of suffering:*

   For men of courage physical sufferings (and privations) are often a test
   of endurance and of strength of soul. But there is a better use to be
   made of them. For me then, may they not be that. May they rather be
   a testimony, loved and felt, of human misery. May I endure them in a
   completely passive manner. Whatever happens, how could I ever think
   an affliction too great, since the wound of an affliction and the abase-
   ment to which those whom it strikes are condemned opens to them
   the knowledge of human misery, knowledge which is the door to all
   wisdom (31)?

6. *Renunciation means submission to God:*

   God gave me being in order that I should give it back to him. . . . Humility is the refusal to exist outside God. It is the queen of virtues (35).

The consequence of this life of renunciation, according to Weil, is that it
leads to wisdom, to knowledge of the truth, to encounter with absolute good.

One additional point that surely follows from the core idea of renunciation
is intellectual humility: being willing to give up cherished notions in order
to learn from others. This virtue is emphasized by the Quakers in their call
to recognize the Light in everyone:

Do you respect that of God in everyone though it may be expressed in
unfamiliar ways or be difficult to discern? . . . Listen patiently and seek the

truth which other peoples' opinions may contain. . . . Think it possible that you may be mistaken.[7]

2.1 Its Paradoxical Nature

The paradoxical nature of an ethic of self-sacrifice or renunciation is captured in Jesus' saying that those who try to make their life secure will lose it, but those who lose their life will keep it (Luke 17:33 NRSV).

The denial of one's own interests at first seems negative and destructive—the way to a distorted humanity rather than the way to fulfillment. There are indeed distortions of this ethic that aim more at manipulation of others than at transformation. Genuine self-sacrifice for the good of the other, however, is the way to open oneself to a greater good: to make generosity the order of the day transforms the situation, totally transcending the miserly ethic of nicely calculated debts and duties. And this way of "giving up" one's own interests is the true way to self-fulfillment. There lies the paradox; yet this has been a central theme in spiritual texts through the ages.

This kind of approach brings about transformation; it overcomes the petty obstacles and impediments one sees from one's limited, self-centered perspective, opening up totally new possibilities that arise if those involved view their situation from a more generous and inclusive view. Working for the greater good of all, forgetting one's own needs and demands, has the potential to generate a corresponding response in others, raising the level of morality of the group and creating a community in which each looks after the other and therefore no one lacks. Responding to the needs and humanity of those outside one's natural circle of caring offers participation in the good available to all. Thus, eventually even the group's enemies are made aware that they need not be excluded; they need not remain enemies.[8]

Thus, (seeming) paradox is central to true morality. One might note here the analogy with fundamental physics: the foundations of quantum mechanics seem at first totally illogical, quite unlike what we expected at first on the basis of ordinary everyday experience, which is totally misleading when we try to understand the foundations of microphysics. Yet the hints are there, and quantum theory has its own discoverable internal logic, which, when comprehended, enables us to understand reality in a more profound way than before. We suggest that the same is true in morality: its true nature is different from what most take it to be, but the hints are there for all to see; and its

---

7. *Quaker Faith and Practice* (Warwick, U.K.: The Yearly Meeting of the Society of Friends in Britain, 1995), Advices and Queries, chap. 1, no. 17.

8. Cf. Parker Palmer, *The Promise of Paradox* (Notre Dame, Ind.: Ave Maria Press, 1980).

apparently paradoxical nature makes perfect sense when once one understands the underlying dynamic.

It is essential that such a morality cannot be imposed by coercion or law; it can only be a guiding principle, an invitation to be freely chosen and accepted (or rejected). This free acceptance is the central nature of morality; moral teaching cannot properly violate the principle being taught. This point is a complete paradox to those who believe that good behavior only comes through coercion. And indeed many of the greatest moral evils over the centuries have come about from those who have tried to impose a self-denying morality by force. Examples are legion, both of a religious nature and of a secular nature (the Great Leap Forward in China, for example). Such means are in contradiction to its very nature, for self-denial cannot be imposed; it has to come from within.

3 RENUNCIATION AS A SOCIAL ETHIC

We mentioned above the distinction between personal and social ethics. Insofar as this distinction can be made, it is noteworthy that all three of the authors quoted above treat renunciation as a personal ethic. So an important task for this chapter is to examine the consequences of our hard core for social and political life. A complete ethical system must have implications for all areas of social life, including interpersonal relations, of course, but also economics, politics, and jurisprudence. The task is to show that *realistic* forms of social life follow from this viewpoint.

It is beyond the scope of this chapter, perhaps even of an entire book, to give a complete account of the ethical system (or an ethical system) that follows from the *telos* of self-renunciation. Our goal will be the more modest one of describing points at which the ethic here considered diverges most radically from more common accounts of morality. We first make some brief comments on implications for the spheres of economics, politics, and law. Then we take up the issue of nonviolence, which we claim is an important implication of the ethic of renunciation in both the political and the interpersonal sphere. We end with brief remarks on renunciation and epistemology.

3.1 Law and Renunciation

Jim Consedine has observed that many Western penal systems operate on the principle of retribution. These are largely systems based on English law, and include those of the United States, South Africa, and New Zealand. An ethic of renunciation calls such systems into question. The task of this section is to show that there are alternative systems, based on moral views compatible with an ethic of renunciation. Such systems have existed in biblical times, in pre-

Norman Celtic societies, and in a variety of Polynesian, African, Asian, and Caribbean cultures.[9]

Howard Zehr, an internationally known expert on criminal justice, writes:

> Throughout most of Western history, crime has been understood as an offence of one person against another person, much like other conflicts and wrongs which are treated as "civil." Throughout most of this history, people have assumed that the central response must be to somehow make things right; restitution and compensation were very common, perhaps normative. Crime created obligations, liabilities, that needed to be taken care of, usually through a process of negotiation. Acts of vengeance could occur, but not, it appears, as frequently as is usually assumed and the functions of vengeance may have been different [from] what we expect. Both victim and offender had a responsibility in this process, as did the community. The state had a role as well, but it was limited and was by necessity responsive to the wishes of victims.
>
> This is a gross simplification, of course, but to some extent our history has been a dialectic between two modes of justice: state justice and community justice. State justice was imposed justice, punitive justice, hierarchical justice. Community justice was negotiated justice, restitutive justice.
>
> State justice has operated in some form during most of Western history. However, community justice predominated until fairly recently. Only in the past few centuries did state justice win out. The state won a monopoly on justice, but only with a great fight. The victory of state justice constituted a legal revolution of tremendous import, but a revolution which has been recognized and studied too infrequently. It is no accident that the birth of prisons—new technology for delivering doses of pain—coincided with this legal revolution.[10]

The process of change in England from community-based, restorative justice to state-based retributive justice has been traced to William the Conqueror and his descendants, who discovered that the legal system could be a highly effective means for increasing political control:

> To this end, William's son, Henry I, issued in 1116 the *Leges Henrici,* creating the idea of the "King's Peace" and asserting royal jurisdiction over certain offences by which it was deemed to have been violated. These included arson, robbery, murder, false coinage and crimes of violence. A violation of the King's Peace was a violation against his person, and thus

---

9. See Jim Consedine, *Restorative Justice: Healing the Effects of Crime* (Lyttelton, N.Z.: Ploughshares Publications, 1995).

10. *Justice: The Restorative Vision,* Mennonite Central Committee, 1989, quoted by Consedine, *Restorative Justice,* 12.

the King became the primary victim in such offences, taking the place of the victim before the law. The actual victim lost his position in the process and the state and the offender were left as the sole concerned parties.

As a result the system, rather than being concerned to make the victim whole, now focused on upholding the authority of the state. It now centered on the offender rather than the victim, since it was concerned with why the law had been broken and how to stop it being broken again. Criminal justice became future-orientated, concerned rather to make the offender and potential offenders law-abiding, than to make them atone for their past offence. Restitution, being past-orientated and concerned with the victim, was gradually abandoned. Monies which would have been paid to the victim were now paid to the state, and thus took on a punitive rather than a compensatory role, becoming what we know as a fine. Many cruel and humiliating forms of corporal punishment were also used.[11]

Consedine, a prison chaplain in New Zealand, supports the contention that most contemporary sentencing has a punitive, retributive intent by detailing the brutality of typical prison systems. For instance, he quotes U.S. Supreme Court Justice Harry A. Blackmun:

> Various kinds of state-sponsored torture and abuse—of the kind ingeniously designed to cause pain but without a telltale "significant injury"—lashing prisoners with leather straps, whipping them with rubber hoses, beating them with naked fists, shocking them with electric currents, asphyxiating them short of death, intentionally exposing them to undue heat or cold, or forcibly injecting them with psychosis-inducing drugs—techniques, commonly thought to be practiced outside this nation's borders, are hardly unknown within this nation's prisons.[12]

Many of us live in societies where the criminal justice system has taken up the "responsibility" of vengeance on behalf of its citizens. And we are currently seeing pressure from citizens in the U.S., Great Britain, and elsewhere to exact higher penalties for crime. California's new "three-strikes" law, requiring twenty-five years to life imprisonment for anyone convicted of a third felony is a case in point.

When the victims of crimes hand over to the state the right to seek retaliation, however, they also lose the right to forgive and seek healing between themselves and offenders. Weil's ethic of renunciation includes the principle of refusing to harm another when we have been harmed. Is a legal system that allows for such a possibility conceivable? Would the institution of a sys-

---

11. Consedine, *Restorative Justice,* 54.
12. *Hudson vs. McMillian,* 25 February 1992; quoted by Consedine, 65.

tem based on (nonpunitive) restoration and forgiveness not lead to social chaos?

Consedine describes a variety of restorative justice systems, past and present. We summarize two: the early Celtic system in Ireland and a current experiment in reinstituting the legal system of the Maori people of New Zealand in children's courts. Our purpose is to show the possibility of legal systems that at least avoid vengeance, intentional harm to the offender, and even make forgiveness and reconciliation possible.

For over a thousand years, before the imposition of the English penal system in the seventeenth century, the Irish had a restorative justice system. Nearly all crimes could be dealt with by means of a fine, which was paid to the victim or victim's family. Other penalties could be added, such as disqualification from holding public office. There were no prisons and hardly any public officials who could be called police.

For particularly vile crimes or for habitual offences, a criminal could be banished. When the fine for homicide could not be paid or when there were special circumstances, the family of the victim could kill the murderer, but this seems to have been a rare occurrence. In general, the aim of the justice system, encoded in texts going back to the writings of Cormac, King of Ireland from 227–266 C.E., was to avoid retaliation and vengeance.[13]

The current restoration of the Maori system of justice in New Zealand children's courts brings together the offender and the victim, as well as the families or support groups of both parties. The judge and other officials of the state are present to facilitate a process that includes an opportunity for the victim to describe in personal terms the suffering and loss that has been occasioned. The families of both victim and offender also speak of their grief. The offender is given a chance to express regret, which happens in approximately 90 percent of cases. In such cases, the victims often forgive the offender. The penalties agreed upon by the participants are aimed only at making restitution to the victims, not at harming the offender.

This system does not mandate the sort of renunciation of which Weil writes; she would refuse any sort of restitution. It does, however, leave open the possibility of such renunciation:

> Sometimes moving gestures of healing come from the victim side. They waive their right to compensation from an unemployed young offender who cannot afford it. They invite them to their home for dinner a week after the conference. They help to find an unemployed young offender a job, a homeless young person a home. In one amazing case, a female victim

---

13. Consedine, *Restorative Justice,* chap. 10.

who had been robbed by a young offender at the point of a gun had the offender live in her home as part of the agreed plan of action.[14]

Consedine emphasizes that similar practices in traditional Maori culture developed to ensure order and the survival of the society. The aim was to restore right relations among community members. Thus, it cannot be said that such a system shows a lack of concern for social order. We look at issues of comparative effectiveness in chapter 7, section 3, below.

3.2   Renunciation in the Economic Sphere

Following established methods for assessing qualitative features in the social sciences,[15] it is possible to create a scale of attitudes and behavior regarding economic sharing. One extreme represents total selfishness and the other a kenotic attitude toward goods, a renunciation of one's own property for the sake of others.

We suggest four levels for this scale. First we define these levels of sharing, then apply them to the operations of businesses, relative to their employees and to the community. Then we consider the role of governmental policies in encouraging one or the other of these levels of sharing in business practices. Finally, in the next section, we consider application of such a scale to the role of government in economic affairs.

At the lowest level of the scale is a purely self-serving use of goods. The basis of ordinary (purely competitive) views is competitive mono-use of limited resources of unchanging quantity. If one person is using a facility (an automobile, a church hall), then another cannot use it. Because the pie is of a given size, the more I have, the less you get. Therefore, each person must compete with the other for a fair share and usually tries to get more than that fair share. In other words, life is considered as a zero-sum game, with winners and losers. Success here is indicated by how much more you can accumulate than the next person. A popular bumper-sticker in Southern California well illustrates this attitude toward material possessions: "The one who dies with the most toys wins."

The notion of sharing begins to change the nature of the transaction: you aim to share with others, so you can use some resource now, I can use it tonight, and we both get satisfaction. This is the next level in the scale. There is a small cost in utility to each individual (I cannot have it available any time I want) in return for a much reduced cost of the amenity per person and an extended availability of its benefits to a greater number of people. This is the basis of most sporting clubs, for example. There are also other pragmatic

---

14. Ibid., 102.

15. See the discussion of ordinal indicators in J. Drewnowski, *On Measuring and Planning the Quality of Life* (The Hague: Mouton, 1974).

gains: in effect one has a larger resource pool, and so economies of scale come into operation. Thus, cooperative economics gain greater benefits from the same facilities than purely competitive policies and can make more efficient use of consumables, thereby in effect increasing their supply. This has the potential to benefit all. This is of course well-known; there is a widespread cooperative movement throughout the world that operates with varying degrees of success, and it is the key element in many cases of uplifting of the rural poor.[16]

The third level in the scale is when I derive pleasure from seeing you use the resource, even when that use excludes me from its benefits. This is the basis of much family life. For example, parents voluntarily give over resources to their children even when doing so demands a degree of sacrifice on their part, and this gives them joy. Thus, family economics envisages the possibility that even though it may result in a smaller share for some people when sharing consumables, they experience an increase of total welfare.

This pattern is part of the paradox of the kenotic ethic. The result can be even more positive, however: once the sharing ethic is in action, it may well be that the pie to be shared will in fact be larger—partly because others will be willing to contribute resources they otherwise would have kept to themselves, including their labor. The cooperative motivation to work hard (on behalf of all of us) is increased in this case; workers may be motivated to produce more when they see it as beneficial to their community as a whole rather than to some group ("bosses") to whom they have no particular allegiance.

Thus, in these circumstances economic transactions are transformed: they are no longer zero-sum games. In economic behavior, as in other areas, motivation is the key. The economics of sharing may or may not produce more goods, but it certainly has the capacity to increase experienced welfare, provided it is partaken of voluntarily and not as the result of coercion. It is crucial to the survival of the poorest people in society.[17]

The final level in this progression is when I am willing to sacrifice goods or other aspects of my own welfare for others who are not my own kin and whose enjoyment will not contribute directly to my own happiness (indeed, I may not even know them). We see this, for example, among those in various environmental movements who sacrifice some measure of their own standard of living for the sake of the ecosystem and for future generations.

16. See Ibrahima Bakhoum et al., *Banking the Unbankable: Bringing Credit to the Poor* (London: Panos Publications, 1989), for examples from Pakistan, Colombia, Kenya, Sri Lanka, Tanzania, Chile, Indonesia, and India.

17. See detailed examples in M. J. Wilsworth, *Strategies for Survival: Transcending the Culture of Poverty in a Black South African Township* (Grahamstown, South Africa: Institute of Social and Economic Research, Rhodes University, 1980).

3.2.1 Organizations and Businesses

We have been speaking here of individual economic behavior, but the point of this section is to consider social applications of our kenotic ethic. An obvious point of application is in business ethics. We suggest that organizations and businesses can be run at any of these four levels, as regards their employees, other organizations, and the community at large.

Currently a body of literature discusses the role of "values" in shaping business management policies. For example, James O'Toole describes two pairs of competing values: liberty versus equality, and efficiency versus community. He argues that understanding these values and their opposition will both shed light on present debates in economics and also provide a context for charting management strategies. This is a useful move for relating both economic theory and business practice to the level of ethics in the hierarchy of the sciences. However (typical of much modern Western thought), O'Toole does not believe it possible to arbitrate among these values; the corporate executive can only hold them in varying sorts of tension. Discussing the role corporations ought to play in the pursuit of the good society, he says: "In the final analysis, we must each make up our own minds about the nature of the society we wish to live in."[18]

A more nuanced approach to business ethics can be developed using the concepts of *virtue* and *internal goods* as defined by Alasdair MacIntyre.[19] It is helpful to consider businesses as social practices, in MacIntyre's technical sense: a complex form of cooperative human activity through which goods internal to that form of activity are realized in the course of trying to achieve those standards of excellence that are appropriate to and partially definitive of that form of activity.[20] MacIntyre argues that there are certain virtues, such as justice, that are necessary to achieve the goods internal to any practice whatsoever. Francis Fukuyama has recently argued that the virtue of *trust* is essential to all business whatsoever. His argument is in large part empirical, based on careful studies of the correlation between levels of interpersonal trust and business success in a variety of cultural contexts. His argument is also based on pointing out the huge "transaction costs" that become necessary when businesses need to try to protect themselves from all possible forms of dishonesty.[21]

Furthermore, looking at business as practices leads us to inquire about the

18. James O'Toole, *The Executive's Compass: Business and the Good Society* (New York: Oxford University Press, 1993), 20–21.

19. See also Michael Goldberg, ed., *Against the Grain: New Approaches to Professional Ethics* (Valley Forge, Pa.: Trinity Press International, 1993).

20. MacIntyre, *After Virtue,* 187.

21. See Francis Fukuyama, *Trust: The Social Virtues and the Creation of Prosperity* (New York: Free Press, 1995).

goods internal to and partially definitive of business in general or any specific business. If one thinks, for instance, of shoe manufacturing, it is clear that the business could not be what it is without the aim of producing shoes. One of the goods at which all healthy practices aim is an improved understanding of the nature of the (other) goods they seek to realize. Thus, the aims of the shoe business can be further defined by considering the purposes of shoes and deciding, say, between high fashion and affordability as aims for this particular factory. So the production of good shoes is a good intrinsic to and partially definitive of the practice of shoe manufacturing.

A second goal toward which all businesses aim is gainful employment. A business's conception of this good can be extended by considering additional aspects such as job security, safe and pleasant working conditions, mental stimulation and sense of responsibility for the employees. In addition, many businesses now see good community relations as intrinsic to their identity.

An important question to raise, now, is whether profit for shareholders is a good internal to the practice of business, or whether it is merely an external good like the money won by a chess master. We do not wish to enter the capitalism-socialism debate here, which is clearly relevant in that socialism in theory has at its heart the concept of sharing. In practice, however, socialism has often failed to produce the goods required, to a great extent because it has been implemented in a centralized and bureaucratic manner that is in fact incompatible with its proclaimed aims. The debate is complex, because while it is often recognized that a work force operating in cooperative fashion is usually happier and so more productive than one working in a purely self-centered mode, it is also claimed that the individual motivation of the capitalist, profit-oriented system is the key feature to most economic growth and success.

Undoubtedly the profit motive has been a major feature in the financial success of many economies; however, it is certainly mistaken to suggest it has been the only ethic operative in these economies. Rather a whole spectrum of purposes is in action. While some economic theories in fact see profit as the supreme good, with all others a distant second, the consideration of businesses as social practices suggests that this cannot be an adequate account of most business, as our example of shoe manufacture illustrates.

We suggest four levels of business operation analogous to the four levels of economic sharing on the personal level described above. The lowest level is a particularly rapacious form of capitalism, which is based on the assumption that making profit is the supreme good and that all other goods need to be subordinated to it. This understanding of business is derived from a combination of the economics of Adam Smith and the sociopolitical individualism of John Stuart Mill.

The second level we call constrained capitalism, that is, business practice

that seeks first to maximize profit, but within limits set by government regu-
lation, union agreements, and so forth. This is a matter of accommodation to
other demands for the sake of efficiency.

The third level we understand as businesses aiming at their own proper
internal goods: production of valuable goods and services, training and care
of employees, and so on. We also include at this level the phenomena of
corporate philanthropy: the diversion of some part of the profit for community service. The goods at which such corporations aim (both internal and
philanthropic) can be within the general scope of a kenotic ethic, since the
company foregoes profits for itself in order to help others. We should like to
make the point that many companies undertake this kind of activity. As examples in the South African context, the Anglo-American Chairman's Fund
is one of the main donors to charities in the country, while the Douglas
Murray Trust of Murray and Roberts (a major construction company) is also
a significant donor to welfare projects.[22]

Finally, the vast nonprofit sector in many countries is aimed at making
some specific contribution to the welfare of others. In many cases these operations are in fact large businesses. CARE and the YWCA are well-known
international examples. We could also include here business operations that
have been created with the specific purpose of philanthropic activity in general, generating profits to be used for the welfare of others in particular. Two
examples are the Scott Bader Commonwealth, a chemical company based on
Quaker principles, with a specific antiwar constitution. This company uses
its profits for welfare purposes (*inter alia* it has supported the Quaker Peace
Centre in Cape Town). A second example is the van Leer Foundation, which
runs a packaging company created with the specific intention of using its
profits for welfare purposes; it has made a large contribution to preschool
education in South Africa.

Our four levels correlate somewhat with the four values O'Toole describes
as guiding business practices. But whereas he presents the four values as equal
competitors, we see in Figure 6.3 a clear hierarchy of goods.

Our conclusion, then, is that business practices, even within a capitalist
system, can range along a spectrum from the purely predatory to the purely
service-oriented. Nonprofit organizations aimed at the good of others and
living up to their own ideals fall within the scope of kenotic practices; for-
profit organizations can fall into that range as well, depending on the goods
at which they aim.

So it simply is not true that all or even most of society regards personal

---

22. See Myra Alperson, *Foundations for New Democracy: Corporate Social Investment* (Randburg,
South Africa: Ravan Press, 1995), for a profile of twenty companies running innovative programs.

Sharing in Business	Values
• non-profit (kenotic)	community
• business aimed at internal goods/	
philanthropic involvement	equality
• constrained capitalism	efficiency
• rapacious capitalism	liberty

Fig. 6.3. A moral hierarchy of business practices.

profit as the prime economic motive, either personally or for organizations within society. Fukuyama estimates that only 80 percent of economic activity can be accounted for in terms of rational economic self-interest. Culture, including ethical commitments, needs to be taken into account to explain the rest.[23] Nor is it true of society as a whole, which often spends large sums on other projects: the erection of monuments and cathedrals, for example, which defy the laws of economics envisaged in terms of personal profit alone. Kenneth Boulding emphasizes that an economy cannot be adequately understood in terms of exchange: one has to consider voluntary giving (a system based on "love") as well. As he writes, "The one-way transfer, far from being something extraneous or extraordinary in the general organization of social life, is an integral and essential part of the system, without which not only community but organization and society itself would be virtually impossible."[24]

3.2.2 Government Role
The economic priorities of society at large inevitably merge with the political. The same spectrum of aims relative to the scale of kenosis in economics applies to the economic activities of government in two broad areas.

First, the government makes choices that shape the environment in which business operates via legislation, tax policies, and other incentives, which will favor one of the four positions over the others. For example, it may or may not allow tax exemption on donations to charity.

Second, the government sets economic priorities for the country as a whole by its own expenditure patterns; for example, by the extent to which it engages in welfare expenditure (unemployment benefits, health care services, etc.) and takes part in foreign aid programs. Monies allocated to these kinds of tasks are not available for other purposes; if no such expenditures are made, then taxes can be reduced. It can also focus expenditure on non-

23. Fukuyama, Trust, 13.
24. The Economy of Love and Fear: A Preface to Grants Economics (Belmont, Calif.: Wadsworth, 1973), 47.

kenotic activities such as boosting the armaments industry or promoting wars in foreign territories. In either case it is making an ethical statement based on some position in the scale of kenotic positions.

Analyzing aid expenditures and policies cannot be done in too simplistic a manner, however, for at least two reasons. First, promoting welfare organizations and other actions to help the poorest in society can represent simply enlightened self-interest rather than unselfishness, because of the relation between poverty, unemployment, and crime. Second, assistance can be given to those in need in ways that build up their esteem and future capacities, or in ways that undermine them and their motivation. This is a difficult area that requires careful thought and creativity. Nevertheless, it can be said that a range of governmental policies, attitudes, and actions on the scale from the self-serving to the kenotic are important in setting the parameters and shaping the tone of public life.

These choices are important statements regarding public aims, and they illustrate interactions among the economic, political, and legal spheres. They relate as well to the issue of nonviolence, due to the tremendous size of many countries' military expenditures. In 1990, the estimated world expenditure on armaments of $676 billion included an expenditure on armaments of $119 billion by developing countries (and $274 billion by the U.S.), as compared with expenditures by the developing countries of $49 billion on health and $116 billion on education. In the same year the developed countries provided $56 billion of economic aid to the developing countries, and exported $36 billion worth of arms to them.[25]

3.3 Renunciation in the Political Sphere

Although the political sphere will inevitably interact with the economic and legal spheres, nevertheless it is distinct and important enough to need assessment in its own right. One can advance an analysis of levels of kenosis similar to that for the economic sphere. It would involve a scale of attitudes and behavior, characterizing how political organizations relate to their members and the community, and a similar scale for a government's relations to its own citizens and to other states.

The lowest level in this scale would include centralized unilateral decision-making enforced by tyrannical methods, with other groups brought into line by coercive methods. The second level would involve broad democratic methods of majority decision-making, but with the minority having to accept the decision of the majority; and power negotiation in relations to outside

---

25. I.R. Sivard, *World Military and Social Expenditures 1993* (Washington, D.C.: World Priorities, 1993).

groups. The third level would involve participatory democracy, arriving at policy on the basis of general agreement, taking into account minority views in arriving at decisions; electing representatives who act on one's behalf and report back; and using methods of persuasion, negotiation, and accommodation in relation to other groups. The fourth level would involve consensus decision-making within the organization, and true political kenosis in outside relations: opening oneself to the opposition and using methods that have the potential of transforming enemies into friends. These higher levels of political kenosis will be developed in detail below.

3.3.1 Organizations Other than the State
No shortage exists of examples of organizations that work in a despotic manner; also many work in more democratic modes (although one must distinguish carefully between the rhetoric of an organization and the methods it actually uses in its own internal and external workings).

Political organizations can operate in a kenotic manner both with regard to their own internal governance and in relations with outsiders. The Religious Society of Friends (the Quakers) provides an example of kenotic internal relations in its use of the consensus method of governance. This model aims always to take seriously the interests and insights of all members. This involves giving up quick decision-making in order to arrive at true consensus. This form of governance is only possible in relatively small-scale structures; nevertheless one can go a long way toward this ideal in larger organizations.

Kenotic political action toward others has been demonstrated in a profound manner in the protest movements against national or local government led by M. K. Gandhi and by Martin Luther King, Jr.; another example is the work of Danilo Dolci in Sicily. These movements demonstrate both the method and the viability of this kind of operation within the political sphere, and its ability to make real changes occur. They also show the cost involved.[26]

3.3.2 Can Governments Practice Renunciation?
Finally the issue arises as to whether a government can operate in a kenotic fashion, either in relation to its own citizens or in relation to other states. We take up the issue of coercion versus consent in the next section, but we offer some general remarks here.

Clearly at this scale consensus is impracticable: a country must have a leader who can act with decisiveness. Nevertheless, as regards its own citizens

---

26. See, for example, James M. Washington, ed., *A Testament of Hope: The Essential Writings of Martin Luther King, Jr.* (San Francisco: Harper and Row, 1986); and Dennis Dalton, *Mahatma Gandhi: Nonviolent Power in Action* (New York: Columbia University Press, 1993).

and organizations in the state apart from the government, some general kenotic principles can be applied: the government can hand over some of its powers to others in order that they can take part in running the state and ordering
their own lives. Two major considerations apply. The first is organizational,
where the key issue is decentralization of powers as far as possible, without
losing overall coherence. This can be done effectively by appropriate organizational design of government structures, with modern technology able to
play a role in making this a reality.[27] This is one of the main reasons for
widespread calls for federal principles to be incorporated in the new South
African Constitution. Current moves in the U.S. to return power to the
states, however, may well result in loss of hard-won federal protections for
the poor and for minorities. Obviously, the issues are too complex to be dealt
with in any sort of adequate way here.

The second issue is attitudinal: the determination on the part of those in
power to run the state in an inclusive manner, moving toward consensus as
far as possible by whatever means are available. The key is that the ruling
party make quite clear by all it does that it is taking into account the concerns
raised by minorities and altering its plans as far as possible to accommodate
them. In such a case, those in power are using power for the benefit of society
as a whole rather than to pursue their own ends; they in fact are giving up
possible self-aggrandizement in favor of common good.

We cite two examples showing that this too is a practicable option: kenotic
methods can be employed and can have a transforming effect, creating a
different quality of government. The examples are the State of Pennsylvania
at the time of its founding,[28] and the role of Nelson Mandela in the recent
South African political transition. The latter example will be developed later
in this chapter.

Relations with other states can again be considered in terms of a scale of
qualities, but now in the context of international politics. The issue is the
degree to which national sovereignty and power are defended and extended
at a cost to others, or are limited and altered in order that other countries
may also flourish and the international order be more stable and peaceful.

Three particular issues arise; the first is foundational to the others. It is the
degree of tolerance and exclusivity: the definition of "us" and "them," insid-
ers versus outsiders. To what degree can the national spirit accept and tolerate
people of other nationalities and ethnic origins? The political foundation of
many wars is the enemy image: they are different from us; they are against

27. See Stafford Beer, *Brain of the Firm*, 2nd ed. (Chichester, U.K.: John Wiley and Sons, 1981);
and *idem, Platform for Change* (London: Wiley, 1978), for penetrating analyses.

28. See Peter Brock, *Pioneers of the Peaceable Kingdom* (Princeton, N.J.: Princeton University
Press, 1968).

us. The opposite is the broader vision that all people are human and have needs, we are all part of one human family, we can work to help them just as we work to help our own people and our own family. Unscrupulous politicians build their power base on exclusive community identity that eventually leads to strife and war; the kenotic politician works on an inclusive basis, a spirit of acceptance and accommodation that lessens conflict and builds common cause. It recognizes the humanity and needs of the outsider as well as the insider and is willing to give to and work for the welfare of the outsider.

The second, related, issue is the degree and nature of support of international bodies, such as the League of Nations and United Nations, that work for international peace and welfare. This priority will naturally follow from the first. It involves a degree of renunciation of national power in favor of such international bodies.[29]

The third issue is the degree of aggression or cooperation and consensus in international relations, and hence the issue of militarism and pacifism: the willingness or not to use military power and methods to achieve national goals. The latter issue is so central to our thesis that we devote the following section to it.

We have offered here only the barest sketch of how the ethic we advocate would look in the political sphere. Even though we are not able to develop or support our contentions, we believe that merely listing some of the possibilities is valuable, since a common objection to an ethic of self-renunciation is that it could never be completely enacted. Our goal is simply to note that there is a vast range of options, political and economic, and that one usually has the option to move some distance in one direction or the other along such a scale or range. The claim that the extreme kenotic end of the scale is unattainable cannot be used as a reason for wholesale rejection of the ethic.

3.4 Nonviolence as Renunciation

We are attempting here to describe a way of life in which one renounces what one holds dear for a higher purpose. The result is often that one nonetheless receives what one has sacrificed and something of incomparably greater worth as well. A central instance of this pattern of renunciation is the practice of nonviolence. Here one renounces one's legitimate right to self-defense for the sake of the freedom and moral worth of the attacker. In the best cases, one achieves one's objectives in the end, and wins reconciliation

---

29. See James Wm. McClendon, Jr., *Biography as Theology: How Life Stories Can Remake Today's Theology*, rev. ed. (Philadelphia, Pa.: Trinity Press International, 1990), for a biography of Dag Hammarskjold, which aptly illustrates both the value of kenotic behavior on the part of public officials and the role of international organizations.

with a former enemy as well. Simone Weil believed that nonviolence was a consequence of self-renunciation, and the role of this specific practice will become clearer as we see that nonviolence requires for its flourishing exactly the personal characteristics (virtues) that constitute an ethic of renunciation.

Because of the role institutions play in enabling practices, an account of the practice of nonviolence will call for a correlative account of the nature of noncoercive institutions and of the changes required to make them a reality. Our entire account stands or falls on whether the development and maintenance of noncoercive institutions are possible.

The practices of nonviolence have become familiar since Gandhi's nonviolent campaign for Indian independence and the civil rights movement in the United States, of which Martin Luther King, Jr.'s nonviolent campaign was an important part. The extensive literature on the topic of nonviolence informs our description of both the phenomena themselves and some of the theory that has grown up to guide and describe the practice.

In speaking of nonviolence it is helpful to distinguish two concepts: nonviolent resistance or "nonresistance," on the one hand, and nonviolent direct action, on the other. "Nonresistance" and "nonviolent resistance" refer to the policy of refraining from retaliation when attacked, and they often include the avoidance of all forms of self-defense. While "nonresistance" is a traditional name for this policy, especially among Christians—this sort of response to attack is often taken to be in accordance with Jesus' command to turn the other cheek, not to return evil for evil—"nonviolent resistance" is probably the better term, since it highlights the fact that we are not dealing here with mere acquiescence, mere passivity, but rather with an act aimed at stopping the abuse or attack and at changing the total situation.

"Nonviolent direct action" refers to planned campaigns aimed to right a wrong, to protect the innocent, to interfere with objectionable processes, using one or more of a variety of nonviolent means. Nonresistance and nonviolent action are often related, in that the objective of a nonviolent direct-action campaign is often to bring the participants into conflict with the opposing forces in such a way as to create the opportunity for the use of nonviolent resistance. It is at this level of organization that we have a full-fledged practice, in MacIntyre's sense. Planning, organizing, and executing a nonviolent direct-action campaign is certainly a complex social activity. The development of a body of literature and of specialists in organizing such campaigns has given the practice international coherence.

To appreciate the goods internal to this form of social activity, it is necessary to look at the theory of nonviolence. The aim of nonviolence, as stated above, is to correct injustice, to protect innocent people, or to interfere with or stop morally objectionable processes. Of course, the goods that *characterize* nonviolence have to do with the means employed—the rejection of any violent tactics.

The rationale for the practice of nonviolence can be considered under two headings: negative and positive. On the negative side, reasons for choosing nonviolence as a strategy have to do with the likely effects of the alternative: a violent response. When violence is met by violence, the violent response retrospectively justifies the original attack. First, it establishes the legitimacy or appropriateness of the resort to violence in general and, second, it adds self-defense as a motive and justification. Consequently, the level of violence escalates—the counter-attack feeds the aggressor's fear, anger, and sense of moral justification. Nonviolence breaks this cycle or prevents it from starting. Richard Gregg describes it as moral jiu-jitsu: it throws the attacker off guard and creates feelings in conflict with the aggressive drive: first, surprise, then sympathy and respect for the one who has been attacked. While the initial effect of the act of nonresistance may be to bring out a greater degree of sadism on the part of the attacker, the conflicting motives created by patient suffering often eventually bring the violence to an end.

The suffering of the nonviolent resister is not incidental to the process; rather, it is a crucial ingredient, since it serves to alter the balance of motives and sympathies on the part of the attacker (and also of bystanders).

The positive reasons for nonviolence have to do with a sense of the moral worth and moral capacities of the attacker. The refusal to resort to violence even when attacked is intended to convey respect for the adversary. It is also expected to be the best way to touch a hardened heart. The goal is to allow the best of the attacker's motives to come to the fore in the hope of reconciliation. Gregg puts it this way:

> As to the outcome of a struggle waged by non-violence, we must understand one point thoroughly. The aim of the non-violent resister is not to injure, or to crush and humiliate his opponent, or to "break his will," as in a violent fight. The aim is to convert the opponent, to change his understanding and his sense of values so that he will join whole-heartedly with the resister in seeking a settlement truly amicable and truly satisfying to both sides. The non-violent resister seeks a solution under which both parties can have complete self-respect and mutual respect, a settlement that will implement the new desires and full energies of both parties. The non-violent resister seeks to help the violent attacker to re-establish his moral balance on a level higher and more secure than that from which he first launched his violent attack. The function of the non-violent type of resistance is not to harm the opponent nor impose a solution against his will,

but to help both parties into a more secure, creative, happy, and truthful re-lationship.[30]

A Quaker rationale for nonviolence goes beyond respect for the humanity of the attacker; it is based on the concept of "that of God in every man," to which the Christian in the presence of evil is called to make an appeal. This approach is presumed, in the long run, to be the most likely to reach the "inward witness" and so "change the evil mind into the right mind."[31]

So the *internal* good at which the practice of nonviolence aims, and which distinguishes it from other justice-seeking practices, is the moral betterment of both oneself and the opponent. And this quest for moral improvement has as its heart the presumption that the solution of interpersonal or social prob-lems requires voluntary cooperation on the part of the opponent. It aims to bring it about that both parties in the conflict seek one another's good as well as their own. If achieved, this will bring about extremely desirable *external* goods as well—remarkably improved general behavior and social climate. This will not always occur. Part of the internal good (moral betterment of the opponent) is extremely difficult to attain and may not often happen. But part of the internal good is definitely attainable and indeed is virtually auto-matic if the practice is carried out faithfully: namely, moral betterment of oneself. In this sense, one cannot lose by adopting this path, for by its very nature it is an admirable route to follow.

Notice the close correspondence between the acquired characteristics (vir-tues) required for the practice of nonviolent direct action and the characteris-tics Weil includes as constitutive of an ethic of renunciation: Participants in nonviolent campaigns need to have developed the willingness to forego the harm to others that would restore their own sense of importance, to renounce their rights (their "imaginary royalty"), to forgive debts. Participants also need to be willing to renounce legitimate desires for life's goods, for example, to accept the financial loss or deprivation entailed by a strike or boycott. Nonviolence requires a willingness to suffer—to suffer on behalf of others—since nonviolence is often met with violence, even with sadism. Finally, it sometimes requires the sacrifice of one's very life.

In addition, we would add that nonviolence requires cultivation of imagi-nation and ingenuity: the ability to imagine peaceful solutions to intractable social problems and the ingenuity to find creative ways to bring about those solutions.

It is important to emphasize that while nonviolence can be used as a mere

---

30. *The Power of Nonviolence,* 2nd, revised ed. (New York: Schocken Books, 1969), 51.
31. *Christian Faith and Practice in the Experience of the Society of Friends* (London: London Yearly Meeting of the Society of Friends, 1960), no. 606.

technique, our goal here is to describe a way of life. The virtues required for the practice of nonviolence must be developed over a lifetime, they must fit into a coherent life-story. Furthermore, nonviolence as a way of life must go beyond the mere avoidance of violence. It must be motivated by a deep respect for the freedom, integrity, and moral worth of all people—however different they may be racially, ethnically, socially—including especially one's enemies. In short, it is the habitual embodiment of the attitude of self-sacrifice for the sake of the other, in the belief or hope that such self-giving can transform the situation, bringing about moral changes that cannot be attained by other means. Yet even this social transformation is not the ultimate good toward which the practice aims. The hard core of our program states that to become this sort of person, to develop this moral character, is not merely a means to an end, but is the central goal of human life.

4 ETHICS AND EPISTEMOLOGY

We end this chapter with a brief excursus on the relation between self-renunciation and the pursuit of knowledge. It has become common since the writings of Karl Marx to argue that certain social locations provide privileged epistemological positions. Liberation theologians of various sorts argue that the oppressed (whether blacks, women, or the poor) have greater insight into the kingdom of God.

In this and a variety of ways, the discipline of ethics is coming to be seen as logically prior to epistemology. Some of the most powerful arguments come from the Nietzschean tradition. Friedrich Nietzsche himself, along with such followers as Michel Foucault and various deconstructionists, argue that knowledge does not so much represent "reality" as it does the interests of the social groups or individuals who have the power to impose their will on others.

While we reject this as a general account of knowledge, we believe it would be naive to suppose that knowledge is not subject to the taint of powerful self-interest. The epistemological consequence that follows from this hermeneutic of suspicion, therefore, is that self-renunciation is not only the key to ethics—to orthopraxis; it is also the key to knowledge—to orthodoxy. Renunciation of the will to power is a prerequisite for seeking the truth.[32]

---

32. At a more prosaic level, one can argue simply that learning requires a willingness to give up what one holds dear, whether this be self-aggrandizing views of reality or simply pet scientific theories. The literature on teaching science contains many reports that confirm the utility of a kenotic approach in underpinning the ability to learn. See, for example, Lillian McDermott, "What We Teach and What Is Learned: Closing the Gap," *American Journal of Physics* 59 (1991): 301–15.

5 CONCLUSION

In this chapter we have described some social arrangements—legal, economic, political—that are consistent with our kenotic ethic. We have concentrated on social consequences because the common objection to an ethic of self-renunciation is that it is only practicable for the few heroic individuals and cannot conceivably be embodied in society as a whole. We hope to have begun to counter this charge; in the next chapter we pursue the counterargument in more detail.

Chapter Seven

Reconfiguration of Social Science in Light of Ethics

I EMPIRICAL CONSEQUENCES OF A KENOTIC ETHIC

We have argued that ethics, conceived as the science of the ultimate good for humankind, has implications for the social sciences. This is for two reasons: First, the application of a moral conception of the good in particular circumstances will require some empirical information about the nature of those circumstances and some judgments about means-end relations, which are amenable to testing via social-scientific and psychological research. But, second, a social-ethics program is the normative side of a thesis about human sociality whose descriptive side is social-scientific. Each of the claims about how people ought to organize their social life is an implicit claim that such arrangements are both possible and conducive to the good life. So an ethic as a whole can be refuted if it can be shown that it calls for a form of life that is simply incapable of social embodiment.

In the preceding chapter (secs. 3.1 through 3.4) we spelled out some of the implications of our ethic for economic, legal, and political arrangements: legal systems ought to be aimed at restoration rather than retribution; economic behavior ought to involve sacrifice for the welfare of others; governments ought to incorporate the marginalized and seek peace with their neighbors; and, finally, all social change ought to be brought about nonviolently. All of these ethical prescriptions entail social-scientific theses to the effect that such states of affairs are possible, along with empirically testable theses regarding means of bringing them about.

Notice that a radical consequence of our treatment of ethics is that the distinction between pure and applied social science disappears. Sociology was originally conceived as the science of social transformation; but in the late modern pluralist West, values and ultimate goals came to be seen as beyond the ken of science. Thus, pure social science must be value-free; applied social science could study means of achieving social ends, but determining those ends was not within its competence.

Yet with an answer to the question of what is the (objective, true) end of human existence, sociology (and its fellow social sciences) can become again the scientific study of the means of social transformation, proposing hypotheses regarding subsidiary ends and effective methods of achieving them and then testing them empirically through the design of social programs. What are currently defined as the "value-free" human sciences (sociology, anthropology, etc.) will be considered in this scheme as the "pure" theoretical side of the discipline proper—a legitimate but restricted part of the fully conceived social sciences. It will be recognized that they can provide helpful and indeed vital studies of the ways things work when values are (for the moment) discounted; but this partial view is simply unable to look at many of the most important issues that the human sciences should address. Alasdair MacIntyre claims that a crucial practice for any society is an ongoing, structured debate that seeks progressive clarification of the concept of the good at which the society aims.[1] This is politics in Aristotle's sense. We envision social sciences engaging in this practice.

In the following sections we sample the sorts of social-scientific analyses that comport with the ethical program we advocate. In effect, we aim to begin replacing what John Milbank calls the "heretical" ethico-theological assumptions of modern social science with assumptions in line with our kenotic ethic.[2] Along the way, we mention some data and anecdotal information that show these claims to be plausible. We concentrate especially on the topic of nonviolence, since we suspect that this will be the most controversial of our proposals. A brief preview of this argument will illustrate the *general* form of our arguments: The core of a kenotic ethic entails the proscription of violence. Thus, nonviolent social structures and social change must be possible. Current sociology and political theory, however, assume that violent

---

1. Alasdair MacIntyre, *After Virtue*, 2nd ed. (Notre Dame, Ind.: University of Notre Dame Press, 1984); and *idem, Whose Justice? Which Rationality?* (Notre Dame, Ind.: University of Notre Dame Press, 1988). See above, chap. 5, sec. 3.

2. John Milbank, *Theology and Social Theory* (Cambridge: Basil Blackwell, 1990). See above, chap. 5, sec. 5.1.

coercion is necessary to preserve social order. We indicate why this assumption is or may be mistaken and provide some positive evidence for the possibility of a society based on nonviolence. The data provide direct confirmation of the social-scientific analyses and *indirect* confirmation for the ethical research program, in that they counter a significant rebuttal to our claims.

Our analyses will of necessity be sketchy in many cases and the data pitifully few. In fact, we do not tread at all in the contested area of empirical support for economic or political theories. Our hope, however, is that these suggestions might in fact lead to the sorts of research needed for adequate confirmation of our theses.

2 CONFIRMATION IN THE INTERPERSONAL SPHERE

The ethic sketched in the preceding chapter has a great deal to say regarding interpersonal relations and, while we have chosen to focus instead on higher levels of social organization, we believe that confirmation for the ethic could be found at this level. We briefly sketch the sort of analysis and empirical research that would be relevant here. The ethic of renunciation proscribes all attempts to coerce or dominate others in interpersonal relations. This entails two sorts of empirical claims: (1) that noncoercive and nondomineering personal relations are an essential aspect of *the good* for human life—that is, they contribute to happiness, success, ultimate effectiveness; and (2) that noncoercive, nondomineering personal relations are possible. Since it is obvious that *some* noncoercive relations are possible, the interesting question is whether and how the sphere of noncoercion, nonviolence, and cooperation can be widened.

A wealth of popular literature in psychology and management suggests that, in fact, successful interpersonal relations *depend on* an openness to the other person and a willingness that each one involved not dominate the interaction.[3] A growing body of research of a more serious academic nature addresses such topics as attitude change, prejudice and attribution, competition and aggression and the effects both of observing violence and of acting violently. All of these studies are relevant to the question whether and how noncoercive, cooperative interpersonal relations can replace aggression, coercion, and domination.[4] All such research on the causes and cures of aggression, prejudice, and violence indirectly supports our ethical thesis in that it

3. See, for example, Anthony Storr, *The Integrity of the Personality* (London: Penguin, 1960); T. Gordon, *P.E.T.: Parent Effectiveness Training* (New York: Plume Books, 1975); R. Fisher and W. Ury, *Getting to Yes: Negotiating Agreement without Giving In* (London: Business Books, 1981).

4. A fine collection of reports on relevant research is found in Elliot Aronson, ed., *Readings about the Social Animal,* 7th ed. (New York: W. H. Freeman, 1995).

rebuts claims that violence is an ineradicable aspect of human nature and therefore not subject to moral sanction.

3 CONFIRMATION IN THE LEGAL SPHERE

We distinguished above (in sec. 3.1 of chap. 6) between two sorts of criminal legal systems—retributive and restorative—and claimed that a restorative system accords with an ethic of renunciation, first, in that it avoids retaliation against the offender and, second, in that some such systems leave open the possibility for victims of crime to renounce even reparation for the wrongs they have suffered—a truly kenotic gesture. The question was raised there whether such a system would preserve public order. If such a system were shown to lead to social chaos, it would count as strong evidence against our claim that restorative systems are more moral than retributive ones. So the burden of this section is to provide some evidence for the workability of restorative systems, thus providing indirect confirmation of our ethical program. Again, we turn to the research compiled by Jim Consedine.

Consedine argues strenuously for the *inefficiency* of retributive penal systems. The ostensible purposes of a retributive system are deterrence and reform. Consedine emphasizes ways in which the prison experience increases offenders' tendencies to commit repeat offenses: (1) Association with other criminals offers opportunities to learn about criminal activities and even to plan crimes for after release. (2) Humiliation and brutality in prison cause anger and resentment, which may be acted out after release. The clear racial inequalities built into many penal systems are especially prone to generate resentment. (3) Former prisoners tend to have a higher rate of homelessness and unemployment after release and thus greater incentives to commit future crimes. The statistical links between unemployment and crime are clear. (5) Punitive prison systems fail to address conditions that increase the likelihood of criminal behavior, such as drug and alcohol addiction, illiteracy, and mental illness.[5]

Consedine presents some data showing a *negative correlation* between tougher sentencing and reform. Here are a few of the numbers he reports:

> In the period 1985–92 incidents of violent crime [in New Zealand] rose by 41 percent, despite a nearly two-thirds increase in the length of prison terms for such offences. Statistics in New Zealand also revealed a 3 percent decrease in overall crime figures in the year ended 30 June 1994. Many

---

5. Jim Consedine, *Restorative Justice: Healing the Effects of Crime* (Lyttelton, N.Z.: Ploughshares Publications, 1995).

areas of criminal offending—traffic, fraud, burglaries, thefts—showed a marked drop in offending rates. The two areas where offending rose substantially against this national trend, violent crime and drug offending, were the two areas where penalties had increased most in the previous 10 years. The rationale behind increasing the penalties at the time was one of deterrence.[6]

The United States imprisons at a rate of 520 per 100,000, four times that of New Zealand, which has the second highest rate; five times that of Britain; sixteen times that of Ireland. Yet a young American man is twenty times more likely to be murdered than an Englishman or a Dane.[7]

Despite the political popularity of the notion that more and harder prison time makes the streets safer, there seems to be a great deal of evidence against this assumption. For the success of the reinstituted Maori system in children's court in New Zealand, the results are as follows: Only 10 percent of youthful offenders go through the regular court system, down from 30 percent. Of the cases handled through the restorative system, 90 percent reach agreements. The rate of youth offenses has dropped from 64 per 1000 to 16 per 1000. The number of prosecutions of defendants aged 17–19 has dropped by 27 percent between 1987 and 1992.[8]

This is fairly clear evidence for the effectiveness of a system for juveniles in one particular culture. However, one could reasonably question whether such a system would work for hardened adult criminals. Research is needed, but at least one could predict that fewer juvenile offenders would become hardened criminals if all societies used a system like that of the Maoris.

In addition, one can argue for the effectiveness of restorative systems simply by pointing out that they seem to have worked for centuries in a variety of cultures: at least 1400 years in Ireland, 40,000 years among Australian Aborigines, unknown centuries among various Polynesian peoples.

Much more research is needed here, but so far there is adequate information to suggest the effectiveness of restorative systems for maintaining public order, and enough information to call into serious question the retributive systems in the U.S., Britain, and elsewhere.

4 NONVIOLENCE AND SOCIAL SCIENCE

While effectiveness is not the criterion by which to evaluate the ethic of renunciation or one of its more striking practices, it is certainly the case that

6. Ibid., 36.
7. Ibid., 69, 67.
8. Ibid., chap. 7.

were the practice of nonviolence totally unworkable, it would count strongly against its moral rightness. That is, while we reject utilitarianism as an adequate theory of ethics, an ethic that consistently leads to the lesser good is surely suspect. Thus, it is necessary to pay attention to the effectiveness of nonviolence in attaining its external goals: to resist evil, stop aggression, fight injustice, and so forth.

In fact, the most damaging arguments against the ethical research program we advocate are not that renunciation at the personal level is immoral, or even that the practice of nonviolence would not be a good thing if it were possible. Rather, it is argued, a society that attempted to institutionalize nonviolence would be unworkable. Nonviolence may be a technique peculiarly suited to individuals and groups outside of the sphere of legitimate power, it is argued; so Jesus could teach nonresistance to his little band of followers. When Christianity became the religion of the empire, however, it needed to legitimate coercion, corporal punishment, and war.

So the question that must be addressed is: is it possible for social and political structures themselves to be nonviolent, or is nonviolence a way of life suited only for individuals or groups outside the mainstream of society? Notice that this is an empirical (social-scientific) question, not one restricted to moral philosophy or ethics as ordinarily understood.

Our treatment of this question involves first examining the opposing programs; second, considering issues that relate to the cogency of the theoretical analyses on both sides; and finally (in the following section) surfacing a variety of empirically testable hypotheses germane to the social sciences and to psychology.

4.1 Competing Socio-Ethical Programs

A variety of thinkers in both sociology and ethics have argued that noncoercive social institutions are not possible, and that violence is simply the ultimate form of coercion. This is then taken to justify the use of violence (even if its use is regarded as distasteful). We reported in chapter 5, section 2.1.2, the views of Max Weber, Reinhold Niebuhr, and Peter Berger on the social necessity of violence. By contrast, we here summarize the views on nonviolence of Richard Gregg and Mahatma Gandhi. Considering these examples enables us to focus more clearly on the issues at stake. In response to Niebuhr, Richard Gregg argues that:

> The statement that human collectives are less moral than the individuals which compose them is a highly doubtful generalization. The ability of a human collective to behave morally depends on such factors as the extent and duration of its organization, the structure of the organization, its size

and the sizes of any component subgroups in it, the interrelationships of the subgroups and the kind of integration among them, the kind of discipline (if any) to which the members have been subject, the duration of that discipline, the clarity of the ideas of the group and the extent of their permeation among the members, the extent and clarity of understanding of the group's purposes among its members, the loftiness of the common ideal, the simplicity or complexity of their general purpose, the quality of leadership, and the moral character of the environment. With so many variables as these, the broad generalization of the immorality of all human collectives is not valid. It disregards too much pertinent evidence. It does not square with the results of a wealth of patient and careful biological experiments and observations.[9]

James W. Douglass reports on Gandhi's rejection of views, such as Weber's, that distinguish sharply between moral ends and immoral but necessary means. Gandhi claimed that "we are merely the instruments of the Almighty Will and are therefore often ignorant of what helps us forward and what acts as an impediment. We must thus rest satisfied with a knowledge only of the means, and if these are pure, we can fearlessly leave the end to take care of itself."[10] According to Douglass, "Gandhi's political ethic made the end of peace realizable by the end's presence in the means themselves. Nevertheless, although Gandhi prosecuted these non-violent means relentlessly, he left the precise character of their ends up to God."[11]

Gandhi often compromised with adversaries at points short of the victory desired by his followers because he believed that reconciliation between adversaries was more important than winning reluctantly granted concessions. "His constant aim therefore was to appeal by suffering love to the humanity of the opponent and to gain not a particular end but the fullness of humanity," says Douglass.[12] Similar points are made by Martin Luther King, Jr., whose careful analysis drew heavily on the thought of Gandhi, as well as by many others in the pacifist tradition.[13]

Gandhi's account of the ultimate goal of political action—raising both sides of the dispute to a higher level of humanity—is to be contrasted with Reinhold Niebuhr's. Niebuhr wrote that "justice rather than unselfishness [is

9. *The Power of Nonviolence*, 2nd revised ed. (Canton, Maine: Greanleaf Books, 1960), 118.

10. M. K. Gandhi, *Satyagraha in South Africa* (Ahmedabad, India: Navajivan Publishing House, 1928), 318; quoted by Douglass, *The Non-Violent Cross: A Theology of Revolution and Peace* (Toronto: Macmillan, 1966), 264.

11. Douglass, *Non-Violent Cross*, 265.

12. Ibid, 265.

13. See, e.g., Stanley Hauerwas, *The Peaceable Kingdom* (Notre Dame, Ind.: University of Notre Dame Press, 1983); John Howard Yoder, *The Politics of Jesus*, 2nd, enlarged ed. (Grand Rapids, Mich.: Eerdmans, 1994).

society's] highest moral ideal,[14] and this realistic social ethic needs to be contrasted with the ethics of religious idealism:

> Society must strive for justice even if it is forced to use means, such as self-assertion, resistance, coercion and perhaps resentment, which cannot gain the moral sanction of the most sensitive moral spirit. The individual must strive to realize his life by losing and finding himself in something greater than himself. These two moral perspectives are not mutually exclusive and the contradiction between them is not absolute. But neither are they easily harmonized.[15]

4.2 The Issues at Stake

This brief discussion of opposing views makes it apparent that three kinds of issues are at stake here. One is the purely empirical issue regarding the psychological, social, and political effects of the use of violent versus nonviolent means. There is evidence on both sides, and this issue cannot be settled without more systematic study. We discuss this further below.

A second kind of issue regards the soundness of the theoretical reasoning involved in each position.

The third kind of issue is theological or metaphysical. We repeat the point made earlier: Ethics (now pertaining to social entities rather than merely to individuals) makes its claims in light of a central vision of the highest good for humankind. For Niebuhr it is justice; for Gandhi it is acting as agents of the Almighty Will to bring about growth of humanity. We claim that the highest good for humankind is self-renunciation, and that an important corollary is that an essential aspect of the good for social groups is to participate in the intellectual and practical pursuit of noncoercive social structures.

This corollary follows from our hard core, along with an analysis of the practices that develop and exercise self-renunciation (e.g., nonviolence) and of the social-institutional setting that makes nonviolence a "practical" practice. (Note that in addition to core theories there are other theological assumptions involved in the positions we have surveyed: Gandhi's thesis makes use of a view about the nature of divine action. Both Weber's and Niebuhr's positions make theological assumptions about the nature of salvation—that it is otherworldly or essentially "beyond history." Niebuhr's pessimism regarding the possibilities of transcending human egoism is also a theological stance—an update of the Augustinian view of fallen human nature, as opposed to that of more perfectionist strands in the Christian tradition.)

If it is not possible to judge rationally among the metaphysical-theological

14. *Moral Man and Immoral Society* (New York: Charles Scribner's Sons, 1932), 258.
15. Ibid., 257.

theories that constitute the cores of these contrasting programs in social ethics, then the modern emotivist assumption about ethics turns out to be true: in the end, moral claims are nothing but statements of personal preference.

In the remainder of this section we hope to contribute to the evaluation of these two sorts of programs, which we shall refer to as realist versus noncoercive. In the next subsection, we provide a few refinements in sociological analysis that help our case. In the following subsections we take up issues of empirical confirmation. This takes us some of the way toward the empirical confirmation of our ethical research program. Our broader goal, however, which can only be met by means of the entire volume, is to provide a cumulative argument for a theology different from Niebuhr's—one leading ultimately to a more positive prognosis for human society than Niebuhr's "realism." This is taken up in the next chapter.

4.3 Refinements in Social Analysis
Our goal in this section is to further the critique of Christian realism by considering two factors that we believe have not been given adequate attention so far: The first is top-down causation. The second is the distinction between levels of persuasion and coercion, considering the probable differences among the effects to be attained by the use of the broad range of means of persuasion and coercion. We go on to present an alternative view of social interaction, which we refer to as kenosis and consent. Finally, we summarize the conclusions reached here in the form of a proposed thesis.

4.3.1 Top-Down Causation
Niebuhr, at least by the time he wrote *The Nature and Destiny of Man*,[16] had a good sense of what we have called "top-down causation" as it pertained to the relation between the higher levels of psychology (self-consciousness, or his preferred terms, "spirit" or "self-transcendence") and the biological level. In his criticism of the romantic conception of human nature he wrote that:

> romanticism errs. . . . in interpreting the vitality of man, of which it constitutes itself the champion. Its error consists not so much in reducing that vitality to bio-mechanical propositions as bourgeois naturalism tends to do. Its basic error lies in the effort to ascribe to the realm of the biological and the organic what is clearly a compound of nature and spirit, of biological impulse and rational and spiritual freedom. Man is never a simple two-layer affair who can be understood from the standpoint of the bottom layer, should efforts to understand him from the standpoint of the top layer fail.

16. *The Nature and Destiny of Man*, 2 vols. (New York: Charles Scribner's Sons, 1943).

If rationalism tends to depreciate the significance, power, inherent order and unity of biological impulse, romanticism tends to appreciate these without recognizing that human nature knows no animal impulse in its pure form. Every biological fact and every animal impulse, however obvious its relation to the world below man, is altered because of its incorporation into the human psyche.[17]

Thus, it is surprising that Niebuhr's earlier argument for the necessity of coercion in social life trades entirely (it seems to us) on a bottom-up view of causation, from the individual to the social level. There Niebuhr treats social realities as mere collections of individuals, such that the capacities and limitations of social groups can be calculated by considering the interplay of a few variables pertaining to the individual level. Individual behavior is the result of a variety of impulses, more or less directed and controlled by reason. One impulse is benevolence, whose reach and strength are largely dependent on face-to-face encounters with its potential objects, as well as on the opposite impulses to egoism or self-assertion. Reason tempers impulse both by calculating the consequences of actions, and also by attempting to impose order on benevolence and egoism in the form of justice, here understood as simple equality.

Social groups cannot be as moral (as unselfish) as individuals, Niebuhr believed, because "the proportion of reason to impulse becomes increasingly negative when we proceed from the life of individuals to that of social groups, among whom a common mind and purpose is always more or less inchoate and transitory and who depend therefore upon a common impulse to bind them together."[18] So group reason and group impulse are being treated simply as sums of individual characteristics. Contradictory impulses within the group cancel one another out; similar impulses reinforce one another. Similarly, the rational elements reinforce or cancel one another. The further assumption that leads to the pessimistic conclusion regarding group morality seems to be that groups always or usually exhibit more similarity among their impulses than among ideas; hence reason is weakened by the summation, while impulse is strengthened.

More generally, Niebuhr's neglect of top-down causation (social to individual) allows him to argue from a fixed account of human nature to sociological conclusions without taking into account the possibility that "human nature" is itself affected by the social environment in which it develops. If top-down causation is a real possibility, then one must ask not only: What are the limitations that human nature as we now know it places on social

17. *Nature and Destiny,* 39–40.
18. Ibid., 35.

morality? but also, What are the possibilities for development of human nature, given changes in social context?

Top-down causation refers to the effects on lower-level entities of entities or structures at higher levels that cannot themselves be analyzed solely in terms of their lower-level constituents. The question that needs to be asked, then, is: what causal effect will the practice of nonviolence have over time on individuals' capacities to cooperate in social institutions without violence or the threat of violence? Recall that the theory of nonviolence involves the thesis that nonviolent resistance to evil changes the character of all of the individuals involved, making them more amenable to persuasion and cooperation.

Thus, we can formulate a first approximation of a hypothesis about the top-down effects of nonviolent practices as follows: *a consistent policy of using the least coercive means possible in each social situation will affect the character of the individuals involved such that less coercion will be needed in future resolution of conflict.*

Notice that this thesis depends on there being meaningful differences among the various forms of coercion. Therefore, it is to the topic of levels of coercion that we now turn.

4.3.2 Levels of Persuasion and Coercion

The functioning of any society is based on the fragile structures that maintain social order and coherence of action. Inevitably some forces will try to destroy it: in any population a fraction of malcontents will resist any order at all. Furthermore, various interest groups will place their own good above those of the rest of the society, and will be prepared to destroy the social structure—or at least those parts of it that are to the benefit of those they see as their "enemies"—in order to attain their goals. Thus, there is reason to assume that an element of coercion is required in order that society not be destroyed by the disruptive forces within it.

Realists tend to emphasize this requirement for sanctions to obtain the consent of the population and, furthermore, to emphasize the similarities among forms of coercion. Peter Berger classifies the kinds of social control as follows:

violence
political and legal controls with the threat of violence as a last resort
economic pressure
persuasion via ridicule, gossip, and opprobrium
systematic opprobrium and ostracism.[19]

19. *Invitation to Sociology* (New York: Doubleday, 1963), 69–73.

Berger claims that this last form of social control is "the most devastating means of punishment at the disposal of a human community."[20] His example is an Amish community shunning a member who has become sexually involved with an outsider. We find this a startling claim. Perhaps Berger's reasoning is based on the supposition that shunning effectively excludes the victim from all human society, and what could be more devastating than exclusion from the human race?

Berger's example, however, belies this line of reasoning: shunning is merely the exclusion of an individual, who has already taken up alternative social relations, from one specific social group. So when Berger says, "It is hard to imagine a more cruel punishment," and quips that "such are the wonders of pacifism," perhaps he merely suffers from lack of imagination—an imagination found in ample supply among the persecutors of pacifists, as the following account of the "punishment" of sixteenth-century Anabaptist leader Michael Sattler illustrates:

> When the judges returned to the room the verdict was read, as follows: "In the matter of the prosecutor of the imperial majesty versus Michael Sattler, it has been found that Michael Sattler should be given into the hands of the hangman, who shall lead him to the square and cut off his tongue, then chain him to a wagon, there tear his body twice with red hot tongs, and again when he is brought before the gate, five more times." When this is done to be burned to powder as a heretic.[21]

If realists tend to downplay the differences among types of coercion and persuasion, theorists of nonviolence are more interested in the differences. William Robert Miller reproduces several valuable classificatory schemes. One is that of Clarence Marsh Case, who distinguishes persuasion, nonviolent coercion, and violent coercion in as Figure 7.1.[22] C. J. Cadoux has diagrammed a much more elaborate spectrum of actions designed to bring about social cooperation (Figure 7.2, page 154).[23] Miller notes that even this scheme could be further elaborated. Note the ingenuity of Sattler's judges in combining all four of Cadoux's most extreme measures.

A common assumption about the relationship between coercion and cooperation is that as coerciveness increases, so does effectiveness in attaining cooperation. Thus, if Cadoux's scale is properly ordered, we should expect a relationship as in Figure 7.3, on page 155.

20. Ibid., 73.

21. John Howard Yoder, ed., *The Legacy of Michael Sattler* (Scottdale, Pa.: Herald Press, 1973), 74–75.

22. In William Robert Miller, *Nonviolence: A Christian Interpretation* (New York: Schocken Books, 1964), 60.

23. In ibid., 59.

PERSUASION
1. By argument.
2. By suffering:
   a) nonresistant martyrdom when suffering is inflicted by the opponent;
   b) self-inflicted, e.g., a hunger strike.

NONVIOLENT COERCION
1. Indirect action: strike, boycott, noncooperation (withdrawal from voluntary cooperation with opponent).
2. Political action through institutions and culture—combining partisan persuasion and impersonal coercion of law and established traditions. This involves the threat or use of force or "legitimated violence" by police, courts and prisons.
3. Social coercion:
   a) ostracism,
   b) collective pressure through passive resistance.

VIOLENT COERCION
1. Threat of violence or force.
2. Use of violence or force.

Fig. 7.1. Clarence Marsh Case's classification of types of persuasion and coercion.

The theory of nonviolence explained above, however, suggests an alternative relation. The negative effects of violence on one's opponent (moral justification for the original attack, sustenance of the energy for combat) and the positive effects of nonviolence (raising the social interaction to a higher moral level) suggest that, in general, the less the violence the more effective will be a social interaction *in the long run*. Thus, we suggest the relation in Figure 7.4, on page 155.

Several arguments can be presented for this expected relationship. First, coercive measures can only succeed if there is a broad consent of the population concerned; if the social order is imposed against the population's will, a widespread negative reaction is possible that can destroy it. Consider, for example, the popular action in South Africa, which quite literally succeeded in making the country ungovernable. The reason is that police forces cannot be everywhere all the time; in fact they can have only a spasmodic presence. One can see this, for example, in jails: guards can function effectively only if the majority of prisoners accept the given order. When such is not the case, riots occur that destroy their ability to function. Similarly, effective functioning of the economic base of the state through payment of taxes depends on the majority of citizens accepting—even if grudgingly—that they should indeed do so. If almost all citizens resist taxation, the state will be in a parlous situation; it will be close to breakdown. Thus, at least a modicum of consent

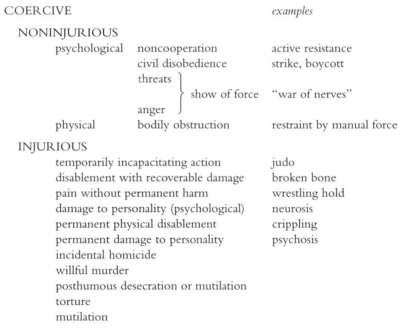

NONCOERCIVE
    personal example
    intercessory prayer
    conciliatory discussion
    direct acts of love
    nonresistance
    unmerited suffering
    self-imposed penance
    arguments and appeals
    mediation
    arbitration
    promises
    rewards
    bribes

COERCIVE   *examples*

  NONINJURIOUS

psychological	noncooperation	active resistance
	civil disobedience	strike, boycott
	threats ⎱ show of force	"war of nerves"
	anger ⎰	
physical	bodily obstruction	restraint by manual force

  INJURIOUS

temporarily incapacitating action	judo
disablement with recoverable damage	broken bone
pain without permanent harm	wrestling hold
damage to personality (psychological)	neurosis
permanent physical disablement	crippling
permanent damage to personality	psychosis
incidental homicide	
willful murder	
posthumous desecration or mutilation	
torture	
mutilation	

Fig. 7.2. C. J. Cadoux's classification of types of persuasion and coercion.

is required of the citizens for the state to function; they must to some degree accept the offered social contract.

So the more coercion that is required, the less effectively the state will function. This is so not only because the citizens will cease to perform as desired by the authorities the moment they are not under surveillance, but also because surveillance and the other apparatus of coercion are very expensive; in a society dominated by discord they absorb a disproportionate amount

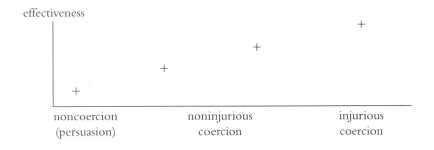

Fig. 7.3. *The "punitive" view of the effectiveness of coercion.*

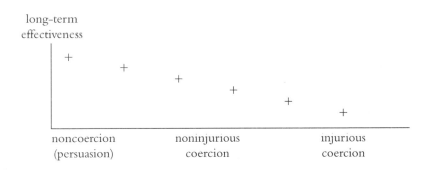

Fig. 7.4. *The "persuasive" view of the effectiveness of coercion.*

of the society's wealth. While there may be a great deal of energy and wealth, very little of it will be usable (cf. the discussion of entropy in chapter 3). Niebuhr himself makes similar arguments:

> If the purpose of a social policy is morally and rationally approved, the choice of means in fulfilling the purpose raises pragmatic issues. . . . Conflict and coercion are manifestly such dangerous instruments. They are so fruitful of the very evils from which society must be saved that an intelligent society will not countenance their indiscriminate use. If reason is to make coercion a tool of the moral ideal it must not only enlist it in the service of the highest causes but it must choose those types of coercion which are most compatible with, and least dangerous to, the rational and moral forces of society. Moral reason must learn how to make coercion its ally without running the risk of a Pyrrhic victory in which the ally exploits and negates the triumph.[24]

24. *Moral Man*, 238.

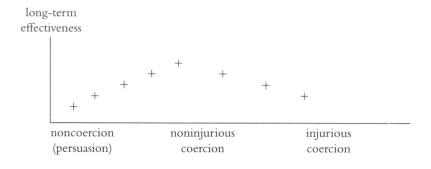

Fig. 7.5. The "mixed view" of the effectiveness of persuasion and coercion.

Speaking of the similarities and differences between violent and nonviolent coercion, Niebuhr observes:

> Non-violent coercion and resistance, in short, is a type of coercion which offers the largest opportunities for a harmonious relationship with the moral and rational factors in social life. It does not destroy the process of a moral and rational adjustment of interest to interest completely during the course of resistance. Resistance to self-assertion easily makes self-assertion more stubborn, and conflict arouses dormant passions which completely obscure the real issues of conflict. Non-violence reduces these dangers to a minimum. It preserves moral, rational and co-operative attitudes within an area of conflict and thus augments the moral forces without destroying them. . . . The technique of nonviolence will, if persisted in. . . . with the same patience and discipline attained by Mr. Gandhi and his followers, achieve a degree of justice which neither pure moral suasion nor violence could gain.[25]

So while Niebuhr does not share our confidence in noncoercive persuasive techniques, he does emphasize the greater ultimate effectiveness of nonviolent coercion, based on arguments similar to the ones we have sketched. He might graph the relations as in Figure 7.5.

4.3.3 Kenosis and Consent

The dynamics of coercion, persuasion, and cooperation are actually more complicated than can be represented by a simple function relating degree of coercion to level of cooperation.

Four elements in Cadoux's list of persuasive techniques—direct acts of love, nonresistance, unmerited suffering, and self-imposed penance—are, in

25. Ibid., 250–51, 254.

a sense, off the scale in terms of their effects. While Cadoux's list suggests that on a scale moving from pure persuasion toward nonviolent coercion, nonresistance falls between conciliatory discussion and argument in its persuasive power, we believe that in terms of effectiveness the scale needs to be amended such that it goes from acts that represent a deliberate sacrificing of self, through noncoercive persuasion, noninjurious coercion, to injurious coercion. We need a term for this end of the scale, and shall employ the same term as for our system of ethics: "kenosis." We noted in chapter 5 that this is a theological term; it was originally used to describe the pre-existent Christ's self-renunciation of divine prerogatives in taking on human nature. However, we shall use it (in chap. 8) especially in connection with Jesus' acquiescence in his crucifixion.

The factor that distinguishes the kenotic category of actions from other noncoercive forms of persuasion is the issue of suffering and of sacrificing oneself for the sake of the other. It includes but is not limited to Gandhi's *ahimsa,* which can be translated as "self-suffering." Notice how this particular form of nonviolent action follows from the core of our program, which focuses on self-renunciation. This is in contrast to uses of nonviolent means for self-serving purposes.

Some theorists of nonviolence believe it is important to distinguish this kind of nonviolent action from the others because of the change it aims to produce in the opponent. Gene Sharp distinguishes three forms or levels of consent resulting from nonviolent action: conversion, accommodation, and nonviolent coercion. "Conversion" means that:

> the opponent, as a result of the actions of the nonviolent person or group, comes around to a new point of view which embraces the ends of the nonviolent actor. This change may be influenced by reason, argumentation and other intellectual efforts. It is doubtful, however, that conversion will be produced solely by intellectual effort. Conversion is more likely to involve the opponent's emotions, beliefs, attitudes and moral system.[26]

"Accommodation" means that:

> the opponent does not agree with the changes (he has not been converted), and he could continue the struggle (he has not been nonviolently coerced), but nevertheless he has concluded that it is best to grant some or all of the demands. He may see the issues as not so important after all, the actionists as not as bad as he had thought, or he may expect to lose more by continuing the struggle than by conceding gracefully.[27]

26. *The Politics of Nonviolent Action* (Boston: Porter Sargent, 1973), 707.
27. Ibid., 706.

"Nonviolent coercion" means that:

> the opponent has not changed his mind on the issues and wants to continue
> the struggle, but is unable to do so; the sources of his power and means of
> control have been taken away from him without the use of violence. This
> may have been done by the nonviolent group or by opposition and nonco-
> operation among his own group (as, mutiny of his troops), or some combi-
> nation of these.[28]

This distinction among kinds of consent makes it possible to state the renun-
ciative position more precisely, and in such a way as to avoid the charge made
by realists such as Niebuhr that nonviolent action is just as much coercion as
violent action and that there is therefore no moral difference between
them—only a pragmatic difference.[29]

Recall our earlier claim that long-term top-down causation needs to be
considered, along with differences among kinds of persuasion and coercion,
in order to predict whether noncoercive social institutions are possible. In
particular, it is necessary to take into account the possibility for character
development in both the nonviolent actors and their opponents, and the
differences such changes might make in possibilities for future social cooperation. Thus, the focus for a social program of nonviolence based on renunciation will be kenotic actions aimed at character change on both sides, including especially conversion of the opponent.

As Sharp explains the rationale for self-suffering, suffering acts as a "shock
treatment" to shatter indifference. The initial reaction is often hatred, so such
campaigns need to be planned for the long term. After a time, however,
sympathy for and identification with the nonviolent actors may be aroused.
A variety of factors have been identified that influence the outcome of a self-
suffering campaign, which will be described below.

The term "conversion" is a useful one here, not because of its religious
connotations, but because it suggests a positive and long-lasting change in the
opponent—a change in character. Sharp mentions changes in perception and
understanding, sometimes involving a change in worldview, and changes in
feelings and attitudes. Self-suffering tends to counteract character defects such
as cruelty, self-interest, and stereotypes.

Richard Gregg understands the effects of kenosis, both self-suffering and
loving actions, in terms of biological models. First, our evolutionary history
is such that the sight of suffering causes an involuntary sympathetic response
in the nervous system of the beholder.[30] Second, he emphasizes the possibility

28. Ibid.
29. Niebuhr, *Moral Man, 238*.
30. Gregg, *The Power of Nonviolence, 53*.

of a small force, often repeated, to produce major changes in systems that are both complex and delicately balanced. In particular, biological systems respond differently to stimuli of different strengths: a weak stimulus produces a weak monophasic response; a medium stimulus produces a stronger effect at the beginning, followed by reversal; a strong stimulus causes an intense effect followed by non-reversible injury. The combination of loving-kindness and nonviolent resistance, he claims, is a weak force that produces an enduring process of growth:

> Thus the believer in nonviolence is convinced that, because the potentiality for good exists in every living person, the potentiality itself is living, [it] is therefore subject to the law of stimulus and response, and hence is capable of growth until, compared with the harmful living factors in any given person, it becomes as strong, or even stronger. This, I think, is what Jesus meant when he told his disciples to forgive seventy times seven—repeating many, many times the gentle stimulus to unity implied in forgiveness.[31]

Gregg's estimates of the effects of repeated "stimuli" of different kinds for producing character change can be represented as in Figures 7.6, 7.7, and 7.8, as shown on the following page.

This leads us to express the relations among forms of social pressure and kinds of responses as in Figure 7.9.

4.3.4 The Thesis Proposed

We have looked at aspects of what might be considered two competing sociopolitical research programs: Niebuhrian realism and our own program based on self-renunciation. Niebuhr's program depends on arguments to the effect that the need for coercion (perhaps even violent coercion) follows from incontestable facts about social groups. Niebuhr's arguments, if correct, undercut our program by showing a priori that no society built on such principles can survive. We, however, proposed additional factors that we believe lead to a more positive view of the possibilities for noncoercive social institutions. Our thesis, in brief, is as follows:

> *A variety of means exist for bringing about social cooperation; the consistent policy of using the lowest degree of coercion needed to be effective will have a cumulative effect, increasing the effectiveness of less coercive means in the long run. Furthermore, the practice of nonviolence, now further specified to focus on what we term kenotic actions, is a social practice aimed at a radical change in the moral character of the participants—a shock treatment to reverse the direction of a deteriorating social situation.*

31. Ibid., 117.

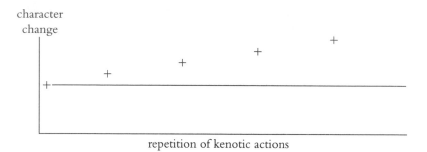

Fig. 7.6. *Effect of kenotic actions on character.*

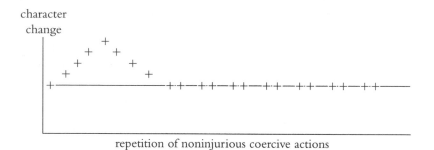

Fig. 7.7. *Effect of noninjurious coercive actions on character.*

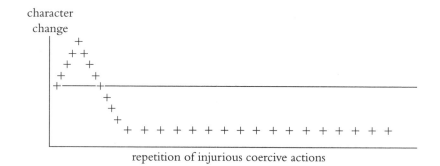

Fig. 7.8. *Effect of injurious coercive actions on character.*

In the process of arguing to this conclusion we have used not only a more elaborate conceptual analysis (top-down causation and more careful distinctions among forms of social sanctions). We have also introduced a variety of hypotheses regarding psychological and sociological effects of various forms of social interaction. The question can now be raised whether these are merely ad hoc hypotheses added to make our case, or whether they are gen-

type of action	kenosis	persuasion	noninjurious coercion	injurious coercion
direction of character change	↑			↓
type of consent	conversion	accommodation	coercion	coercion

Fig. 7.9. Type of character change and consent associated with various forms of action.

erally true. Thus, it is time to move from theoretical analysis to the question of empirical testability.

4.4 The Effectiveness of Nonviolence

A simple, if crude, sort of test of our ethic would be to ask, simply, does nonviolence work? Proponents of nonviolence have collected a vast number of accounts of effective uses of a variety of nonviolent techniques. They have certainly shown that nonviolence works some of the time. We mentioned Gandhi's and King's campaigns. It is often said that they succeeded only because of the high moral development of their opponents. Yet the rich literature documenting effective nonviolent campaigns includes a variety of successes against the Nazis.[32] There are, of course, many instances of failure to be recorded also. In *Moral Man and Immoral Society,* Niebuhr mentioned two groups whose nonviolent movements failed miserably: socialists in Italy during the rise of fascism and Tolstoy's disciples in czarist Russia. Since there is evidence on both sides, this kind of scorekeeping is not especially meaningful. More structured research is needed now, not only to collect instances, but also to begin isolating factors that can be shown empirically to contribute to positive and negative outcomes.

Most of the instances of the use of nonviolence so far have been episodic: people coming together for a specific campaign with limited objectives. So an important ingredient in the assessment of an ethic involving nonviolence would be to study communities that are committed to nonviolence as a way of life. Two such communities are the sixteenth-century Anabaptists (along with their contemporary heirs, the Mennonites, Amish, and Brethren), and the Society of Friends (Quakers).

---

32. Gene Sharp's *Politics of Nonviolent Action* is a 900-page volume including descriptions of 198 types of action, with a number of historical examples of each. See also Mulford Q. Sibley, *The Quiet Battle: Writings on the Theory and Practice of Non-Violent Resistance* (Boston: Beacon Press, 1963); William Robert Miller, *Nonviolence: A Christian Interpretation* (New York: Schocken Books, 1966); Douglas Johnston and Cynthia Sampson, eds., *Religion: The Missing Dimension of Statecraft* (New York: Oxford University Press, 1994).

One of the seven distinctives around which the Anabaptist movement organized itself (after several disastrous attempts by fringe groups at violent revolution) was rejection of "the sword." In particular, this meant the refusal of military service and of any government jobs that involved the administration of capital punishment. The origin of this view (in addition to their reading of the New Testament) was the judgment that coerced religious conformity was of no value. To use terms from our previous discussion, conversion mattered; accommodation and coercion were valueless in the eyes of God. But if the sword was not to be used by Christians to compel assent in this most important of issues, neither should it be used for lesser ends.

The Anabaptists took Jesus' admonition recorded in Matthew 18:15ff. as guidance for ultimate community discipline: If repeated attempts to persuade the offender fail, then "let him be to you as a Gentile and a tax collector" (Matt 18:17). This was the source of the practice of the ban, the exclusion of the offender from the religious community.

If physical survival is the test of success for such a community, the Anabaptists did not fare well. It has been estimated that more Anabaptists were put to death by the state churches during the Reformation than the total number of martyrs in the first three hundred years of Christian history. But if adoption of one's teachings is a criterion, it is important to notice that none of the Christian bodies today advocate corporal punishment, much less the death penalty, for religious nonconformity.

Studies of the general quality of life for dedicated members of groups such as the Quakers and Mennonites would be enlightening. How do these subcommunities fare in psychological health, effective social institutions, and so forth, as compared with typical inhabitants of our Western societies, which by all accounts are becoming increasingly more violent?

This latter question suggests a third mode of evaluation. Any assessment of the effectiveness of nonviolence must surely look at the consequences of the alternative—of a violent response. We live in a world torn by strife. As we write, roughly one out of every 114 persons on the face of the globe is a refugee; most of them have been displaced by war or war-related famine.[33] Conflicts rage in Rwanda, Bosnia, Afghanistan, Azerbaijan, Somalia, Angola, Mozambique, Sudan, Tadjikistan, Sri Lanka, India, Iraq, Israel, Northern Ireland, and elsewhere. When one inquires into the reasons for the conflict, in the former Yugoslavia, for instance, a major component of the explanation often turns out to be the surfacing of long-standing resentment of former injustices, even atrocities. Violence and other hate crimes beget more of the same. How do such cycles come to an end? Early empires attempted to end them by exterminating one of the people-groups involved—killing them,

---

33. *New York Times,* August 8, 1994.

selling them into slavery, outlawing their language, razing their cities, sowing salt in their fields.

Perhaps in some instances this strategy has worked, but in the main it seems to have been surprisingly ineffective in halting cycles of hate and violence.[34] Thus, nonviolent practices do not need to show a very impressive record to pass a utilitarian test.

Our judgment, however, is that while much of value can be learned from pursuing the global sorts of questions raised in this subsection, there is too much room for the researchers' attitudes to affect their conclusions. Thus, it is more helpful to investigate smaller-scale hypotheses that form a part of our socio-ethical research program.

4.5 Confirmation of Specific Auxiliary Hypotheses

Recall that in the course of defending a priori a key auxiliary hypothesis of our program—the moral rightness of the practice of nonviolence—we resorted to a conceptual elaboration that involved distinguishing among different kinds of nonviolent behavior and different kinds of consent, and that the workability of some kinds of noncoercive social interaction was predicated on lower-level hypotheses regarding psychological mechanisms and responses, laws of social behavior, and likely outcomes. In general these hypotheses are readily testable. Several examples of such testable hypotheses are the following:

Courageous suffering changes subjects' attitudes toward the sufferer in the direction of greater respect.

Consistent avoidance of signs of hostility reduces the opponent's level of fear.

Reduced fear increases one's reasoning ability and susceptibility to persuasion.

Of special interest here is the question, under what circumstances does kenotic behavior affect the conversion of the opponent? Theorists such as Gandhi and Gregg who emphasize this form of nonviolence have provided a substantial list of factors that affect the outcome of such actions, all of which are empirically testable. Sharp lists these factors under two headings: external factors pertaining to the context in which the action takes place, and internal factors under the actionists' control:[35]

---

34. L. F. Richardson, for example, has collected data showing that, contrary to the view that arms build-ups deter aggression, they actually make war more likely. See Quincy Wright and C. C. Lienau, eds., *Statistics of Deadly Quarrels* (Pittsburgh and Chicago: Quadrangle Presses, 1942).

35. Sharp, *Politics of Nonviolent Action*, 726–30.

External factors

1. The degree of conflict of interest. If the issues at stake are of great importance to the opponent, conversion will be more difficult.
2. Social distance—the degree to which the opponents see the sufferers as members of the moral order rather than outsiders, traitors to the moral order, inferiors, or even nonhuman. Having established the role of social distance, one can then study the factors that are hypothesized to decrease social distance: working to alleviate fear, prolonged contact between the two groups, actions on the part of the sufferers to remove traits in themselves that are seen as undesirable. One of the most important tools for reducing social distance is thought to be the courage with which the nonviolent actors face suffering.[36]
3. The personality structure of the opponent. Some types of personalities are more resistant to conversion than others.[37]
4. Beliefs and norms. If the opponents and actionists share a belief system, conversion is more likely.
5. The role of third parties. Whether the opponents care about the responses of third parties, and how these third parties respond, will influence the outcome.

Internal factors

6. Refraining from violence and hostility.
7. Attempting to gain the opponent's trust by truthfulness, openness concerning intentions, personal appearance and manners, chivalry (meaning consideration for the opponent, such as calling off actions on the opponent's holy days).
8. Refraining from humiliating the opponent.
9. Making visible sacrifices for one's cause.
10. Carrying on constructive work.
11. Maintaining personal contact with the opponent.
12. Demonstrating trust of the opponent.
13. Developing empathy, good will, and patience toward the opponent.

In addition to these psychological and sociological hypotheses, Gregg has suggested that measurable biological effects are involved in the use of nonvio-

36. This suggests that nonviolent campaigns by Germany's own "Aryans" against the Nazis would have been much more effective than such action by Jews. The way had been prepared for "the final solution" by an intense propaganda campaign aimed at dehumanizing the Jews.

37. Efficient totalitarian organizations place unsympathetic characters on the front lines. Efficient response requires both aiming the campaign at the less "thuggish" organizers but also mounting patient and often fruitless attempts to improve the moral character of the thugs on the front lines.

lence: physiological reactions to the sight of suffering, for instance. G. Simon Harek has proposed a broader thesis, that all virtues, being habitual responses of an embodied agent, are realized in changes at the biological level.[38] If it can be shown that altered behavioral and affective responses are encoded physiologically, it would add dramatic confirmation to the claim that character change (as opposed to mere episodic changes in response) is a real possibility.

Thus, our ethical hard core has been shown to yield testable hypotheses that fall mainly within the levels of sociology and psychology, but conceivably within the level of biology as well. Therefore, we believe we can say at this point that we have attained one goal of this chapter, namely, to show that a program in ethics is subject to empirical confirmation and, insofar as it is, it deserves to be counted a science.

Furthermore, while we do not have a great deal of such confirmation in hand, we believe we can claim that the empirical hypotheses we have surfaced in the course of our discussion have some a priori plausibility, as well as some degree of anecdotal evidence to support them. Thus, we claim to have provided some weak support for the content of this specific ethical program as well, which was the second goal of this chapter.

5 SOCIAL CHANGE

We have argued for the possibility of the social embodiment of our kenotic ethic, and much of our argument depends on the feasibility of massive social changes. For example, we recognize that police in U.S. cities cannot simply trade their weapons for night sticks, but rather that the whole character of American society needs to change.

The question of the possibility of genuine social change is a vexing one. In light of Charles Darwin's theories, the West saw a phase of optimism regarding moral progress in history, but changed its collective mind after the two World Wars. As we have indicated above, theories on this subject are heavily influenced by theology. When the kingdom of God was identified by nineteenth-century liberal Protestants with human progress in history, their optimism seemed backed by divine authority. But then the neo-orthodox reaction removed the kingdom of God to beyond history.

In addition to these disagreements over eschatology, discussions of nature and grace play a role. Our arguments for the possibility of social planning leading to more peaceful societies, and our emphasis on virtue, will appear Pelagian to some. Let us simply state here that in our view, every positive change in human history is both an act of God (whether understood in terms of grace or the action of the Holy Spirit) and an event amenable to social-

---

38. *Virtuous Passions: The Formation of Christian Character* (New York: Paulist Press, 1993).

scientific investigation. This is an implication of our placing theology in the hierarchy of the sciences: theology and science provide descriptions of the same reality from different levels of analysis.

Although we discuss the role of the church in social change in the following chapter, we certainly cannot settle the issues. Here we present one case study, involving massive and rather sudden social change, and argue that the kenotic behavior of one man was a crucial factor in making the change possible.

5.1 A Case Study: South Africa

The recent dramatic political changes in South Africa, often described as a miracle, are an example of change that could not have taken place without a significant kenotic element in the political action.[39]

The elements of white supremacy were firmly in place long before the National Party came into power in 1948 and created the apartheid philosophy as its official ideology.[40]

The African resistance movement in South Africa started off peaceably, a classic example being Albert Luthuli, a president of the African National Congress (ANC), who consistently maintained a policy of nonviolence and cooperation between white and black despite harassment, banning, and various arrests. His autobiography reproduces a statement, issued jointly by the, ANC and Natal Indian Congress in November 1953, after his dismissal as chief because of opposition to government policy, in which he defended his nonviolent passive resistance. It concludes with the statement: "The Road to Freedom is via the Cross."[41] (He was awarded the Nobel Peace Prize in 1961.)

This peaceful approach was met with iron resistance by the Afrikaner government, so eventually the main black opposition decided they had no alternative but violence in order to attain their freedom. Explains Nelson Mandela, "For 50 years the ANC had treated non-violence as a core principle, beyond question or debate. Henceforth the ANC would be a different kind of organization. We were embarking on a new and more dangerous path, a path of organized violence, the results of which we did not and could not know."[42] Similarly the Pan-Africanist Congress (PAC) adopted a military strategy after the Sharpeville massacre.

---

39. The broad sweep of these events is described in Alastair Sparks, *Tomorrow Is Another Country* (Sandton, South Africa: Struik, 1995).

40. See Leo Marquard, *The Peoples and Policies of South Africa* (Oxford: Oxford University Press, 1962); M. Wilson and L. Thompson, eds., *The Oxford History of South Africa*, 2 vols. (Oxford: Oxford University Press, 1971).

41. *Let My People Go* (London: Fontana, 1970), 210.

42. Nelson Mandela, *Long Walk to Freedom* (Randburg, South Africa: McDonald Purnell, 1994), 261.

The military wing of the ANC was Umkhonto we Sizwe ("Spear of the Nation"). It undertook limited military action that was, frankly, not very threatening to the South African state; however, the state reaction was overwhelmingly militaristic and destructive in its nature, aiming at a total militarization of South African society.[43] The government was apparently operating on the broad principle of ten eyes for an eye and fifty teeth for a tooth. It won support from the white electorate by a propaganda campaign propagating the idea of "total onslaught" on South Africa by the communist menace.

Together with the systematic exclusion of blacks from mainstream economic life and their displacement and resettlement through the Group Areas Act, the harassment accompanying the military response generated massive black resistance to the government and all its policies. The ANC was forced to operate mainly from abroad, with military camps in neighboring countries; consequently the South African Defense Force (SADF) initiated massive reprisals against those countries, both through covert destabilization operations and through blatant invasion.[44] The border war waged by the SADF in South West Africa started to take a significant toll in South African lives but failed to stop the attainment of independence by that country, then renamed Namibia.

While this was going on, an active peaceful protest movement was waged inside the country by various liberal organizations, which, one after the other, were banned by the government and then replaced by new ones. The Communist Party and Liberal Party were banned, but the Progressive Party remained actively committed to a reversal of government policies and had the support of a significant part of the electorate. It used the parliamentary machinery with skill to make the government reveal many of its hidden activities. The Black Sash, a remarkable group of committed white women, vigorously protested government policy and provided support to blacks through advice offices. The End Conscription Campaign was formed to campaign against conscription of young white men into the armed forces, which were increasingly being used to back up the police suppression of the population at large. They were supported by liberal newspapers, which were constantly under government fire, and by various lawyers' groups, which also published evidence about torture in prison and deaths in detentions. The opposition churches formed the Christian Institute, which was banned, followed by the

43. K. W. Grundy, *The Militarization of South African Politics* (Oxford: Oxford University Press, 1988); J. Cock and L. Nathan, eds., *War and Society: The Militarization of South Africa* (Cape Town: David Philip, 1989).

44. See P. Johnson and D. Martin, eds., *Destructive Engagement: Southern Africa at War* (Harare: Zimbabwe Publishing House, 1986), and *Frontline South Africa: Destructive Engagement* (New York: Four Walls Eight Windows, 1988); J. Hanlon, *Beggar Your Neighbours: Apartheid Power in South Africa* (London: Catholic Institute for International Relations, 1988).

South African Council of Churches, which formed a major base for nonviolent resistance through the apartheid years, as did the four white liberal universities.

The spirit of this peaceful movement against the forces of apartheid was particularly captured in the person of Bishop Desmond Tutu, who courageously stood for black aspirations and also for reconciliation of white and black. The award of the Nobel Peace Prize to him in 1984 was richly deserved.

The real forces that would undermine the government, however, were the combined sport and economic boycotts of South Africa from overseas, the latter hitting the South African economy hard—this coupled with internal pressure from the increasingly restive black and colored youth. Violent resistance to use of Afrikaans as a language of instruction in black schools escalated into a campaign to make the country ungovernable, which together with the declining economic situation, some bomb attacks within the country, and increasing troop losses on the border, started to make the white majority seek some way toward peace. It became increasingly clear to the government that its attempts to withhold some form of power from the black majority could not be maintained undiluted without the quality of life of whites in the country declining disastrously.

The government, therefore, had to turn to Nelson Mandela, leader of the banned ANC, who had been imprisoned on Robben Island and then in Pollsmoor Prison for twenty-seven years. Mandela had developed a reputation for reconciliatory actions while on Robben Island, acting to heal rifts between the various liberation movements and also acting without rancor toward his jailers. He was released and negotiations commenced.

The motivation of President F. W. de Klerk in initiating the transition are not fully clear. One view is that this was an amazing kenotic action, the first recorded time in modern political history when a dominant government negotiated itself peacefully out of power in order that the greater good could triumph. Indeed, the event is remarkable in terms of what happened, and de Klerk certainly showed great courage in pursuing policies for the greater good of the country that led to this transition.

An alternative view of de Klerk's motives is that when he initiated negotiations, he thought he could control them by various means so that a full transition would not take place. Rather the Afrikaner Volk ("the people") would manage largely to maintain control of what was happening, as they had done in the "independent" states of Transkei, Ciskei, and Bophutatswana. The transition would be apparent but not real.

This question is yet to be clarified. Even if not truly kenotic—a possibility, but regrettably probably not the real story—de Klerk's move was courageous and ultimately emerged as a more or less voluntary giving up of power, an act with kenotic elements, even if not fully intended.

The key point is that in the negotiations that led to a change of government, Mandela firmly and consistently took an inclusive stance, at all times trying to accommodate all factions in the country, including those who had treated his followers most cruelly. Thus, in order to promote a peaceful accommodation, he was willing to work with all and to accommodate in the government of National Unity all parties with a significant following in the country. In contrast, "the PAC was a reluctant negotiator and peacemaker, continuing with war talk even as the war ended, and never succeeded in presenting an alternative vision to the ANC's policy of reconciliation and compromise."[45] Consequently, it fared dismally in the elections, as against the massive support obtained by the ANC.

As talks leading to the transition of power continued, a determined and ruthless segment of the right wing initiated an internal destabilization campaign in an attempt to disrupt the negotiations. It instigated massacres of blacks on trains and in taxi stands, and spread mayhem through black townships by training and arming Zulu warriors and supporting them in murderous township rampages. After one particularly outrageous attack, Mandela withdrew from the talks, returning only when steps had been taken to curb this destabilizing activity.

In fact, the campaign continued right to the end of the election period, and was ended only by two events. First, a right-wing foray into Bophutatswana in an attempt to bolster the local black dictator came unstuck after the raiders went on a rampage, killing local blacks; two of them were in turn killed by black troops in a public way (the killing was televised and broadcast over and over), resulting in the sudden realization that these stormtroopers were not invulnerable and were as likely to be killed as to kill. Second, a government-appointed inquiry finally identified some police generals as responsible for the destabilization campaign in a much publicized report, so that the government had to fire them in order to retain any credibility. It must be said, however, that the government did so only at the last minute and under great pressure; indeed, it never appeared as if they were in any great hurry to identify those behind this campaign (this is the reason that President de Klerk's motivation has to be considered as debatable).

The truly remarkable feature, then, is that Mandela continued his path of inclusivity and peace despite all this, and even included in his Government of National Unity and cabinet some of those who were either actively in-

---

45. Anton Harber and Barbara Ludman, eds., *Weekly Mail and Guardian A-Z of South African Politics* (London: Penguin, 1995), 271.

volved in this campaign, or at least did not stop it when they had the power to do so. It is this political magnanimity that transformed the situation, so that at his remarkable inauguration at the Union Buildings in Pretoria the nation became one; and the right-wing Afrikaner resistance, which had threatened to submerge the country in a blood-bath, evaporated away. The true nature of Mandela's magnanimity became apparent to even his most bitter opponents. It completely took the wind out of the sails of the propaganda campaign against him and the ANC that had underpinned right-wing resistance.

The kind of imaginative, conciliatory step that has made this possible was later demonstrated when Mandela invited to a tea party political widows from all parties. So he had at the same function black women whose husbands had been murdered by the security forces or had died in detention, together with white widows of previous Nationalist politicians who had vowed that black politicians would never run the country—and had been in power when the police were killing prisoners in detention and sending out hit squads to kill black opposition leaders. Thus, he was exercising restorative politics, in the same spirit as the restorative justice described in a previous section.

Thus, the South African political miracle of a largely peaceful transfer to power (15,000 people—most black—were killed in the course of the destabilization activities in the country; but there was no civil war, as in Algeria, Bosnia, Rwanda, Nigeria) was possible because of the reconciliatory and magnanimous way Nelson Mandela handled it. By opening up his government to previous enemies and giving up retribution in favor of restoration, he led an exercise in nation-building that has succeeded to an astonishing degree. One can claim that this was a demonstration of the transformative nature of kenotic methods in action.

5.2 Initiating and Sustaining Kenotic Action

We believe such case histories show that kenotic action is indeed possible and practicable in the real world. The final point we wish to make is that there are two different aspects to this: initiating kenotic action and sustaining it.

Initiation of kenotic action is not easy, but the steps are relatively clear. One has somehow to propagate an inspirational message that can build up commitment to the proposed course of action; this involves setting agreed goals and also agreed methods that are compatible with each other, and both of a kenotic nature. By the very nature of what is intended one can only use methods of persuasion—some disastrous situations have been caused by people intent on a kenotic type of program who for one reason or another have tried to propagate it by coercive methods. This method simply cannot work, because it negates what one is trying to achieve. Having attained consensus on the proposed action, one needs detailed and realistic planning, and then initiation of the action. Many examples are at hand, such as in the campaigns by Mahatma Gandhi and Martin Luther King, Jr.

The much more difficult part is maintaining kenotic action. One can generate enthusiasm for the first few days, months, even years. But the real challenge is to keep it going on a long-term basis. One faces the problem of tired workers, decaying inspiration, a vision that fades away; and so there is a need for continual renewal. We do not comment on this except to say that this is a standard problem in all of spiritual life, and the problem arises because kenotic action is in essence a spiritual type of action. One needs the same kinds of methods here as elsewhere in spiritual nurturing: quiet times, retreats, ceremonies of renewal, and so on.

Thus, we identify the problem of sustainable kenosis. It is difficult to keep the original fire burning, but there is evidence one can keep a lower-intensity flame burning for long periods of time; we refer to such groups as the Franciscans and the Religious Society of Friends, who have to some degree managed to maintain a broadly kenotic kind of action over the course of some centuries. We suspect that such long-term action of a kenotic kind is only possible with some kind of religious or spiritual base.

These problems suggest that the answers to long-term human social problems are beyond the scope of purely human solutions. Thus, it is appropriate to turn to the next level in the hierarchical description of reality—to the theological.

6 CONCLUSION: THE PROGRAM AND OBJECTIONS

We have developed one small segment of an ethical research program. Our goal has been twofold: to show that an ethical program is amenable to empirical (scientific) confirmation, and to begin to provide some confirmation for a particular view of ethics.

We developed the research program as follows. From our hard core, "renunciation is humankind's highest good," we derived several important auxiliary hypotheses: that social groups ought to engage in the practice of nonviolence, that retributive penal systems ought to be replaced by restorative systems, that individuals and groups ought to use both power and economic resources for the welfare of others. In the process of defending the auxiliary hypothesis regarding nonviolence we elaborated it considerably, distinguishing among various kinds of nonviolent action and refining our conception of the internal good at which the practice of nonviolence aims, along with a list of virtues required for its success.

We then claimed, following Alasdair MacIntyre, that if such a practice is indeed an aspect of the good life, then it must be possible to embody it in some conceivable social order. Thus, we explored reasons for thinking that nonviolence is a workable lifestyle, capable of being embodied in social institutions. In the process, a variety of lower-level auxiliary hypotheses surfaced that are amenable to testing and confirmation by means of social-scientific and psychological research.

We also suggested sketches of the sorts of empirical confirmation that may be available to support our other economic, legal, and political auxiliary hypotheses. We have thereby shown that adoption of ethics into the hierarchy of the social sciences enables ethical positions to have a top-down influence on not only the content but the very nature of the social sciences. We recognize this is not a modest proposal, but we make it because we believe it provides essential clarification of how the social sciences should function.

Two objections are likely to be raised at this point. One is that while we have, in a sense, shown that our ethical program can be confirmed by confirming some of the factual statements that are incorporated into it, we have still not touched the problem of showing the "moral rightness" of our central moral claims. This is a fair objection. The moral rightness of a form of life does go beyond its workability—otherwise we are assuming a crude sort of pragmatism. Any core theory (any theory at all) is underdetermined by its data, however, so an important further step will be to show additional support for our core theory from above—from theology. We turn to this task in the next chapter.

A second objection may be that the vision of society we have sketched in this chapter is utopian.[46] We cannot counter this charge without the pursuit of all of the changes in science and society that we are advocating. The charge is to a small extent refuted by some of the small-scale idealist societies already in existence. A final consideration is the element of self-fulfilling prophecy. Niebuhr believed that there is a role for idealists in society, especially religious idealists, in that while their visions are utopian, they have positive effects on believers, inspiring them to work for the improvements in society that are in fact capable of achievement (even though these are less than the inspiring ideals).

We do not intend to justify our program in this manner but rather to point to the deleterious effects a Niebuhrian realism can have (and we believe, has had) when it acts as a negative self-fulfilling prophecy regarding social policy. This in itself serves as evidence against that viewpoint.[47]

46. There are also much more vehement criticisms. We find it an interesting (and probably significant) fact that pacifists so often meet with more hostility than is usually expressed in academia. We do not know what to make of this phenomenon, however.

47. See photo of Dresden on the cover of the book.

Chapter Eight

Ethics and Theories of God

---

1 THE NEED FOR A RELATED THEOLOGY

In the previous chapters we sketched an ethic based on the concept of self-renunciation. We paid attention to the effects of such a lifestyle, especially to the effects of the particular form of nonviolent social interaction that we characterized as kenotic. Confirmation of our ethical program required this attention to effectiveness, not because pragmatism is our theory of ethical truth or utilitarianism our theory of the good, but in order to rebut the charge that such an ethic is only conceivable for the heroic individual in face-to-face relationships or for minority groups who have no access to normal channels of power. We believe that we have shown that this ethic is capable of social embodiment.

We also attended to the testability of social-scientific auxiliary hypotheses incorporated into our program and to the way in which the whole program could become subject to empirical confirmation *from below* insofar as the ethic suggests new research programs in the social sciences themselves. Yet, despite all of this attention to confirmation, something is still missing. We ask:

> What is it that confirms the *moral rightness* of this way of life (if not its efficacy or fruitfulness for social-science research)?

One of the premises of this book is that an ethical core theory, *qua* ethics, can only be confirmed *from above,* in that it follows from a theological or metaphysical conception of ultimate reality. Thus, in this chapter we present a theological research program from which the core of our ethics follows as a logical implication.

More specifically, we shall present a theology congruent with one strand of the Christian tradition. While our presentation is largely shaped by the writings of John Howard Yoder, similar accounts could be put together from the writings of other authors, such as Walter Wink, Stanley Hauerwas, James Wm. McClendon, Jr., Paul Fiddes, Jürgen Moltmann, and Martin Luther King, Jr. We recognize that some readers may see this as a dogmatic imposition of our own beliefs, but, while we happily confess our commitment to this version of Christianity, we will not present it in a dogmatic way. Rather our goal is to show that it (as opposed to other, more widely accepted Christian views) is not only consistent in its own right but also is capable of supporting the ethical stance just described. In the following chapter, we show that it also coheres with some of the findings of the natural sciences. Therefore, we present this theology not as dogma but as hypothesis to be tested according to the usual standards for theology and also by its ability to form a link between the natural and human-science branches of the hierarchy of the sciences.

Any polemics in our presentation will be aimed at our fellow Christians, not at adherents of other religions. We suspect, but are not able to substantiate here, that within each of the major religions there is a strand—a minority strand—that would legitimate an ethic surprisingly similar to the one we described in chapter 6. Preliminary evidence for this is found in the fact that Mahatma Gandhi, one of the most important contributors to this understanding of right living, found justification and guidance in his own Hindu tradition and was able to make a case for it among his Buddhist and Muslim followers. We hope we may be excused, due to lack of space and expertise, from exploring these other traditions. We also hope that adherents of these other traditions will be inspired by our work to develop similar projects to which ours could then be compared.

2 KENOTIC CONCEPTIONS OF GOD

In this chapter we point to a particular sort of theory of the divine that can account for the kenotic ethic. In short, the most plausible explanation of the rightness of a kenotic ethic is a kenotic doctrine of God. The connection is that such a way of life is imitation, reflection of the character of God. Only if kenosis is somehow in harmony with the ultimate character of reality should it be regarded as expected to be anything but foolishness.

Several authors use "kenosis" explicitly to describe the nature of God;

others do not use the term but have contributed to an understanding of God that is compatible with such language. While the origin of the term was in Christology—it was used to explain how the divine nature could be reconciled with Jesus' humanness—it is now used to refer to God's self-limitation and self-sacrifice and to God's involvement in the suffering of creation. This view of God is often contrasted with "traditional theism," according to which God is *impassible*—that is, unable to be affected by created beings. This latter view seemed necessary in order to uphold God's perfection during the centuries when Greek-influenced philosophy identified all change with imperfection.

Contemporary process theology has provided an alternative to God's impassibility by developing Alfred North Whitehead's conception of a dipolar God into a more Christian form. One of the implications of God's having a "consequent nature" is that God is intrinsically open to influence by what happens in the universe.

Jürgen Moltmann has contributed significantly to a rethinking of the character of God in his book, *The Crucified God*.[1] He reviews and augments the arguments of theologians (Karl Barth, Karl Rahner, Hans Küng, and others) who claim that Jesus' death on the cross shows the very nature of God. The question, then, is what is the *meaning* of Jesus' death? Here Moltmann focuses on Jesus' cry of dereliction—"My God, my God, why have you forsaken me?" (Matt 27:46)—and argues that from this theological insight there follows an ethic of concern for the godforsaken of the world.

Arthur Peacocke has also developed the theme of God's kenosis. He speaks of the self-emptying of God in terms of God's omniscience and omnipotence. God voluntarily accepts limited knowledge of the future, due to the creation of free agents and open-ended processes whose future states are unpredictable. God's omnipotence is limited by God's creation of a world in which there are processes over which God has chosen not to have control. The expression of God "in the restricted human personhood of Jesus" is a revelation of the perennial self-limiting, self-giving relation of God to the created world.[2] In short, William Placher suggests, the notion of God's vulnerability has become the new theological orthodoxy.[3]

Peacocke uses the notion of kenosis in its traditional Christological sense despite the fact that he recognizes the exegetical problems connected with its

1. Jürgen Moltmann, *The Crucified God: The Cross of Christ as the Foundation and Criticism of Christian Theology*, trans. by R. A. Wilson and John Bowden (New York: Harper and Row, 1974).

2. See Arthur Peacocke, *Theology for a Scientific Age: Being and Becoming—Natural, Divine, and Human*, 2nd, enlarged ed. (Minneapolis: Fortress Press, 1993), pp. 121–24.

3. See William Placher, *Narratives of a Vulnerable God: Christ, Theology, and Scripture* (Louisville, Ky.: Westminster John Knox Press, 1994), 6.

supposed grounding in Philippians 2. Our plan, however, is to show that a proper reading of Philippians 2 gives a different account of what it means to say that Jesus' self-emptying reveals the character of God, and hence of how we must live in order to be children of God.

2.1 The Christology of Philippians 2:5–11

> Take to heart among yourselves what you find in Christ Jesus:
>> He was in the form of God;
>> yet he laid no claim to equality with God,
>> but made himself nothing,
>> assuming the form of a slave.
>> Bearing the human likeness,
>> sharing the human lot,
>> he humbled himself,
>> and was obedient,
>> even to the point of death,
>>> death on a cross!
>> Therefore God raised him to the heights
>> and bestowed on him the name above all names,
>> that at the name of Jesus
>> every knee should bow—
>> in heaven, on earth, and in the depths—
>> and every tongue acclaim,
>> "Jesus Christ is Lord,"
>> to the glory of God the Father. (Phil 2:5–11 REB)

This passage is widely recognized to be an early hymn to Christ, incorporated almost verbatim into Paul's letter ("death on a cross" is apparently Paul's addition). In the nineteenth century it was taken to speak of a heavenly being who emptied himself, the pre-existent Christ, who divested himself of the "form" of God in order to take up human form. In accordance with the long theological tradition's conception of the attributes of God, that of which the Son emptied himself was his omnipotence, omnipresence, and omniscience. This theory allowed nineteeth-century theologians to hold on to the notion of incarnation while fully crediting historical-critical recognition of the genuine humanness of Jesus, even to the point of his making mistakes.

There is now a growing recognition, however, that this interpretation of the hymn reads later concerns back into Paul's letter. James Wm. McClendon, Jr., argues that Paul's real concern can best be perceived by the way he uses the hymn to parallel, with regard to Christ, a point he makes about himself in the following chapter: he counts as rubbish all the prerogatives he has renounced for Christ's sake—his race, his tribe, being of the right school of thought, and exhibiting impeccable zeal (3:5–10). Both cases, Christ's emptying himself and Paul's renunciation of high social status, are presented as models for the Philippians, who are to empty themselves of "selfish ambition and vanity" (2:3).

Thus, McClendon argues that Jesus' decision not to grasp after "the form of God" means in this context that he rejected, not metaphysical perfections but the earthly temptations to kingship, in favor of identification with servants and outcasts, even though that identification would lead to his death. Noting that the incarnational theology of the Bible translators has affected their rendering of the Greek, McClendon offers his own translation as follows:

> Take to heart among yourselves your being in Christ Jesus: who, mirroring God *on earth,* turned back the temptation to rival God and poured out his life, taking a servant role. Bearing the likeness of *Adam's* race, sharing the human lot, he brought his life low, obedient to death (death by a cross).[4]

John Howard Yoder relates the passage to Paul's interpretation of Christ as the new Adam, and reaches a conclusion similar to McClendon's. "Being in God's likeness" does not mean being God. Eve and Adam were made in God's likeness but were tempted to grasp at a more lofty godlikeness—the root act of rebellion. Jesus met the same tempter: "If you are the Son of God" (Matt 4:3), then claim your kingdom—make bread, leap into the temple court, make a deal with me. When the tempter said, "If you are the Son of God," however, that did not mean "If you are the Second Person of the Trinity." Says Yoder, "It meant far more concretely, humanly, politically, 'If you are the anointed one, if you are the awaited liberator, if you are the one designated to rule these people and to free them, *then* do these things I offer you.'. . . Seize power!"[5] Jesus chose not to do so in the desert, and again in Gethsemane. Paul's (probable) addition, "death on a cross," underscores the *political* significance of the hymn: crucifixion was the penalty the Romans reserved for political rebels.

If this reading of Philippians 2 is correct (and we believe it is)[6] we must ask: what is the real meaning of a kenotic conception of God if Jesus' kenosis is *sociopolitical* rather than *metaphysical?*[7] Fortunately for us, the theological im-

---

4. James Wm. McClendon, Jr., *Doctrine: Systematic Theology, Volume II* (Nashville, Tenn.: Abingdon Press, 1994), 268. Italics, as in the KJV, show exegetical assumptions.

5. *He Came Preaching Peace* (Scottdale, Pa.: Herald Press, 1985), 91.

6. See also James D. G. Dunn, *Christology in the Making: A New Testament Inquiry into the Origins of the Doctrine of the Incarnation* (London: SCM, 1989).

7. Our argument does not fail if this reading is rejected, however. It would still be possible to argue that the metaphysical kenosis of the pre-existing divine being sets a moral pattern of political

plications (and ethical implications as well) have already been worked out in some detail by Yoder.

3 JOHN HOWARD YODER'S RESEARCH PROGRAM

Before attending to the content of Yoder's theology it will be useful to set out the formal structure we shall use for organization. In keeping with our conception of theology as a science, we must be able to show that it fits the form of a scientific research program. This means that we must be able to isolate a core theory—a central thesis from which all the rest of the theoretical structure (the network of auxiliary hypotheses) follows. These lower-level theories must be supported by appropriate sorts of data. In addition the system as a whole must show development over time; and ideally that development ought to be governed by a positive heuristic, a coherent plan for elaborations and refinements of the theoretical content.

Thus, in the rest of this section we discuss Yoder's theology under headings derived from this model of scientific reasoning. The goal will be twofold. First, we show how an ethic like the one we presented in chapter 6 follows from Yoder's theology. Second, we hope to make some headway in showing the acceptability of the theological program itself.

3.1 The Hard Core

David Kelsey has written that the use one makes of Scripture in grounding theological claims depends on a prior "single, synoptic judgment" in which one attempts to "catch up what Christianity is basically all about."[8] John Howard Yoder's best-known work, and his most systematic to date, is *The Politics of Jesus.*[9] In the preface to the second edition he writes that the book is intended to show that the total moral witness of the New Testament texts is political. We believe one could go further and say that, for Yoder, the point of the New Testament witness, *tout court,* is first of all moral and political (as opposed to metaphysical, doctrinal, mystical). We venture to sum up Yoder's program as follows:

> *The moral character of God is revealed in Jesus' vulnerable enemy love and renunciation of dominion. Imitation of Jesus in this regard constitutes a* social ethic.

---

kenosis for Jesus' followers (and, in fact, is a necessary presupposition, if one begins with a high Christology), but the argument would not be as direct. Our reading has a further advantage in that it is not obviated by a low Christology.

8. David R. Kelsey, *The Uses of Scripture in Recent Theology* (Philadelphia: Fortress Press, 1975), 159.

9. *The Politics of Jesus,* 2nd ed. (Grand Rapids, Mich.: Eerdmans, 1994. First publ. 1972).

We shall take this to be the hard core of Yoder's theology. In the following subsections we present auxiliary hypotheses that fill out the program.

3.2 Relating the Core to Ethics

The first aspect of the program that we shall examine is the line of reasoning by which Yoder's social ethic is developed and related to the description of God in the hard core.

The rationale for ethics, not only for Yoder but for many Christian ethicists, is the requirement to imitate the character of God. Yoder claims that sharing in the divine nature is "the definition of Christian existence"[10] and cites texts from throughout the New Testament as grounds (Matt 5:43–48; 6:12,14–15; Luke 6:32–36; 11:4; Eph 4:24; Col 3:9,13; 1 John 1:5–7; 3:1–3; 4:17; 1 Pet 1:15–16).

Because the moral character of God is revealed in Jesus, the definition of Christian existence can also be expressed as "being in Christ": loving as he loved, serving as he served. Yoder, however, argues that in only one respect are Christians specifically called to *imitate* Christ, and that is in taking up the cross.[11] So (just as in Moltmann's theology) a crucial question is how to interpret the cross. The Christian's cross, Yoder argues, does not represent any and every kind of suffering; it is the price of social nonconformity. Jesus' warning to expect persecution is a statement about:

> the relation of our social obedience to the messianity of Jesus. Representing as he did the divine order now at hand, accessible; renouncing as he did the legitimate use of violence and the accrediting of the existing authorities; renouncing as well the ritual purity of noninvolvement, his people will encounter in ways analogous to his own the hostility of the old order.[12]

Yoder's elaboration of his ethical views involves drawing conclusions from his core theory in conjunction with sociopolitical insights. One of the ways in which Yoder's work contrasts with that of many other Christian ethicists is in the requirement he places upon himself to draw his sociopolitical analyses themselves from Scripture.

The most significant contribution that Yoder's reading of Scripture makes to political analysis is his use of the Pauline doctrine of the "principalities and powers." Yoder raises the question: if Jesus' ministry is to be understood in political terms, where in the New Testament do we find the equivalent of the concepts of *power* or *structures* as these are used by contemporary social scientists? Yoder cites New Testament exegetical research by G. B. Caird,

10. Ibid., 115.
11. Ibid., 94–95.
12. Ibid., 96.

Hendrik Berkhof, and others exploring the meaning of a set of terms used by Paul and his school: "principalities and powers," "thrones and dominations," "angels and archangels," "elements," "heights and depths," "law" and "knowledge." In the intervening centuries many of these ancient terms were taken to apply to demons and angelic beings and thus came to be ignored in the modern period. The New Testament concept of the powers apparently developed from concepts of the alien gods of other nations in Old Testament understanding—hence there is a lingering sense of their being spiritual realities. Their most significant function, however, is in application to what we would now call power structures: human traditions, the state, class and economic structures, and religious institutions, to name a few.[13]

If we can draw this connection between Paul's peculiar set of powers and our contemporary concept of power structures, then we are in a position to appreciate Paul's sociopolitical theory and to see Jesus' relation to the power structures. The powers were created by God for good purposes, since human social life is impossible without them. They are "fallen," however, in the sense that they do not serve the good of humankind for which they were created but seek instead their own self-aggrandizement.[14] They have become idols in that they require individuals to serve them as though they are of absolute value.

Jesus' role in relation to the powers was to destroy their idolatrous claims. In his public ministry he showed that it was possible to live a genuinely free life in spite of the powers. He conquered the powers through his death, in that the most worthy representatives of Jewish religion and the Roman state conspired to put him to death and thus revealed their true colors. Christ "disarmed the principalities and powers" by stripping them of their ability to create an illusion of absolute legitimacy; he made a public spectacle of them and thereby triumphed over them (cf. Col 2:15).

In the time between Jesus' victory on the cross and the eschaton, the powers linger on, but their absolute sway over Christians is broken. With our Western heritage of freedom of dissent (a legacy largely of the Radical Reformation, or Free-Church tradition) it is difficult for us to imagine the liberating effect that Jesus' "defeat" of the powers must have had in a tradi-

---

13. Walter Wink has written extensively on the powers. He claims that the spiritual realities are the "interiorities" (we might say, the analogue of personalities) of sociopolitical entities. See *Naming the Powers* (Philadelphia: Fortress Press, 1984); *Unmasking the Powers* (Philadelphia: Fortress Press, 1986); and *Engaging the Powers* (Minneapolis: Fortress Press, 1992).

14. This aspect of the doctrine of the powers relates to Reinhold Niebuhr's claim that social entities are necessarily less moral than their members because they must do unsavory things in order to ensure their survival. The difference is that Niebuhr sees this as a simple fact about all social organizations; Yoder's reading of Paul sees this as a sign of fallenness capable of at least partial and temporary remedy—redemption—prior to the end of history.

tional society in which social class, gender roles, family, religion, and nation placed absolute demands on the individual.

The ethical conclusions that follow from this analysis, along with the injunction derived from Yoder's core hypothesis to follow Jesus to the cross are as follows: Power structures are a reality, and they serve essential purposes in human life. Their claims, however, cannot be granted ultimacy in that the powers are "fallen." Thus, the Christian must sometimes refuse cooperation. The refusal to cooperate is a *sign* of the (truly) ultimate claim of God on human life and helps to liberate others from slavish obedience to the powers. The cost of defying the powers, especially when it effectively undercuts their idolatrous claims, is suffering—sometimes even to the point of death. This, precisely, is the meaning of bearing one's cross:

> What Jesus refers to in his call to cross-bearing is rather the seeming defeat of that strategy of obedience which is no strategy, the inevitable suffering of those whose only goal is to be faithful to that love which puts one at the mercy of one's neighbor, which abandons claims to justice for oneself and for one's own in an overriding concern for the reconciling of the adversary and the estranged.[15]

Here we see Yoder's connection of the theme of cross-bearing with that of renunciation, explored in chapter 6. He makes the same point as Simone Weil when he claims that vengeance or retaliation for harm restores one's self-esteem.[16] Thus, the acceptance of injustice requires self-renunciation.

The Pauline analysis of the principalities and powers draws us back, as well, to questions raised in chapters 6 and 7 about possibilities for the moral improvement of social structures and about the relation between a self-sacrificial ethic of love and political realism. These questions, however, are better addressed after we survey more of Yoder's theology.

3.3 Methodological Auxiliary Hypotheses

We have already alluded to an auxiliary hypothesis of a methodological sort that shapes Yoder's program: the requirement to make use of the sociopolitical analyses that can be found in Scripture, rather than analyses based on other sources.

Another methodological auxiliary is Yoder's rejection of individualism. We would term this the recognition of top-down causation between the social and the individual levels. The way he puts it is this: The ethical tradition tells us that we must choose between the individual and the social. "But Jesus

---

15. Yoder, *Politics,* 236.
16. John Howard Yoder, "A Theological Critique of Violence," *New Conversations* (Fall 1994), 9.

doesn't know anything about radical personalism." The personhood Jesus proclaims is a call to be integrated into a new, healing sort of community. "The idea of Jesus as an individualist or a teacher of radical personalism could arise only in the (Protestant, post-Pietist, rationalist) context that it did. . . . "[17]

Yoder's preference for understanding the relation of individual to community in a way that he attributes to Jesus (as opposed to that of modern Protestantism) is an instance of preferring the sociological analysis of Scripture over that of other sources.

3.4 The Positive Heuristic

Imre Lakatos invented the term "positive heuristic" to discriminate between scientific research programs that develop a unified vision of their subject matter and those that progress by means of accidental accretion of theoretical insights. The positive heuristic, then, is a plan, either consciously formulated or implicit, that directs the growth of a scientific research program. Nancey Murphy has suggested that the positive heuristic of a theological program will be the plan to elaborate the central vision in such a way as to cover all of the traditional theological loci in a manner consistent with the hard core of the program and in accordance with any other binding constraints.[18] For example, the positive heuristic of an existentialist theological program would be to reinterpret the traditional Christian doctrines in terms of the existentialist account of the nature of human existence.

The positive heuristic of Yoder's program would be the plan to interpret the standard Christian doctrines in a way consistent with his core theory and with his political reading of Jesus' ministry, and subject to the methodological assumptions just mentioned. A more thorough account of Yoder's program would also address his more technical exegetical assumptions. Yoder does not intend to write as a systematic theologian, so he would disavow any such conscious plan. We argue, though, that no one could hope to promote a view of Jesus that differs so radically from the standard account without expecting it to be possible to work out the theological consequences of this view within the usual theological battlegrounds (loci). In the following subsections we see the fruit of this heuristic for Christian doctrine.

3.5 Doctrinal Auxiliary Hypotheses

The best way to interpret the epistemological status of theological doctrines is to see them as auxiliary hypotheses contributing to a research program in

---

17. Yoder, *Politics*, 108.

18. Nancey Murphy, *Theology in the Age of Scientific Reasoning* (Ithaca, N.Y.: Cornell University Press, 1990), 185–86.

theology.[19] Accordingly, we now proceed to examine the doctrinal positions that make up the theological content of Yoder's program.

3.5.1 Christology and Trinity

Yoder's accounts of the *content* of Christology and the doctrine of the Trinity are not unusual. Where his account differs from the standard account is in his justification of these doctrines. Both are justified insofar as they attribute to Jesus the "metaphysical" status he must have in order that the church be justified in worshiping *and obeying* him as absolute LORD. So the doctrinal affirmations are justified hypothetico deductively: they are hypotheses which, if true, explain *why* the ethic taught by Jesus is morally binding:

> When the later, more "theological" New Testament writings formulated the claim to preexistence and cosmic preeminence for the divine Son or Word (John 1:1–4; Col 1:15ff.; Heb 1:2ff.) the intent of this language was not to consecrate beside Jesus some other way of perceiving the eternal Word, through reason or history or nature, but rather to affirm the exclusivity of the revelation claim they were making for Jesus. The same must be said of the later development of the classic ideas of the Trinity and the Incarnation. "Incarnation" does not originally mean (as it tends to today in some theologies of history, and in some kinds of Anglican theology) that God took all of human nature as it was, put his seal of approval on it, and thereby ratified nature as revelation. The point is just the opposite; that God broke through the borders of our standard definition of what is human, and gave a new, formative definition in Jesus. "Trinity" did not originally mean, as it does for some later, that there are three kinds of revelation, the Father speaking through creation and the Spirit through experience, by which the words and example of the Son must be corrected; it meant rather that language must be found and definitions created so that Christians, who believe in only one God, can affirm that that God is most adequately and bindingly known in Jesus.[20]

So the divinity and the unity of the Son with the Father are the guarantees that no other claims can be more binding on humankind than those of Jesus.[21] There is no other redeemer figure whose claims take precedence over those

---

19. Murphy, *Theology in the Age of Scientific Reasoning.*

20. Yoder, *Politics,* 99.

21. Note that this is not to reduce the theological claims to mere expressions of the ethic, any more than a scientific theory can be reduced to the data that support it. Instrumentalists in the philosophy of science attempted to argue for such a reduction of scientific theories, but most today would judge the move to be incoherent. The only way a theory, either scientific or theological, can be justified is by means of its explanatory power. If the theory is deprived of any ontological import, it loses all explanatory power.

of Jesus Messiah; there can be no other source of divine revelation that contradicts Jesus' teaching. Conversely, doctrinal heresies are defective insofar as they lead to the rejection of Jesus' ethic. Ebionitic heresies (denying Christ's divinity) thereby deny his right to moral lordship. Docetism (denying the full humanity of Christ) calls into question the possibility, and thus the requirement for, mere humans to imitate Jesus' faithfulness.

3.5.2 Atonement, Sin, and Justification

When we come to the doctrines of atonement and justification, Christian anthropology and sin, we reach the point where Yoder's theology is most clearly divergent from the standard account of Christian doctrine. By the standard account, we mean especially Augustinian forms of Christianity, whose features include a doctrine of the fall as a key to understanding human nature, a major emphasis on the substitutionary theory of atonement, and justification as imputed righteousness.

It has become common since the publication of Gustaf Aulén's *Christus Victor*[22] to speak of three types of atonement theories: the Anselmian or substitutionary theories; the Abelardian or moral influence theories; and the "classical" ransom or conflict theories, according to which the work of Christ is interpreted in terms of conflict with and triumph over cosmic evil powers. A variety of versions were developed during the early centuries of the Church: Christ as a ransom paid to the devil, a transaction wherein God used Christ as "bait" to deceive the devil, and a political form in which the devil lost his rightful dominion over sinful humankind by abusing the sinless Christ.

While the classical theory clearly has New Testament support, it has been seen as objectionable because it involves the concept of the devil, which many now take to require "demythologization." Aulén had argued that the mythological language of the conflict theory could simply be dropped, leaving the theory intact. But then it is no longer clear what is meant by "cosmic evil powers."

Yoder's central understanding of atonement fits the classical model and fills the gap left by the excision of a mythical devil by means of the interpretation of the "principalities and powers" described above. These superhuman power structures are the forces with which Jesus came into conflict, and from which he has freed humankind, both by his example (and here the moral influence theory gets its due) and by stripping them of the illusion of absolute legitimacy, precisely because their most worthy representatives abused him in his innocence. The cross has as much significance in this theory as it does in the substitution theory, but for different reasons.

---

22. Gustaf Aulén, *Christus Victor*, trans. by A. G. Herbert (New York: Macmillan, 1931).

Yoder does not ignore personal sinfulness, but he gives it neither the significance nor the inevitability that it has in Augustinian Christianity. His focus instead is on institutionalized sin; the remedy for it is found in freedom from bondage to the principalities and powers, and especially in the creation of a new social order, the church. Yoder's account of justification, also, is sociopolitical:

> Let us set aside for purposes of discussion the assumption that the righteousness of God and the righteousness of humanity are most fundamentally located on the individual level. . . . Let us posit as at least thinkable the alternate hypothesis that for Paul righteousness, either in God or in human beings, might more appropriately be conceived of as having cosmic or social dimensions. Such larger dimensions would not negate the personal character of the righteousness God imputes to those who believe; but by englobing the personal salvation in a fuller reality they would negate the individualism with which we understand such reconciliation.[23]

Yoder argues that justification (being set right with God) is accomplished when Christians are set right with one another. In Paul's ministry, the reconciling of Jews and Gentiles was primary. The "new creation" is a new "race" of humans in which the Jewish law no longer forms a barrier between Jew and Gentile and in which gender and economic differences are reconciled as well:

> But it is *par excellence* with reference to enmity between peoples, the extension of neighbor love to the enemy, and the renunciation of violence even in the most righteous cause, that this promise takes on flesh in the most original, the most authentic, and most frightening and scandalous, and therefore the most evangelical way. It is the Good News that my enemy and I are united, through no merit or work of our own, in a new humanity that forbids henceforth my ever taking his or her life in my hands.[24]

All of this—a primarily social concept of sin and justification, and a conflict view of atonement suitably politicized—contributes to a complete reinterpretation of the main features of New Testament theology, especially of the Pauline corpus, which, since Martin Luther, has been taken to focus instead on imputed personal righteousness before God on the grounds of faith.

3.5.3 Excursus: Walter Wink on the Domination System
New Testament scholar Walter Wink has expanded on Yoder's claim that the principalities and powers form a system. In its fallen state, Wink calls this

23. Yoder, *Politics*, 215.
24. Ibid., 226.

the "Domination System." Wink's analysis strengthens Yoder's position in several ways.

First, this conceptual move explains the integral relationship between an ethic of nonviolence and an ethic of social and economic justice. That is, Yoder, Weil, and many others recognize that social justice and nonviolence "go together." Why? Wink provides a sociological-historical explanation.

The domination system arose in the Middle East sometime between 4000 and 3000 B.C.E. Before this period, archaeological evidence shows, there were many peaceful civilizations—cities with no walls, no armies, no weapons for battle. After 3000 B.C.E., warfare proliferates dramatically.[25] By this same date, autocracy was the accepted order of things: the social system was rigidly hierarchical, authoritarian, and patriarchal. Power lost by men through submission to the ruling elite was compensated by power over women, children, hired workers, slaves, and the land. Power inequalities permitted economic inequalities, and amassing wealth became necessary for the support of large armies.

The domination system has its own myth of origins in the *Enuma Elish* (from around 1250 B.C.E., but based on much older traditions), in which the universe is said to have been created out of the body of a murdered goddess. The gods themselves set the pattern of domination and warfare. The implication is that the very substance of which humans are created is tinged with violence. Furthermore, warfare and domination are necessary to prevent the cosmos from reverting to the chaos from which it was created.

So here is the story that gives meaning to mainline Western culture. It was repeated in Greek and Roman mythology. It continues today in nearly all of the literature and television programming used to socialize children: it is the story of the good guy preserving order by means of violence. It lies behind the social-scientific research programs unmasked by John Milbank, the deep thesis of which is an "ontology of violence." Unfortunately, we claim, it has had all too deep an influence on mainstream Christianity, showing up thinly disguised in the "just-war" tradition from Augustine to the present, as well as in Reinhold Niebuhr's "Christian realism."

The contribution that Wink's historical research makes to Yoder's theological program, then, is first to explain historically and sociologically the intrinsic connections between social justice and nonviolence: they are related in what they oppose. Second, Wink's work makes all the more plausible Yoder's claim that God's response to evil must be at the social level, not just the level of personal sin. Once a single society falls prey to the mythology of the domination system, it forces its neighbors to do likewise, and individuals

25. Wink, *Engaging the Powers*, 36.

within the societies lose their freedom to object. Consequently, the solution must be to instigate (or reinstigate) a whole new model of sociality (the church); to unmask the idolatrous pretensions of the domination system (cf. Col 2:15); and to teach individuals that resistance to the system is possible (the example of Jesus).

Finally, Wink's claim that domination is not coeval with civilization provides strong evidence against theological positions that root it in a constant human sinfulness extending all the way back to the fall at the beginning of human history (or, we might add, in our genetic endowment). This, in turn, makes more plausible our claim (in chap. 6) that there is hope for progressively decreasing the levels of violence, coercion, and economic inequality in contemporary societies.

3.5.4 Excursus: A Progressive Problemshift

René Girard has published a study on the relation between violence and religious ritual that can be used to eliminate an anomaly from Yoder's program.[26] Yoder claims that he does not intend to reject the standard account of the work of Christ, but simply to place it in a social and cosmic setting. Yet readers are likely to object that he needs to give some positive account of New Testament passages that use the language of temple sacrifice to interpret the atoning work of Christ. Girard's conclusions regarding religious sacrifice allow us to do just that. Properly interpreted, the sacrificial atonement motifs exactly reinforce Yoder's own interpretation of what Christianity is basically all about.

Girard's thesis is that religious rites of sacrifice, both animal and human, are devices to quell violence among members of a community. "If left unappeased," he says, "violence will accumulate until it overflows its confines and floods the surrounding area. The role of sacrifice is to stem this rising tide of indiscriminate substitutions and redirect violence into 'proper' channels."[27] Thus, the ritual restores the harmony of the community and reinforces its social fabric. The victim used for the sacrifice is a surrogate for members of the community who have excited the animosity of their fellows. The victim, Girard points out, always shares some characteristics identifying it with the community. For example, the Nuer, who sacrifice cattle, describe the "society" of the herd in the same terms that they use for their own human relations. Yet the victims cannot be of the same class as the community itself—human victims are always marginal or distinguished in some way—so that

---

26. René Girard, *Violence and the Sacred,* trans. Patrick Gregory (Baltimore: Johns Hopkins University Press, 1977).

27. Ibid., 10.

their death does not incur any responsibility for vengeance on the part of community members. Thus, ritual sacrifice allows for the venting of aggression without the "interminable, infinitely repetitive process" of vengeance, which, whenever it turns up in some part of the community, "threatens to involve the whole social body."[28]

Girard notes that sacrifice is generally seen as an act of mediation between a sacrificer and a deity, and he argues that the sacrificial process requires a degree of *misunderstanding*. If the celebrants comprehended the true role of the sacrificial act (as Girard describes it), then it would lose its effectiveness. The participants must suppose that it is the god who demands the victim. The reason, Girard speculates, is that "men can dispose of their violence more efficiently if they regard the process not as something emanating from within themselves, but as a necessity imposed from without."[29]

If Girard's anthropology can help us think our way back to a society ordered by a code of vengeance, rather than by a modern legal system,[30] it becomes clear that the sacrificial atonement motif is not an alternative to Yoder's account of Christian theology in terms of nonviolence and reconciliation. Now we can see Christ, the lamb of God, as the one victim whose sacrificial death is permanently efficacious for ridding the community of violence (cf. Heb 7:27).

The parallels with Girard's account of ritual sacrifice are startling: The victim must be similar enough to suffer on behalf of community members, yet different enough not to be confused with other, nonsacrificeable members. So Jesus is described as both fully human and as the unique Son of God. The moral ambiguity of the sacrificial victim is found here as well. Jesus is described as the wholly sinless one, yet "reckoned among the transgressors." The symbolism of the Last Supper even maintains a hint of the cannibalism that is so often incorporated in sacrifice. We even find in cruder versions of this atonement theology the "necessary degree of misunderstanding": the claim that God the Father required the death of his Son as satisfaction for sin.

So if Girard is correct, the point of the interpretation of Christ's death as the once-for-all sacrifice for sin, for communities in which ritual sacrifice was still an effective control on the cycle of vengeance and violence, would have been to say that violence and vengeance within the community are henceforth prohibited. And against this background we can see more clearly the importance of Paul's (and Yoder's) emphasis on the new humanity that

28. Ibid., 14–15.
29. Ibid., 14.
30. And both Old and New Testament societies were still largely of this type; see Bruce J. Malina, *The New Testament World: Insights from Cultural Anthropology* (Atlanta: John Knox, 1981).

refuses to count any class of people as outside of the community thus protected from violence by the sacrifice of "the Lamb."

What does the sacrificial imagery mean, then, for us who are far removed from cultures where propitiatory sacrifice makes sense? For us, Girard suggests, war and the legal system with its punishments are the primary means of redirecting violence away from protected community members. We would add, as well, that civil religion with its explicit description of loss of life in battle as "sacrifice" maintains the necessary degree of misunderstanding—the illusion that the innocent lives lost on the battlefield are not victims of the citizens' own aggression but are demanded by a righteous god. It may not be pure cynicism when commentators attribute America's small wars to the need to unify the citizens at home for the *domestic* political agenda.

The obvious application of sacrificial atonement imagery to our contemporary situation is to call for a permanent end to violence, both spontaneous and institutionalized. Christ for us, too, is the one victim whose death should be permanently efficacious in ridding our present-day communities of violence. Yoder's image for the work of Christ and of his followers is that of *absorbing evil;* stopping the "eternal, infinitely repetitive process" of violence (Girard) by refusing to retaliate. And, we would add, by refusing as well to find a scapegoat from the margins of our community.

The misunderstanding that it is God who required the death of Jesus as scapegoat for sinners has all too often contributed to the view that God also demands the death of others as payment for sin.[31] Demythologization of atonement imagery requires recognition that it is not God but our own human principalities and powers that demand the death of criminals and the "sacrifice" of young men on the battlefield. High Christology demands that we recognize God's voice not in the powers demanding sacrificial death but rather in the one whose life was sacrificed on the cross.

Thus, the addition of Girard's anthropology to this theological program allows it to overcome what would be called an anomaly in science—a datum that cannot be reconciled with the theory. The anomaly here is the sacrificial language used in the New Testament to interpret the death of Jesus. This language has led to the development of theories of the work of Christ that

31. It may be that interpretations of sacrifice different from Girard's might also serve to reconcile the sacrificial atonement motif with Yoder's kenotic theology. For instance, some scholars argue that the point of sacrifice in the Old Testament was not related to the idea of the scapegoat but rather to the idea that the blood of the animal was released to be a bond among those entering into a covenant and thus creating new bonds of unity. (Arthur Peacocke pointed this out in private conversation.) Alternatively, the emphasis could be placed on the claim that it is God-in-Christ suffering on the cross that reveals the character of God. History, however, does show that it is difficult to avoid reinforcing the conflicting view that God is to be identified with the wrathful one demanding payment for sin.

are at least different from Yoder's interpretation and in some cases actually opposed to it. We have used Girard's thesis regarding the social function of ritual sacrifice as an auxiliary hypothesis to interpret the anomalous data in a way that is not only consistent with Yoder's program but adds additional confirmation.[32]

3.5.5 Church, World, and Eschatology

We deferred the question of moral improvement in social structures until we should have seen more of Yoder's theology. It is appropriate to take up this question in conjunction with the doctrines of the church and eschatology.

An important thesis for Yoder, as well as for other theologians in the Anabaptist tradition, is the recognition that "the church is not the world." The sixteenth-century Anabaptists' most distinctive feature was their rejection of the state-church arrangement, which identified the boundaries of the church first with the empire and then with the nation state. The "ana-baptists" (that is, re-baptizers) rejected infant baptism in part because it was the means by which the incorporation of all citizens into the state church was effected.

When Yoder distinguishes the church from the world, he means to say that there is a system—a set of interconnected power structures—that is opposed to the work of Christ. The question regarding moral improvement of social institutions, then, needs to be recast as a set of questions regarding the possibilities for change within both the church and the world, and especially how the church can affect the world.

The church, according to Yoder, is an alternative social reality in the midst of the world. By its very existence it unmasks the principalities and powers, exposing the illegitimate claims of family, privileged social class, and nation. In a variety of ways this unmasking frees church members to lead agapic lives. For example, Christians are *freed from* requirements to avenge injuries to family members' honor.

The church is a laboratory for imagining and practicing new forms of social life. Where it had once been unimaginable that Jews could live in community with pagans, within a generation that "new creature" became a reality. Christians are even now trying to imagine a community in which there is no such thing as male and female (cf. Gal 3:28).

Within the church, social practices are, to a degree, healed of their sinfulness. The powers themselves can be redeemed—they can accept their role as servants of God in support of human sociality. For example, leadership becomes a form of service. Economic practices are not primarily for the

---

32. Yoder himself makes similar moves in an essay published after this chapter was written. See "A Theological Critique of Violence."

amassing of wealth but for the production of something to share. Housekeeping aims at hospitality to the stranger.

In addition, the church has developed unique social practices that aim at maintaining and improving the moral character of the community. One of these is the practice of "binding and loosing" that Jesus is said to have taught his disciples:

> If your brother does wrong, go and take the matter up with him, strictly between yourselves. If he listens to you, you have won your brother over. But if he will not listen, take one or two others with you, so that every case may be settled on the evidence of two or three witnesses. If he refuses to listen to them, report the matter to the congregation; and if he will not listen even to the congregation, then treat him as you would a pagan or a tax-collector. Truly I tell you: Whatever you forbid on earth shall be forbidden in heaven, and whatever you allow on earth shall be allowed in heaven. (Matt 18:15–18 REB)

This practice not only has the potential for supporting individuals in their faithfulness to the community's teaching but also offers opportunity for healing personal grievances and for productive discussions on matters of conduct.[33] When it does involve reevaluation of the community's moral standards, it becomes an instance of a second Christian practice, that of communal discernment. Yoder calls this practice the rule of Paul, since its justification in all of the new Protestant movements during the Reformation referred to Paul's First Letter to the Corinthians (chap. 14).

The idea behind this practice is that God's Spirit will lead the community in making decisions about doctrine and moral issues through the consensus that arises out of open conversation. The Quakers, says Yoder, have worked out most thoroughly and self-consciously an understanding of how the Spirit shapes and guides the church.[34]

We claim that the practice of discernment can be a powerful tool for cumulative moral development within the church. The practice of discernment itself (like any MacIntyrean practice) is open to development: development of the virtues required for its success, development of skill in applying the church's formative texts to current situations, and development in the very concept of the good at which the practice aims.

Furthermore, the practice of discernment provides for the community what the virtue of *phronēsis* (practical wisdom) provided in Aristotle's *polis*. The individual with the virtue of *phronēsis* could use it to assist the citizens of

---

33. See John Howard Yoder, *Body Politics: Five Practices of the Community before the Watching World* (Nashville, Tenn.: Discipleship Resources, 1992), chap. 1.

34. Ibid., chap. 5.

the *polis* in ordering the various goods toward which they aimed. The practice of discernment institutionalizes this crucial form of reflection on the priorities and goals of the community. Rather than relying on a single leader, though, it allows all members with insights to share them, encourages the use of guidance from Scripture, and most importantly, opens the community to the guiding impulses of the wisdom of God.

All of these features of the church suggest that conscientious pursuit of the good can and will lead to cumulative moral development, both of Christlike character among the members and of noncoercive, virtue-enhancing institutions and practices.

Religious institutions themselves, however, easily become quite powerful and they are especially prone to become idolatrous. It would be difficult to overemphasize this point. So there can be no smug expectation of inevitable moral progress. The prophet will always be needed to call the church to focus critical moral discernment on itself.

The church as it is meant to be acts as an agent of change in the world by showing the world alternatives to its coercive practices. While it is simply a fact that the world does not and cannot operate as the church does, there are still vast differences among the powers in terms of the degree to which they approximate the will of God. The church, as an ethical laboratory, can teach the world better ways. For instance, many attribute modern forms of democratic government to skill and lessons learned in free-church polity. The ideas of public education and hospitals came from church institutions.

It would be difficult to say that Yoder's analysis of social institutions is any less *realistic* than Reinhold Niebuhr's, yet there is an optimism in Yoder's thought that is missing in Niebuhr's; Yoder avoids the note of acquiescence in evil that we find in Niebuhr's thought. What accounts for the difference is different views of eschatology (i.e., the doctrine of last things). More specifically, these two theorists have different views of the relation between history and the kingdom of God.

Niebuhr points out that while all Christians look forward to the *parousia,* the triumphant return of Christ, some interpret this event as a future happening *within* the temporal-historical process; others as necessarily outside of or *beyond* history. Because he sets up the question in terms of the problem of the temporal and the eternal (the claim is that the eternal can never be actualized in the temporal), Niebuhr is forced to side with those whose eschatology transcends history. This, in turn, leads to his conclusion that guilt and moral ambiguity are permanent features of the interim. Christ's overcoming of the world can only mean that Christians know the meaning of history, not that history itself is transformed:

Such an understanding of faith means that the world is in a sense already "overcome"; for none of the corruptions of history, its fanaticisms and conflicts, its imperial lusts and ambitions, its catastrophes and tragedies, can take the faithful completely unaware. The light of revelation into the meaning of life illumines the darkness of history's self-contradictions, its fragmentary realizations of meaning and its premature and false completions.[35]

Yoder claims that the New Testament sees our present age, from Pentecost to the *parousia,* as a period of the overlapping of two aeons. These are not distinct periods of time, for they exist simultaneously:

They differ rather in nature or in direction; one points backwards to human history outside of (before) Christ; the other points forward to the fullness of the kingdom of God, of which it is a foretaste. Each aeon has a social manifestation: the former in the "world," the latter in the church or the body of Christ.[36]

The new aeon was inaugurated by Jesus; Jesus is a mover of history, not merely a teacher of how to understand history's moral ambiguity.[37] The meaning of history is found in the work of the church;[38] the church by its obedience is used by God to bring about the fullness of the kingdom, of which the church is a foretaste.

The resurrection of Jesus is God's guarantee that the new aeon will ultimately prevail. This entails that the means Jesus chose for participation in history are the right ones: the cross and not the sword, suffering and not brute power determine the meaning of history. One need not choose between *agape* and effectiveness.[39]

So the ultimate effectiveness of self-renunciation and kenosis are guaranteed; yet their rightness is not based on effectiveness but on the fact that they anticipate the victory of the Lamb.[40] This ethic makes sense only if Jesus' choice not to rule violently is the surfacing of an eternal divine decision; if

35. Reinhold Niebuhr, *The Nature and Destiny of Man,* 2 vols. (New York: Charles Scribner's Sons, 1943), 2:288.

36. John Howard Yoder, *The Original Revolution: Essays on Christian Pacifism* (Scottdale, Pa.: Herald Press, 1971), 55.

37. Yoder, *Politics,* 233.

38. Yoder, *Original Revolution,* 61.

39. Yoder, *Politics,* 232, 109. Note that this use of the resurrection presumes that it actually happened. If the New Testament witness to the resurrection is merely an odd way of expressing the church's "resurrection faith," then the resurrection cannot serve as grounding for any such faith.

40. Yoder, *Original Revolution,* 61.

self-emptying is not only what Jesus did, but is the very nature of God.[41] As Yoder elaborates:

> This conception of participation in the character of God's struggle with a rebellious world, which early Quakerism referred to as "the war of the lamb," has the peculiar disadvantage—or advantage, depending upon one's point of view—of being meaningful only if Christ be he who Christians claim him to be, the Master. Almost every other kind of ethical approach espoused by Christians, pacifist or otherwise, will continue to make sense to the non-Christian as well. Whether Jesus be the Christ or not, whether Jesus the Christ be Lord or not, whether this kind of religious language be meaningful or not, most types of ethical approach will keep on functioning just the same. For their true foundation is in some reading of the human situation or some ethical insight which is claimed to be generally accessible to all people of good-will. The same is not true for this vision of "completing in our bodies that which was lacking in the suffering of Christ" (Col 1:24). If Jesus Christ was not who historical Christianity confesses he was, the revelation in the life of a real man of the character of God himself, then this one argument for pacifism collapses.[42]

3.5.6 Kenotic Response to God

We have argued that God's nature is essentially kenotic, as is demonstrated in the life and teaching of Jesus and in particular by his death on the cross. The implication is that there should be a kenotic response by men and women, who are made in the image of God, mirroring this kenotic nature and reflecting it in their relations to each other and to God.

We have discussed in previous chapters how this should lead to a kenotic ordering of social relations—ethics being determined in a top-down manner by theology. One aspect of this kenotic ethic was barely mentioned in chapter 6: there is ultimately a more important task for the believer, which indeed forms the proper basis for such social relations; this is a kenotic response to God.

Humility is one of the oldest themes in Christian spirituality. We are given our talents by God and are not responsible for that gift; it is our heritage, the basis from which we proceed into the world. What we are able to do, we do by use of these talents and through our own free will, but this is only possible because of the grace of God, the motivation and inspiration to which we respond freely because we have a God-given disposition to do so. Proceeding in our efforts to act in the best way we can in response to the inspiration we

---

41. Yoder, *He Came Preaching Peace*, 93.
42. Yoder, *Politics*, 237.

are given, we naturally are proud of what we have done, and are tempted to take all the credit to ourselves, to forget that it is only through the grace of God that we can do anything good. So we become proud in our achievements and start to regard ourselves as self-sufficient. Soon we look to those around us for praise and reward for what we have done, then start to praise ourselves for our own wisdom and bravery. We allow our own selves to be central in our lives, a position that really belongs to God. Or we fashion creations of many kinds—beautiful art, abstract theories, legal systems, public institutions (the state, the social fabric of the church), which we claim are infallible and worthy of worship—that is, we set ourselves up as creators equal to God. Hence we fall into idolatry—creating things that we set up as equal to God, or even claiming for ourselves infallibility and the kind of reverence that is due only to God. These pretensions become dear to us, so we protect our status by means that are quite unacceptable. We fall into the deadly sin of pride.

We do not usually literally set ourselves up as equal to God but either set up some of our creations as infallible and worthy of worship, or behave toward others in a way that implicitly makes claims of superiority rather than of creaturely equality in the eyes of God. Such idolatry appears in the way we relate to others, strangers and loved ones (e.g., we do not listen to them because we think what we have to say is more valuable; we do not give our children their freedom because we lay on them claims to which only their Creator is entitled). So half of the battle is in our daily lives and encounters with those around—for this reflects whether our relation to ourselves and to God is kenotic.

The saints through the ages have fought this ever-recurring cycle of pride and humility. The truly devilish feature is that when we come to our senses, see the error of our ways, regret what we have done, and prostrate ourselves before the awful power, beauty, and might of God—indeed, we truly behave humbly—then we become proud of our humility.

The problem is to empty ourselves of pride daily, to walk humbly with God—achieving things in God's name, doing God's will, but being humble while we do so, not setting ourselves up as superior to others or equal to God, no matter what we achieve. This is the kenotic road for the believer, one of the core features of true spirituality and the foundation on which kenotic ethics can be built. It is the proper response to the kenotic nature of God.[43]

43. See Rex Chapman, "Humility," in Gordon S. Wakefield, ed., *A Dictionary of Christian Spirituality* (London: SCM Press, 1983), 200–201; W. H. Vanstone, *Love's Endeavour, Love's Expense: The Response of Being to the Love of God* (London: Darton, Longman and Todd, 1977); K. M. Kronin, *Kenosis: Emptying Self and the Path of Christian Service* (Rockport, Mass.: Element, 1992).

We do not presume to advise here how to handle this problem on a daily basis—that is the domain of spiritual counseling, of prayer and meditation, of continual awareness and watchfulness—except to say that awareness of the problem is half the battle. The point, then, is that the proper response to a kenotic God is a kenotic relation to God and to all of God's creation. It begins as a theological attitude, an awareness of our status relative to God, that enables an emptying of our pride in relation to our work, our achievements, and the fellow humans we encounter in our lives. This awareness is ultimately what makes a kenotic ethic achievable.

3.6 Confirmation

Different theological research programs call for different kinds of supporting data. This difference is analogous to the different kinds of support that are relevant to, say, different programs in psychology: B. F. Skinner's reinforcement schedules versus Sigmund Freud's dream analyses and slips of the tongue.

Yoder's central thesis is about the proper interpretation of the meaning of Jesus and about what Jesus means for history and ethics. Since the Scriptures are the only significant source of information about Jesus, it stands to reason that these texts should provide an important body of data for Yoder, along with other historical texts and traces that are relevant for assisting in their interpretation. Yoder's more systematic works, such as *Politics of Jesus,* contain sophisticated arguments to the effect that his line of interpretation is more faithful to the texts, more fruitful for interpreting obscure passages, than others. Yoder has provided additional scriptural confirmation of his program in published sermons and occasional essays. In this body of literature he has worked through a surprising variety of texts, in each case providing a reading that confirms his interpretation of the life and teaching of Jesus.

However, the other aspect of Yoder's thesis, that Jesus (thus understood) is the ultimate revelation of the character of God and thus of the meaning and purpose of human history, cannot be confirmed merely by Scripture studies without begging the question. The purely theological thesis, the theory about the character of God, can only be fully confirmed eschatologically, although it can acquire some plausibility for Christians from their relations with God in prayer. A historiographical thesis embedded in Yoder's theology, however, may be testable in the interim. Yoder has stated it as follows: "If *kenosis* is the shape of God's own self-sending, then any strategy of Lordship, like that of the kings of this world, is . . . a strategic mistake, likely to backfire. . . ."[44]

---

44. John Howard Yoder, *The Priestly Kingdom: Social Ethics as Gospel* (Notre Dame, Ind.: University of Notre Dame Press, 1984), 145.

Yoder pays some attention, as we did in the previous chapter, to the relative effectiveness of nonviolent versus violent means of social and political action. But his more intriguing contribution is the suggestion that his version of ethics leads to (what we would call) a new research program in the study of history, a part of which is the examination of the effects of violence and nonviolence:

> We now turn to asking . . . whether this "messianic" orientation will have particular implications for history as an intellectual discipline, i.e., for historiography, the recounting of events and the discerning of meanings. Can one gain new light upon the relevance of a Free Church vision of ethics by claiming that it also leads to a new way of interpreting events in the past? Decision in the present is often very much the product of how the past has been recounted to us. If we are then to open up a new future it must be the extension of a rereading of the past. Historiography must be rehabilitated by being taken back from the grasp of the military historians and the chroniclers of battles and dynasties, and informed by other criteria to judge a society's sickness or health.
>
> Instead of reading history as proof of a theory of political science, i.e., the definition *sine qua non* of the state as its monopoly of physical coercion, could we study the story with some openness to the hypothesis that genuine power is always correlated with the consent of the governed or legitimized in some other way? Is there such a thing as a "peace church historiography"?[45]

Yoder mentions a variety of auxiliary hypotheses that follow from this reorientation of historiographic assumptions; each suitable for testing:

1. The sword is not the source of creativity.
    1.1 Theological considerations make a major contribution to the spirit of an age and to political developments.
    1.2 History may be more affected by quiet ministry than by princes.
2. Manhood is not brutality.
    2.1 History and conflict cannot be understood on a simple model of good guys and bad guys.
3. If you wish peace, prepare for it.
    3.1 Preparing for war brings conflict.
    3.2 Practice of constructive methods of conflict resolution will help to undermine unjust institutions and build healthy ones.

45. Yoder, *Original Revolution*, 160–61.

4. War is not a way to save a culture.
5. Social creativity is a minority function.
     5.1 The person in power is not always free or strong.
     5.2 Minority groups have more freedom to experiment with new forms of social life.
6. Rulers are not necessarily society's benefactors.

In short, Yoder's claim is that "world history," the historiography of "the world" produces a distortion of the past, which then provides justification for further coercive practices. Perhaps an equally credible narrative could be constructed, a narrative that is in fact more accurate, which will make it clear that the real historical force is suffering love.

3.7 Rebutting Counter-evidence

Two sorts of possible counter-evidence could be particularly damaging to the theological program sketched here: the complicity of the church in the worst evils of history, and biblical passages that appear to condone or require violence.

The well-known sins not only of individual Christians but especially of the institutional churches themselves rightly raise doubts about Christianity's truth claims, although this is not straightforward falsification, owing to the fact that one of Christianity's central claims has always been its doctrine of sin. The more appropriate approach is to ask whether the observed patterns of goodness and evil are roughly what theological teaching should lead us to expect, and here we have to distinguish among theological traditions. For the Catholic tradition, with its teaching on the non-defectability of the church, sinful church practices constitute a major anomaly; this is much less the case for the Protestant tradition, according to which the church must be *semper reformanda* (always needing to be reformed).

Yoder's version of the Anabaptist tradition is even less damaged by the sin of the church: not only can he predict it, he can specify its main cause. The church is a power; all powers are subject to corruption when they seek their own good over service to God. When the churches become involved in Constantinian arrangements with the great powers of empire or state, they have much more to protect and will inevitably become corrupted. Thus, the church itself must always be on guard against grasping for power (as the Protestant tradition emphasizes) and *in particular* it must eschew state–church status (as the Reformers failed to do).

A second advantage of the Anabaptist tradition for answering the problem of corruption in the church is its teaching on church discipline. Much discredit is brought upon Christian teaching by the behavior of individual members of churches (Mafiosi at Mass, for example). However, Anabaptist church discipline was founded on Matthew 18, and when this practice is followed, members' conduct is either brought into accord with church teaching or they are excluded from worship.

So our claim is that while evil within and by the churches is indeed a terrible scandal, it presents less of an anomaly for the Anabaptist tradition than for others. Persistently sinful individuals do not count as church members in "believers' churches"; the most heinous institutional sins of Christendom (predictably, according to the Anabaptists) have been committed by churches that have made compromises with the empire or the state.

Several passages in the New Testament are regularly used to attempt to rebut pacifist interpretations of Jesus' mission and teaching.[46] Romans 13:1: "Every person must submit to the authorities in power, for all authority comes from God, and the existing authorities are instituted by him" is often cited as proof that Christians have a responsibility to serve in the military. However, such a reading ignores the context, both of the text—the preceding and subsequent verses—and the social setting of the original readers. It is very unlikely that Paul meant to send his Roman readers to join the army, since most Christians then would not have been Roman citizens and thus would have been ineligible for military service.

Verse 13 follows a passage calling for peace and nonresistance to evil:

> Never pay back evil for evil. Let your aims be such as all count honourable. If possible, so far as it lies with you, live at peace with all. My dear friends, do not seek revenge, but leave a place for divine retribution; for there is a text which reads, "Vengeance is mine, says the Lord, I will repay." But there is another text: "If your enemy is hungry, feed him; if he is thirsty, give him a drink; by doing this you will heap live coals on his head." Do not let evil conquer you, but use good to conquer evil (Rom 12:17–21 REB).

We should not be deceived by chapter breaks, added much later, into separating this passage from Romans 13:1, which immediately follows it.

The Revised English Bible's translation of the following verse is: "It follows that anyone who rebels against authority is resisting a divine institution. . . ." All of this makes it much more likely that Paul is cautioning Roman Christians *against* taking up arms; that is, against joining in the armed rebellion against the government!

---

46. We will not attempt to deal with the question of warfare in the Old Testament since the sort of approach one takes depends largely on a prior judgment about the status of the Old Testament revelation. We recommend Millard C. Lind, *Yahweh Is a Warrior* (Scottdale, Pa.: Herald Press, 1980).

There is a puzzling passage in Luke's Gospel in which Jesus, on the way to his arrest, tells his disciples to provide swords:

> He said to them, "when I sent you out barefoot without purse or pack, were you ever short of anything?" "No," they answered. "It is different now," he said; "whoever has a purse had better take it with him, and his pack, too; and if he has no sword, let him sell his cloak and buy one. For scripture says, 'And he was reckoned among transgressors,' and this, I tell you, must be fulfilled in me; indeed, all that is written of me is reaching its fulfilment." "Lord," they said, "we have two swords here." "Enough!" he replied (Luke 22:35–38 REB).

This passage has been used frequently in the pacifism debate: If Jesus had not meant his disciples to kill, why would he have told them now to arm themselves? Is he not preparing them for legitimate self-defense after Pentecost? But, Yoder asks, how could two swords be "enough" for twelve disciples travelling two by two?[47]

One possible reading of Jesus' motives in arming his disciples is to take him at his word: it is to fulfill the prophecy found in Isaiah:

> Therefore I shall allot him a portion with the great, and he will share the spoil with the mighty, because he exposed himself to death and was reckoned among transgressors, for he bore the sins of many and interceded for transgressors (Isaiah 53:12 REB).

If Jesus was to be taken as a criminal, to be executed by crucifixion, the punishment for insurrection, the symbols of armed rebellion in the hands of his followers would be appropriate. Two swords might not be enough for defense, but plenty for conviction.

Another passage often used is the Johannine story of Jesus "cleansing the temple" (John 2:13–17). The usefulness of this text for justifying violence depends on a once common but now generally rejected translation. According to the King James Version, Jesus, "when he had made a scourge of small cords, he drove them all [the money changers and those that sold oxen, sheep, and doves] out of the temple, and the sheep and the oxen . . ." (v. 15). This act of physical violence by Jesus is then said to set a precedent for his followers. More recent translations, however, make it only the animals that are driven out: "Making a whip of cords, he drove all of them out of the temple, both the sheep and the cattle" (NRSV).[48]

So these passages, long used as proof texts against pacifists, support contrary readings that are at least as plausible, and perhaps more so.

---

47. Yoder, *Politics*, 45, n.44.
48. For a discussion of the problematic aspects of the Greek grammar, see ibid., chap. 10.

4 THEOLOGY AND COSMOLOGY

Yoder claims that the ministry of Jesus has not only social-ethical and historical significance, but *cosmic* significance:

> Then to follow Jesus does not mean renouncing effectiveness. . . . It means
> that in Jesus we have a clue to which kinds of causation, which kinds of
> community-building, which kinds of conflict management, go with the
> grain of the cosmos, of which we know, as Caesar does not, that Jesus is
> both the Word (the inner logic of things) and the Lord ("sitting at the right
> hand"). It is not that we begin with a mechanistic universe and then look
> for cracks and chinks where a little creative freedom might sneak in (for
> which we would then give God credit): it is that we confess the determinis-
> tic world to be enclosed within, smaller than, the sovereignty of the God
> of the Resurrection and Ascension. . . . "Cross and resurrection" desig-
> nates not only a few days' events in first-century Jerusalem but also the
> shape of the cosmos.[49]

Yoder points out that cosmological language of the first century would
have referred to the sociopolitical world in its metaphysical-religious setting,
rather than to the natural world. Yet we cannot help asking what difference
it makes to our view of the *physical* cosmos if the affirmation of John's Prologue is true: if this Jesus is the Word through whom all things came to be.[50]
Is there any sense in which this kenotic conception of God, revealed in the
cross and resurrection of Jesus, finds confirmation in contemporary scientific
cosmology? To this question we turn in the next chapter.

49. Ibid., 246, 160.
50. For Yoder's reflection on the Prologue, see *He Came Preaching Peace*, chap. 6.

Chapter Nine

Ethics, Cosmology, and Theories of God

i OVERVIEW OF THE ARGUMENT

It may be good at this point to remind the reader of the shape of our argument. After establishing a branching hierarchical model for relating the sciences to one another, we turned to contemporary cosmology, asking what it alone could tell us about the nature of ultimate reality. We claimed that the intriguing issue of fine-tuning raises but cannot answer the question of design.

We then turned to the human sciences and argued that these disciplines are essentially incomplete without ethics. But for ethics to fulfill this need, it must possess a degree of objectivity that goes beyond evolutionary programming or mere projection of human value-choices. For this to be the case, there must be an answer to the question, what is the true purpose of human life? This question is best answered theologically. Thus, we have argued that ultimately the social sciences require theology for their completion. Along the way, we have staked a claim for a particular account of the nature of God and for a consequent kenotic view of ethics. The kenotic ethico-theology was (weakly) supported by considerations from the social sciences.

In this chapter we turn back to the natural-science hierarchy in order to show the consequences of our ethico-theological position for issues in these fields. In so doing we intend to show that cosmology, in particular, provides *post hoc* confirmation for both the ethic and the theology. We argue that in light of a theological account of ultimate reality, which includes God's *moral* purposes for the universe, the anthropic features of the universe (i.e., features tending toward the appearance of humans) can now be interpreted as the necessary conditions not only for life but for intelligence and freedom. The anthropic universe is seen to be, more precisely, a moral universe. Once the universe is seen as a moral universe, it becomes possible to explain added cosmological features that other (nontheistic) accounts of the anthropic features cannot explain: Why is there a universe at all? and, Why is it lawlike? Thus, while the purpose of creating free creatures cannot be "read off" from cosmology alone, both life and the lawlike behavior of the nonhuman universe are necessary conditions for freedom. The fact that an ethico-theological account of the fine-tuning provides an answer to the questions *why* the universe is lawlike, and *why* it was suited from the beginning for life provides, via hypothetico-deductive reasoning, confirmation for this view of God.

So far our argument pertains to any theological account that places an emphasis on human moral response. The next step will be to survey factors from the natural sciences that are especially consistent with our kenotic account of God and of morality. We can see hints of these patterns at lower levels of the hierarchy of the natural sciences. In biology, the suffering of nonhuman life can be seen as a "non-moral harbinger" of conscious self-sacrifice.[1] In physics, a theory of divine action as noncoercive can be made consistent with quantum theory, wherein the indeterminacy of quantum events serves as an analogue for human freedom.

Finally, having constructed a logical bridge, via theology, between the natural sciences and ethics, we consider some of the factors from natural science that condition the moral sphere. The following figures represent the structure of our argument. Our simplest representation is Figure 9.1, where the logical relations are hypothetico-deductive.

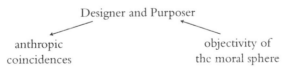

Designer and Purposer

anthropic coincidences   objectivity of the moral sphere

Fig. 9.1. Hypothetico-deductive relations in our argument.

A more complex representation of our argument follows in Figure 9.2 where the single arrows represent consistency relations and the double arrows represent hypothetico-deductive relations.

We can describe the structure of our argument as follows: We argued that,

1. Holmes Rolston, III, "Does Nature Need to Be Redeemed?" *Zygon* 29, no. 2 (June, 1994): 205–29.

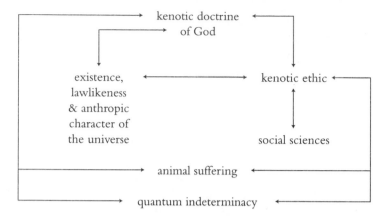

Fig. 9.2. Consistency relations added to the argument.

on the one hand, the hierarchy of the natural sciences was incomplete without a top layer of a metaphysical nature (chap. 3); and on the other, that the hierarchy of the human and applied sciences was incomplete without a moral layer above, which in turn needed a metaphysical or, preferably, theological layer on top (chaps. 4–8). We now take the obvious step of unifying the explanation by supposing that these two metaphysical/theological layers might be the same, since each branch of the hierarchy seems to call for some account of *purpose* for its completion. A single theory of divine purpose answers the ultimate questions arising from each branch of the hierarchy. (See Figure 9.3)

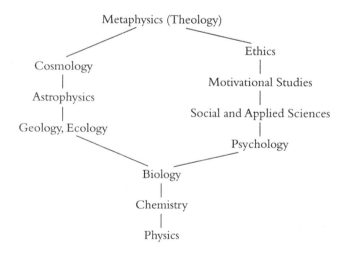

Fig. 9.3. Hierarchy of the natural and human sciences, including cosmology, completed by a metaphysical/theological layer.

This final figure, completing the hierarchical picture, immediately leads to interesting consequences. On requiring that this scheme as a whole be consistent, one sees that the moral nature of the universe, based in its ultimate purpose, constrains its physical nature—and vice-versa. These are the relations we explore in this chapter.

We deal with the question of the justification of our system in the following chapter, but a few remarks are in order here. It is an argument best described by holist epistemology, according to which the support for any thesis consists in the degree of logical interconnection between it and other beliefs that one has no good reason to call into question. The logical links are either hypothetico-deductive or relations of mere coherence and consistency. The overall form might also be designated a cumulative case argument, in that no single piece of evidence carries much weight in itself, but the combined force of all the pieces is increased, due to the fact that each piece makes one of a variety of possible interpretations of each other piece more probable.

2 THEOLOGY AND COSMOLOGY

First, we determine implications for the physical universe of assuming it was created in order that humankind (or at least ethically aware self-conscious beings) might exist. From a materialist viewpoint this is a grossly anthropocentric view of the nature of the universe for—materialistically considered—the human species is an insignificant feature in the vast realms of space, filled with vast numbers of galaxies, each of which is made of vast numbers of stars. On this view, however, it is precisely the highest levels of order in the known universe—the extraordinary structure and function of the human body, making possible moral and religious understanding—that gives the whole its ultimate meaning and, indeed, its rationale for existence.

This claim does not necessarily mean that the whole enterprise is concentrated on humankind specifically (that is, on the species that has evolved on the particular planet Earth in our particular galaxy) but rather that it has its meaning through laws of physics and chemistry that will allow development of intelligent and responsive life, wherever it may evolve. If we accept even the pessimistic assumptions of Barrow and Tipler,[2] there is one advanced civilization in each galaxy, and so about 10^{11} in the observable region of the universe (and conceivably many more in the part that is unobservable). It is the total moral and religious response of all these beings that reflects the underlying purpose. Thus, the viewpoint is not anthropocentric in a pre-

---

2. John D. Barrow and Frank J. Tipler, *The Anthropic Cosmological Principle* (Oxford: Oxford University Press, 1986).

Copernican sense of being limited to our particular existence alone but incorporates that existence into a broader and more "democratic" view of the value of all intelligent life in the universe (which almost certainly exists in many other places as well).

The point we emphasize here is that this assumption of the moral purpose of the universe explains the anthropic features of the universe; at the same time it also provides for cosmology the missing answers to metaphysical questions that physical science itself is unable to answer: Why is there a universe at all? Why does the universe behave in a lawlike manner? Thus, this explanation of the anthropic features of the universe is broader in scope than any of the other possibilities surveyed in chapter 3 and serves to complete the hierarchy of the physical sciences.

The usefulness of a divine creator for explaining the existence of the universe needs no further comment here. The proposed moral purpose of the universe places two kinds of constraints on physical science: (1) the lawlike character of the universe, and (2) the existence of effective free will. We look at each of these in turn.

2.1 The Lawlike Character of the Universe

If the ultimate purpose of the universe is to make possible free, moral response to the creator, then there is a need for the creation of a universe where ordered patterns of events occur, for without this order free will is meaningless. If there were no rules governing natural phenomena or reliable patterns of events, it would not be possible to have a meaningful moral response to events, since one could not predict the outcome of one's actions. Thus, the material world, through which sentient beings are to be realized, needs to exhibit repeatable and understandable patterns of events.

Of course, one might argue that for there to be a cosmos at all (*cosmos* means order) there must be regularity and thus laws. But, as Paul Davies points out,[3] these regularities need not have been simple or obvious enough for the limited human mind to perceive them. The issue of why they should be describable in mathematical terms is a deep one, but the answer is not essential to the further argument here.

One way of attaining the requisite regularity is through physical laws. A difficult question is whether this is the only way to attain such repeatable patterns of behavior; the answer is not clear. This is partly because we do not understand the underlying basis of physical laws, in the sense of knowing how the behavior they characterize is embodied in matter: Is there in some sense a mathematical formulation of these laws embodied in reality? Is there some

---

3. *The Mind of God* (New York: Simon and Schuster, 1992).

kind of template for each kind of particle, embodying its physical behavior but not described in a mathematical sense? Is the behavior the result of the creator simply imaging the desired results and requiring the realized structure to conform, or, finally, is it the result of divine action immanent in the elementary constituents of the universe?[4] In any case, it seems likely that in whatever way order is realized ontologically, the appearance will be that of "laws" underlying the regularity.

For want of a better understanding, we envisage the creator at all times maintaining the nature and processes of the physical world so that a chosen set of laws of physics *describe* its evolution. It must be emphasized that once this choice has been made, providing it is adhered to (as will be assumed), then the action of laws will be seen by us as absolute and rigorously determining the behavior of matter. One can then act freely within the confines of the laws, but the laws themselves cannot be altered by any human action.

2.2 The Anthropic Universe and Free Will

A moral universe requires much more than lawlike regularity, however; it is necessary that the laws and regularities within the physical universe allow for the existence of *intelligent* beings who can sense and react in a conscious way and who have *free will*. This means that whatever the underlying mechanisms governing the human brain, there must be meaningful freedom of choice that can be exercised in a responsible way. We here touch on issues that science has not seriously begun to comprehend: we do not understand the nature of consciousness nor the "free will" we experience, notwithstanding the advances made in this direction, as mentioned in chapter 2. We assume freedom of action, albeit constrained by many biological, psychological, and social factors, for without this the concept of morality is meaningless.

If we consider, then, necessary prerequisites concerning physical laws for the existence of beings with free will, we presume acceptance of the conclusions of the anthropic discussion of chapter 3, section 2.2. The Strong Anthropic Principle would in effect be realized, but without the need for a basis imposed by physical theory; and necessarily all the restrictions implied by the W.A.P. as conditions for the existence of life (e.g., restrictions on the nature

---

4. See W. R. Stoeger, "Contemporary Physics and the Ontological Status of the Laws of Nature," in Robert J. Russell, Nancey Murphy, and C. J. Isham, eds., *Quantum Cosmology and the Laws of Nature: Scientific Perspectives on Divine Action* (Vatican City State and Berkeley, Calif.: Vatican Observatory and Center for Theology and the Natural Sciences, 1993), 209–34; and Nancey Murphy, "Divine Action in the Natural Order: Buridan's Ass and Schrödinger's Cat," in Robert J. Russell, Nancey Murphy, and Arthur Peacocke, eds., *Chaos and Complexity: Scientific Perspectives on Divine Action* (Vatican City State and Berkeley, Calif.: Vatican Observatory and Center for Theology and the Natural Sciences, 1995), 325–57.

of physical laws and limits on the value of the fine structure constant) must be fulfilled. The strictly scientific criteria of the W.A.P. come into play and provide observable consequences regarding the nature of the physical universe in the region we can observe (e.g., that there must be times and places where the background temperature is lower than 3000K, above which a living body could not exist because all atoms would be ionized).

The additional conditions required to attain free will are not normally emphasized in discussions of the anthropic principle. We emphasized in the previous section that a lawlike universe is necessary in order to make free choice *meaningful,* yet those very laws must be such as to permit *undetermined* human actions. We do not know definitively what these conditions are, except that they probably involve the efficacy of top-down causation. It is possible that a fundamental physical indeterminacy at the microlevel, such as we have discovered in quantum mechanics, is needed also. This is, however, highly debatable (cf. section 5.1 below). Thus, we envisage the creator choosing such a framework for the universe (so giving up all the other possibilities allowed by divine power).

From this viewpoint the fine-tuning that is the central puzzle addressed by the anthropic principle is not regarded as *direct* evidence for a universal designer, but rather is seen as a *consequence* of the aim of a designer whose existence we are postulating. Thus, the relation between the concept of a designer and the fine-tuning is hypothetico-deductive. That is, while the fine-tuning does not logically require the assumption of a designer, the existence of a God with the intentions so described provides a suitable explanation of fine-tuning. The fact that the designer hypothesis explains the fine-tuning as well as broader features of the universe means that these features of the universe provide (partial) confirmation for the designer's existence.[5]

3 COSMOLOGY AND THE KENOTIC UNIVERSE

Any moral response requires an ordered and predictable universe, as well as creatures with free will. Not all moral systems, however, place respect for the other's freedom at the very center of the system. Recall the claim of chapter 6 that the reason for insisting on nonviolence as essential to morality is that it is the ultimate form of noncoercion. That is, most ethical systems permit (or even require) the use of coercion in extreme circumstances—that "greater" good might come—and the ultimate form of coercion is violence. In Christian ethics this feature goes back to Augustine's judgment that it is

---

5. See Nancey Murphy, "Evidence of Design in the Fine-Tuning of the Universe," in *Quantum Cosmology.*

better to coerce the body than to lose the soul to eternal damnation. But the Anabaptists objected that a coerced response to God is of no value.

Thus, our account of ethics, with noncoercion at its core, counts freedom of response an ultimate good, one not to be sacrificed for other ends. We now begin to look at the necessary conditions in the natural world for our claim that the ultimate purpose of the universe is to allow for this uncoerced response to the creator, and thus for an ethic we have termed "kenotic."

The first consequence is that we are able to respond to a countercharge that might be raised against a theistic explanation of the fine-tuning of the universe; namely, if the universe is the product of intentional design, then why is the evidence for the existence of a designer so ambiguous? We respond that there are two important features required of the universe by the further specification of a *noncoercive* relation between God and creatures: (1) the provident universe, and (2) the hidden nature of ultimate reality. A further requirement, the possibility of revelation, will be considered in section 5. We look at traces of our kenotic account in biology and quantum physics in the following two sections.

3.1 The Provident Universe

Given the existence of creatures who possess free will, one can still imagine universes arranged in such a way that choice is essentially constrained. That is, it is perfectly conceivable that the universe should be so ordered that comfort or even survival should be dependent on obedience to God. Recall from chapter 7 (section 3.3.2) that there is a wide range of forms of persuasion and coercion. Cadoux includes promises, rewards, and bribes as noncoercive forms of persuasion. If we imagine a God, however, with power to withhold all physical support (reward) in the case of noncompliance, this surely falls within the category of coercion.

Jesus makes it clear, however, that it is not God's will that the universe be arranged in such a manner: the heavenly Father "causes the sun to rise on good and bad alike, and sends the rain on the innocent and the wicked" (Matt 5:45 NEB). The context of this passage is Jesus' explanation of why his disciples must love enemies and pray for persecutors. Thus, Jesus is depicted here as basing his ethic of self-renunciation and nonviolence on what later ethicists would call the "orders of creation."

It is also possible to interpret Jesus' temptations, both in the desert at the beginning of his ministry and in Gethsemane at the end, as temptations to compel cooperation with his political agenda by providing material comfort to his potential followers ("Tell these stones to become bread" [Matt 4:3 NEB]) or by force ("Put up your sword. Do you suppose that I cannot appeal for help to my Father and at once be sent more than twelve legions of angels?" [Matt 26:52–53 NEB]). He rejects these possibilities, thus adopting an ethic of kenosis.[6]

So what we see in nature is that the impartial operation of the laws of physics, chemistry, and biology offers to all persons alike the bounty of nature, irrespective of their beliefs or moral condition. The major requirement is that the laws of physics allow the growth of food for all humankind in an impartial way—their religious observance or obedience does not affect this provision (as they are taken to do in many of the older religions). This does not impose further physical conditions; rather it follows from the basic anthropic under-standing just explained, for humankind could not evolve were this not the case. Thus, the very existence of humanity, in a world governed by physical laws, guarantees the satisfaction of this requirement. This mode of operation of the physical world thus fulfills the condition of freeing people from a need for obedience to God in order to survive, and so makes a free and uncon-strained response possible.

3.2 The Hidden Nature of Ultimate Reality

The question why, in our atheistic age, the evidence for God's existence seems so weak and ambiguous has led to the suggestion by John Hick that a further requirement must be satisfied to enable the free response envisaged by Jesus.[7] This is the requirement of epistemic distance—that the created world not be so dominated by God that belief in the existence and nature of God would be forced on everyone, with a resulting demand on their behav-ior. This would be the case, for example, if there were some kind of explicit marks in the creation making clear that there had to be a creator.[8]

While Hick's position might be overstated,[9] it is at least the case that such direct proof of God's existence and nature would eliminate the necessity for moral discernment. Furthermore, such direct insight into the ultimate cost of disobedience would invite only a grudging allegiance to God's ways.

The requisite hiddenness of God is satisfied through the nature of creation as we see it, apparently governed by impartial physical laws, which neverthe-less allow hints as to God's existence and true nature. Sufficient evidence is given for knowledge of God's existence and an outline of God's will, but this

---

6. See Yoder's commentary in *The Politics of Jesus,* 2d ed. (Grand Rapids, Mich.: 1994), chap. 2.

7. John Hick, *Evil and the God of Love* (New York: Harper and Row, 1966). Also, John Yoder interprets Jesus' refusal to throw himself off the parapet of the temple (Matt 4:5–7) as refusal to give an overwhelming sign of his divine prerogatives. See *Politics,* chap. 2.

8. Cf. for example, Carl Sagan's novel, *Contact* (London: Arrow Books, 1985), where a message to humankind is hidden in the digits of the fundamental number π.

9. For a critique, see J. L. Schellenberg, *Divine Hiddenness and Human Reason* (Ithaca, N.Y.: Cor-nell University Press, 1993).

evidence is not overwhelming; human sinfulness (self-interest) can make us see without seeing and hear without hearing. The ability to see the truth is dependent on readiness to listen and openness to the message (John 3:3).

4 ECHOES OF KENOSIS IN BIOLOGY

If the view of God and morality developed in the previous chapters is correct, one might expect to find echoes of this kenotic idea in various aspects of the physical world. We have emphasized the costliness to God of God's decision to cooperate with human creatures rather than to overrule them by sheer power. The view here presented agrees exactly with what is described by William Temple: "What we find is power in complete subordination to love."[10] For on this view, the possible exercise of creative power by the creator is voluntarily restricted to that which enables a universe where a free and loving response by humankind is possible, despite the costs and sacrifice entailed.

But there is also a costliness for God's human creatures in imitating this character of God. Holmes Rolston has extended this insight to the world of nature. Rolston's thesis is that suffering in the natural world is, in a sense, redemptive. It is a necessary byproduct of the features of life that allow for the emergence of something higher. And just as God suffers in and with human suffering to bring forth greater good, God suffers, as well, in and with all of life.[11] We quote Rolston's inimitable prose at length:

> The Earth is a divine creation and scene of providence. The whole natural history is somehow contained in God, God's doing, and that includes even suffering, which, if it is difficult to say simply that it is immediately from God, is not ultimately outside of God's plan and redemptive control. God absorbs suffering and transforms it into goodness. . . .
>
> Nature is. . . . cruciform. The world is not a paradise of hedonistic ease, but a theater where life is learned and earned by labor, a drama where even the evils drive us to make sense of things. Life is advanced not only by thought and action, but by suffering, not only by logic but by pathos. . . .
>
> This pathetic element in nature is seen in faith to be at the deepest logical level the pathos in God. God is not in a simple way the Benevolent Architect, but is rather the Suffering Redeemer. The whole of the earthen metabolism needs to be understood as having this character. The God met in physics as the divine wellspring from which matter-energy bubbles up . . . is in biology the suffering and resurrecting power that redeems life out of chaos. . . .

10. See *Readings in St. John's Gospel* (London: Macmillan, 1961).
11. Cf. the gospel of all creatures, below, chap. 10, sec. 4.1.

The secret of life is seen now to lie not so much in the heredity molecules, not so much in natural selection and the survival of the fittest, not so much in life's informational, cybernetic learning. The secret of life is that it is a passion play. Things perish in tragedy. The religions knew that full well, before biology arose to reconfirm it. But things perish with a passing over in which the sacrificed individual also flows in the river of life. Each of the suffering creatures is delivered over as an innocent sacrificed to preserve a line, a blood sacrifice perishing that others may live. We have a kind of "slaughter of the innocents," a nonmoral, naturalistic harbinger of the slaughter of the innocents at the birth of the Christ, all perhaps vignettes hinting of the innocent lamb slain from the foundation of the world. They share the labor of the divinity. In their lives, beautiful, tragic, and perpetually incomplete, they speak for God; they prophesy as they participate in the divine pathos. All have "borne our griefs and carried our sorrows."

The abundant life that Jesus exemplifies and offers to his disciples is that of a sacrificial suffering through to something higher. There is something divine about the power to suffer through to something higher. The Spirit of God is the genius that makes alive, that redeems life from its evils. The cruciform creation is, in the end, deiform, godly, just because of this element of struggle, not in spite of it. There is a great divine "yes" hidden behind and within every "no" of crushing nature. God, who is the lure toward rationality and sentience in the upcurrents of the biological pyramid, is also the compassionate lure in, with, and under all purchasing of life at the cost of sacrifice. God rescues from suffering, but the Judeo-Christian faith never teaches that God eschews suffering in the achievement of the divine purposes. To the contrary, seen in the paradigm of the cross, God too suffers, not less than his creatures, in order to gain for his creatures a more abundant life.[12]

In more prosaic terms, a central feature of biological life is the recycling of materials through many generations, taking place through the major resource cycles: the carbon cycle, oxygen cycle, nitrogen cycle, for example.[13] Thus, we are lent the materials of our body to use for a while and then return to nature; after a while the same materials are lent to other living organisms, and so on. Indeed, the materials out of which each of us is made have already been incorporated in thousands of animals and plants before us (the great majority, very simple organisms: bacteria and algae, for example), and will be so incorporated again after we die. There is even a similar pattern in astro-

12. Rolston, "Does Nature Need to Be Redeemed? quotation, 218–20 *passim.*

13. See Paul R. Ehrlich and Anne H. Ehrlich, *Population, Resources, Environment: Issues in Human Ecology* (San Francisco: W. H. Freeman, 1972).

physics: the first generation of stars must "die" in order that elements formed in them might be incorporated into new stars, these second-generation stars then having the right elements to form the planets.

Thus, in a physical sense we are part of a great chain of being, not only in terms of our genetic inheritance, which records hundreds of millions of years of evolutionary history and shapes our bodies in conformity with that history, but also through the very materials of our bodies, which are only temporarily bound in each particular expression of their capacity for life.

So the necessity for death is founded in the way our particular universe works, specifically in the way life is constructed from its microphysical foundations, with associated entropic decay. The question then arises: Are these features necessary? Could there be a universe with life but without death or pain? The anthropic arguments show how narrow the options are for a life-supporting universe. The very regularities that make life possible, by their very nature, severely restrict other possibilities. Hence it seems quite unlikely that there could be a universe with life but without the long-term recycling of materials that necessitates the death of living organisms.

Are pain and suffering, then, a necessary component of any life-bearing universe? Again, the regularities that make life possible also severely restrict the capacities of living organisms, and it is often these limits, coming up against the inexorable processes of physical nature, that result in injury, pain, and suffering. Pain seems to be necessary in any universe that involves freedom, since it protects the higher organisms from self-destructive behavior.

In short, all living things must participate not only in the taking of life in order to live but also in the painful *giving* of their lives that others might live. It has been common since the development of evolutionary biology to emphasize the necessary taking of life (and from this has developed social Darwinist theories of ethics and politics). Rolston's imaginative construal of the biological processes, however, invites us to focus as well on the equally prominent pattern in nature of the giving of one's life. Whether one takes one's moral cues from "nature red in tooth and claw" or from Rolston's presentation of "cruciform creation" cannot be determined from biology alone, but only from seeing biology in the context of a broader worldview. Within this context, we argue, Rolston's can be seen as the correct reading.

5 NONCOERCIVE DIVINE ACTION AND PHYSICAL REALITY

We suggested above (in chap. 2) that it may be necessary that the lowest level of the hierarchy of complexity, the quantum level, exhibit indeterminacy in order that genuine top-down action be possible. Another way of putting this same point with regard to human behavior is that the indeterminacy of quantum events in the brain may be a necessary prerequisite for freedom of the will. So far, all of this is highly speculative.

Elsewhere we have argued that quantum indeterminacy provides the best possibility for giving an account of noninterventionist (noncoercive) divine action.[14] Here we reverse the direction of our arguments and claim that the theological requirement for a noncoercive mode of divine action provides an *explanation* (in the sense of a reason, not a cause) for indeterminacy at the lowest level of the hierarchy of complexity. In this section we consider two related topics: divine action at the quantum level, and the role of indeterminacy in revelation.

5.1 Divine Action at the Quantum Level
We claim that any account of divine action throughout the hierarchy of levels of complexity must show forth God's consistency. If the paradigm of divine activity for Christians is found in the story of Jesus, we should expect that same divine moral character to be manifested, analogously, in God's action within subhuman orders. The relevant feature of God's action is its self-sacrificial and noncoercive character.

We have just argued above that the self-sacrifice and suffering occasioned by choosing noncoercion over domination finds its nonmoral analogue at the biological level. Here we argue that God's noncoercive dealings with human creatures finds a nonmoral analogue at the quantum level.

One of the most pervasive theological problems since the rise of modern science has been the problem of divine action. Deists and many theologians on the liberal end of the spectrum have rejected interventionist accounts of divine action, largely because of the apparent irrationality of a God who would both ordain the laws of nature and then violate those very laws.

We, too, reject interventionist accounts, but on the basis of God's morality, not God's rationality: it is inconsistent with God's refusal to overrule or dominate creatures.[15] We argue that God grants each creature the "right" to be itself. (This is also an important thesis for answering the problem of evil—

---

14. See Murphy, "Divine Action in the Natural Order"; and George F. R. Ellis, "Ordinary and Extraordinary Divine Action," both in *Chaos and Complexity.*

15. Bernard J. F. Lonergan speaks of "intervention's implication of violence." See *Grace and Freedom: Operative Grace in the Thought of St. Thomas Aquinas,* ed. J. Patout Burns (London: Darton, Longman and Todd, 1971), 43; Gordon Kaufman also rejects divine intervention, describing it as God "violently ripping into the fabric of history," in "On the Meaning of 'Act of God,'" in Owen C. Thomas, ed., *God's Activity in the World: The Contemporary Problem* (Chico, Calif.: Scholars Press, 1983), 137–61; quotation p. 157. We think it odd that theologians who so vehemently reject a conception of divine intervention in the natural world do not consistently reject human "intervention." However, Kaufman, a pacifist, is consistent on this point.

see below, chap. 10.) The peculiarity of quantum events or entities, as far as current science can tell us, however, is that they are intrinsically indeterminate in certain respects. Thus, for God to manipulate them (within strict limits) is not inconsistent with the decision to respect their "rights" to be themselves; there is no self-determination in (certain aspects of) their behavior, which God over-rules.

Thus, from a theological point of view, we can say that something like this indeterminacy could have been predicted on the basis of a theory of noncoercive divine action in the subhuman world. This openness is needed at the bottom level of the hierarchical structuring to enable noninterventionist divine action.

We shall not attempt here to specify the extent of divine influence on macroscopic events that this account of divine action allows us to envision; for example, how and whether it explains biblical miracle accounts.[16] There is one kind of divine action, however, that it is our express intention to address, namely, revelation.

5.2 Quantum Indeterminacy and Revelation

The final physical requirement for our worldview to be coherent is that there be a means or channel for divine revelation. That is, despite the hidden nature of underlying reality, it must be open to those who wish to do so to discern its true nature (indeed, on the view taken here, it is God's intention that they should do so) and, further, to receive encouragement to follow the kenotic way that is indicated by this ultimate reality. There is a double requirement here, both for knowledge of God and for knowledge of right and wrong (conscience).

There are two broad types of views on the nature of revelation: One emphasizes the ability of humans to survey the processes of nature and history and to perceive for themselves the patterns of God's intentions. This sort of theory arose in the modern period, and we see it as an attempt to circumvent the problem of explaining how divine action can occur in a closed causal order.[17] For example, Maurice Wiles is one of the advocates of a theory of divine action wherein God is understood to enact the entire creative process

16. See, however, Robert J. Russell's account of divine action through quantum events in the process of evolution. This is a valuable approach in an area where the problem is to explain how God is at work in a process that manifests so little evidence of divine design. See "Theistic Evolution and Special Providence: Does God Really Act in Nature?" in Russell, William R. Stoeger, and Francisco J. Ayala, eds., *Biological Evolution: Scientific Perspectives on Divine Action* (Vatican City State and Berkeley, Calif.: Vatican Observatory and Center for Theology and the Natural Sciences, forthcoming).

17. See Nancey Murphy, *Beyond Liberalism and Fundamentalism: How Modern and Postmodern Philosophy Set the Theological Agenda* (Valley Forge, Pa.: Trinity Press International, 1996), chap. 3.

of the universe, but there are no events that are in any special sense particular acts of God. He relates this view of divine action to the recognition of problems with a "God of the gaps" strategy for understanding divine action. The question arises how the Scriptures can be authoritative for theology if they are not the product of special revelation. His answer depends on special abilities of some people to perceive what God is doing within the whole historical process:

> Now it is an inevitable feature of the variety to be found within human history that some people by virtue of their personality and of their situation are more fully responsive to the divine action than others. Their words and actions in turn will provide a particularly important focus for calling out such responses from others who follow them. And since that quality of life in them to which those others will respond was itself grounded in responsiveness to the divine action, we may rightly speak of the events of their lives as acts of God in a special sense towards those of us who are influenced by them. In calling them special acts of God we would not be implying that there was any fundamental difference in the relation of the divine action to the particular worldly occurrences of their situation; we would be referring to the depth of response and the creative potential for eliciting further response from others embodied in those particular lives or those particular events.[18]

It is interesting that Arthur Peacocke gives even clearer expression to this theory of revelation, despite the fact that one of the main goals of his work is to provide an account of special (but noninterventionist) divine acts:

> It is as if the Creator has endowed matter-energy-space-time, the stuff of the universe, with a propensity now actualized in humanity to discern the meaning in the cosmic process which its Creator has written into it. For in humanity, the stuff of the world has acquired a form and functionality that makes it capable of reading those meanings in existence which are the immanence of the transcendent God of the whole cosmic process.[19]

The other broad sort of theory emphasizes God's active self-revelation— in Ronald Thiemann's terms, God's prevenience.[20] Our theory is of the second sort. We contend that some provision must be made, for those who wish to do so, to obtain an understanding of the full nature of reality in order that

---

18. Maurice Wiles, "Religious Authority and Divine Action," in Thomas, *God's Activity in the World*, 181–94; quotation, 188.

19. Arthur Peacocke, *Theology for a Scientific Age: Being and Becoming—Natural, Human, and Divine*, 2nd, enlarged ed. (Minneapolis: Fortress Press, 1993), 179.

20. See Ronald F. Thiemann, *Revelation and Theology* (Notre Dame, Ind.: University of Notre Dame Press, 1985).

they can properly realize God's plan. Part of the Christian answer to the need for revelation is to claim that this is precisely what the life of Jesus was about; and this does indeed provide a revolutionary answer to the problem of revelation in light of an account of nature based on physical law. This does not fully resolve the problem, however; for if Jesus was fully human, how then did he obtain his vision of reality? The same issue arises in this case as in the case of the prophets and saints, and indeed for the ordinary believer.

Thus, we will assume that there must be a channel through which God can act, in a noninterventionist manner, in order to make available visions of ultimate reality to persons open to them—allowing the nature of that transcendent reality to make itself known, making available to us new patterns of understanding, and providing encouragement and strength to follow these visions. This feature (corresponding to the Quaker notion of "the light within") is clearly related to the issue of the immanence of God, for this kind of feature allows a truly immanent (effective) presence of God in the world.

A possible physical basis for this kind of communication lies in quantum indeterminacy.[21] We suggest that divine action at the quantum level within the human nervous system might indeed provide a means for divine communication, by stimulating the visions and other religious experiences described in religious literature, or perhaps more simply by supplying positive or negative impulses associated with a person's own thoughts or intentions.

George Tyrrell, a Catholic theologian writing a century ago, devoted a great deal of attention to the "how" of revelation. In his early work he suggested that revelation is indeed knowledge derived from God, but indirectly. "What alone is directly given from above . . . is the spiritual craving or impulse with its specific determination, with its sympathetic and antipathetic responses to the suggestions, practical or explanatory, that are presented to it."[22] Later he provided a more full-bodied account of the effects of divine revelation: "It is an experience made up of feelings and impulses and imaginings; which reverberates in every corner of the soul and leaves its impress everywhere."[23]

The argument from quantum physics (along with the supposition that quantum events are implicated in the production of human experiences) shows that accounts of revelation such as Tyrrell's are conceivable without contradicting the laws of physics—without invoking a God of the gaps.

Undoubtedly this attempt to relate religious theories of revelation and divine action to science is controversial. We believe, however, that religious

21. See George F. R. Ellis, "The Theology of the Anthropic Principle," in *Quantum Cosmology.*

22. George Tyrrell, "The Rights and Limits of Theology," *Quarterly Review* (Oct. 1905); reprinted in *Through Scylla and Charybdis* (London: Longmans, Green, 1907), 207.

23. Ibid., 282.

experience itself is an important experience, a datum, to be taken into account in any worldview. Without some such account as ours it is in danger of being explained reductively—that is, in purely psychological terms. Furthermore, an "activist" account of divine revelation is essential to avoid the conclusion that religion is merely a human projection, merely a subjective search for meaning. It is also needed to avoid a correlative account of morality as mere human invention, with attendant cultural relativism, or alternatively as merely the result of blind evolutionary processes.

6 CONSISTENCY WITH THE SCIENTIFIC PICTURE

It should be noted that nothing we have said is in contradiction to the usual physical understanding of the universe. Rather, what we have is an extra layer of explanation offered for the physical world we see around us, providing a kind of rationale for the need for the physical universe to have some of the general features that science reveals.

Physicists can simply claim that there is no need for this extra layer of explanation in order to understand the physical world, and they will be right—provided we attempt to explain only physical reality, accept without question the given nature of physical laws, and ignore the question of the ontological status of those laws, *as well as* all the issues raised by the existence of a moral or ethical order, by religious experience, and, indeed, also by the aesthetic dimension of life encompassed in great art and music. When we try to make sense of these extra dimensions of existence, the simple physical explanation is woefully lacking; something like that offered here is much more profound and satisfying.

This point can be understood in terms of the hierarchy of complexity discussed in chapter 2, where it was made clear that, when viewed in terms of lower-level concepts alone, the higher-level concepts simply do not apply; they cannot even be defined in terms of the lower-level language. That is the situation here: the hierarchy, including its higher levels, is a complete and compelling system. If one insists on viewing it only from a perspective that excludes consideration of the issues and kinds of explanation described at the higher-levels of the hierarchical structure, then these levels do appear superfluous and, indeed, meaningless. So the issue is how complete a worldview or explanatory scheme one wishes to have.

If we include a highest level of explanation, of the specific nature discussed above, we attain a picture that unites the two branches of the hierarchy of the sciences, with a single metaphysical account of the purpose of the whole serving to create a coherent system.

7 THE NATURAL-SCIENTIFIC CONTEXT FOR MORALITY

So far in this chapter we have considered ways in which our ethico-theological account sheds light on features of the cosmos known from the natural sciences. In this section we look at a few of the ways in which physical reality constrains the moral sphere by shaping the context in which it operates. Thus, in terms of the structure of thought represented in Figure 9.3, the left-hand branch of the hierarchy partially shapes the right.

This shaping happens, first, by making moral activity possible at all (as just discussed, by allowing for life, intelligence, free will, and predictability), but also through determining basic features of the physical world such as the conservation of matter. This conservation is needed for the temporary stability of our existence, but it also causes the scarcities of resources that shape much of our physical and social lives (cf. chap. 3).[24] This is the context within which generosity and sharing are needed; if we could conjure resources out of nowhere, such behavior would not be required. If we could reconstitute and repair injured bodies merely by thought, medicine would not be necessary and bodily harm would not be a serious crime. Thus, physical reality in turn plays an important role in shaping the context and needs of moral behavior.

In this context, too, death plays a role. As explained above, death is an expression of intergenerational sharing; but also it is of fundamental importance for our moral lives, both by providing finite time limits on those lives (if we lived eternally, we would always have more time to correct our actions; nothing would ever be final), and by providing the final context for limits on our actions—the fact that we are able to affect the physical existence of humans (ourselves and others).

8 CONCLUSIONS

We have now completed the exposition of our argument. Our claim is that while each of the disciplines considered here is, for many purposes, complete in itself, there arise questions or problems ("boundary questions") that can only be answered by moving to another level of discourse. Modern thinkers emphasized the search downward in the hierarchy of the sciences (reductionism). We emphasize the search upward. The highest level of understand-

---

24. See also Robert J. Russell, "Entropy and Evil," *Zygon* 19, no. 4 (Dec. 1984): 449–68; James Wm. McClendon, Jr., *Ethics: Systematic Theology, Volume One* (Nashville, Tenn.: Abingdon Press, 1986), chap. 3.

ing is the theological. We claim (1) that certain aspects of reality require the context of a vision of the purpose of the whole in order to be fully intelligible, and (2) that the context of the whole, most adequately addressed theologically, provides an intellectual "bridge" whereby the natural sciences and the human sciences (including ethics) mutually illumine one another.

Yet, not just any theology (nor just any ethic) is compatible with the findings of science; we have presented a particular account of the moral nature of God and of God's will for human life that we believe is uniquely fitted to the universe as we now understand it, and that in turn places features of that universe in a more intelligible perspective.

It is also the case that not just any account of the *nature* of theology (and of ethics) will do. There are some views of religion according to which theology is merely an *interpretation* of reality, a perception of "meaning." But if these meanings are merely human projections, it is clear that such an account will not do here, for human projections cannot be in any sense *explanations* of the nature of the physical cosmos, which precedes the first human religious awareness by some billions of years. Thus, we are making claims not merely about better ways to interpret reality, but about the nature of reality itself.

The completion of our project requires an epistemological evaluation of our claims, to which we turn in the next and final chapter.

Chapter Ten

Epistemological Evaluation

I SCOPE OF THE EVALUATION

The purpose of this chapter is to provide an epistemological assessment of the system sketched in the previous chapters. In so doing, we shall make use of the three theories of rationality described in chapter 1. We began with the fine structure of scientific theories and the logical relations between a theory and its confirming evidence, as described by Carl Hempel and others (the hypothetico–deductive method). We then turned to the methodology of Imre Lakatos for a picture both of the organization of scientific knowledge and of the evaluation of vast networks of theory and data (research programs). While both Lakatos and Hempel meant to speak only of the criteria for evaluating scientific theories, we have claimed that these standards of evaluation are applicable (with slight modifications) to theology and ethics, as well.

Finally, we turned to the work of Alasdair MacIntyre for an account of the coarse structure of knowledge. MacIntyre provided a technical definition of a "tradition," and also provided criteria for adjudicating between competing traditions on the basis of their ability to incorporate competitors or solve problems that were insoluble with the resources of the competitor alone. We will follow this progression from small to large scale now, in marshalling support for our position.

To see where each of these levels of analysis and evaluation applies, we review the epistemological structure of our program. In essence, we have set out to establish the claim that Christian belief, especially as articulated in one particular strand of the Christian tradition (the Anabaptist or Radical-Reformation strand) is capable of elaboration in such a way as to take account of current developments in science. A major reason for its effectiveness in this regard is its ethical component—a component that relates a theory of the moral character of God to an ethical program for humankind.

That there be a strong moral component in the total system was shown to be important in that the applied and human sciences are essentially incomplete without an objective account of human purpose or "values." The particular account of the character of God and of God's purposes that we endorsed is especially valuable, we claimed, in that it not only provides the necessary ethical grounding for the social sciences but also explains features of the world known from the natural sciences.

The three theories of rationality just mentioned apply to our system on three levels of scale. The logical relations between theory and data (and also between higher- and lower-level theories) are hypothetico-deductive. In previous chapters we have mentioned some of the relevant data that our set of hypotheses is intended to explain, and we shall provide an overview below.

At each level of the hierarchy of the sciences, now elaborated to include both ethics and theology, the epistemological structure is that of a research program (or a set of interrelated research programs). That is, we presented a theological research program in chapter 8, an ethical program in chapter 6, and these in turn were related (hypothetico-deductively at various points) to a variety of natural- and social-scientific research programs located below them in the hierarchy of the sciences.

Along the way we have paid some attention to Lakatosian-style evaluation of the research programs concerned. In particular we indicated reasons for believing that our theological program is progressive. We shall pursue this further below.

To perform a thorough evaluation of our contribution at this level would require an exhaustive examination of all of the competing research programs at the various levels. That is, we would have to compare our theological proposal to all major theological competitors, both historical and current: process theology, various forms of liberation theology, neo-orthodoxy, an assortment of programs growing out of the liberal tradition, Evangelical theology, and so on.

An even greater undertaking would be the evaluation of our ethical program. This would be more challenging because it would require a thorough reconceiving of each of the competitors, since (with the exception of MacIntyre) current ethicists, both theological and philosophical, do not see themselves as developing research programs (in this sense) at all.

Finally, we have claimed that it would be possible to develop new research programs in the human sciences that incorporate in their hard cores the assumption that the development of noncoercive social structures and nonviolent, self-sacrificing personalities is both achievable and of ultimate value. At present, we believe there is a scattering of relevant research, but the development and testing of such programs is but a hope for the future.

The foregoing, of course, is beyond the scope of any one volume: it is a program for the continued development of a large-scale *tradition,* in MacIntyre's sense of the term.

While this detailed evaluation is not possible, it *is* possible to make some meaningful comments regarding the strength of our total system using both Lakatos's and MacIntyre's criteria for the rational evaluation of competing traditions. After reviewing the fragmentary fine-scale evidence for the various parts of our program, we shall turn to this task.

2 FINE-SCALE EVALUATION: OVERVIEW OF THE DATA

Recall that the essential insight of Hempel's methodology is that a theory or hypothesis is confirmed (made credible) in virtue of the fact that it explains (better than any others) a set of data (facts, observations). So our most basic claim here is that our hierarchically ordered system of theories explains (better than any other such system) a set of data. While a vast number of unrelated bits of data could be mentioned here, we call attention to four *domains* of data that are particularly relevant for supporting our total scheme.

First are the data from the natural sciences described in the previous chapter, such as the lawlike and anthropic character of the universe. (These are themselves actually very high-level inductive generalizations based on myriad lower-level observations, measurements, and calculations.) Our point of departure was an *interpretation* of the meaning of particular scientific findings. This interpretation is one step removed from pure scientific theory, and therefore twice removed from direct empirical confirmation. The scientific data upon which it draws are somewhat contestable at various points; however, it is highly unlikely that the general picture of the fine-tuned universe will be overturned. So here our major worry is competing interpretations.

Most of the discoveries of science are neutral as far as our interpretation is concerned—they neither confirm nor disprove it. However, we can certainly say from the physics side that physics makes free will possible, and so has built into it the foundations of the possibility of moral choice. This is in fact a far-reaching statement: as is clear from the discussion of the anthropic principle, it reaches to many areas of physics, chemistry, and biochemistry. Again, by itself this tells us little; but it is supportive of the proposed theory when viewed from the standpoint of that theory.

We emphasize again that while one could not have argued from these facts alone to our conception of God, they nonetheless provide important post-hoc confirmation for the theological and ethical hypotheses derived from other sources. We need say no more about these data here.

Another class of data previously mentioned are the results of "experiments" in nonviolence and other forms of self-sacrifice. Our suspicion is that there is a great deal more evidence for the effectiveness and deeply satisfying nature of such a lifestyle than most people imagine. What is needed now is intentional, methodical comparison of results of programs of action that are and are not based on a kenotic ethic.

A third class of "data" are scriptural texts. This will be taken by many to be an unusual claim, to say the least—even by Christian theologians. We have made general arguments elsewhere for the reasonableness of treating Scripture as a source of data for theological research programs,[1] but specific arguments depend in each case on how one construes theology, and especially on the sort of documents one takes the scriptural texts to be. Recall that the core of our theological program includes the assertion that Jesus reveals the moral character of God. It follows, then, that knowledge about God (theology) can come most directly from knowledge of the moral character of Jesus, and this, in turn, will be revealed in Jesus' behavior and teaching. Thus, the New Testament texts function as witnesses to the character of Jesus and, as such, provide the most relevant sort of *data* for theology.

We were able to give some indication of the extent to which John Howard Yoder has drawn support for our shared theological program from a variety of New Testament texts. Yet there is a widespread suspicion that any claim can be grounded biblically if one is allowed to be selective enough in choosing and interpreting texts. Thus, a better way to look at the issue of textual support is not to ask whether there are (any) supportive texts, but rather to consider which of the various theories about the essence of Christianity does a better job in accounting for the whole of the New Testament. Yoder, in his life's work of preaching, lecturing, and writing history, theology, and ethics, has dealt with a vast array of passages, primarily from the New Testament (but without neglecting the Old). He has surely come close to testing his thesis against the whole of the New Testament witness, and has dealt with some of the more threatening rebuttals based on the Old Testament.

In speaking this way about the New Testament evidence, we have, of

---

1. See Nancey Murphy, *Theology in the Age of Scientific Reasoning* (Ithaca, N.Y.: Cornell University Press, 1990), especially chap. 6.

course, raised the question of what counts as a *better* explanation of the set of data—the issue that Lakatos's methodology is intended to address.

Finally, a fourth domain of data that deserves mention here is what we shall designate simply as morality. That is, we claim that the very fact that most people in most cultures, in most historical periods have some sense of moral obligation, and to some extent attempt to live accordingly, is an important *fact* about the world that needs to be explained.[2]

Traditionally, explanations of morality have been top-down: usually theological, but sometimes (as in the thought of Plato and Aristotle) metaphysical. The modern and postmodern rejection of both ancient realist metaphysics and theological accounts has led to the development of bottom-up explanations: First came psychological and sociological accounts arguing that morality is enforced by internalization during childhood because it promotes the survival of social groups. More recently, biological accounts have been suggested in which nature selects for altruistic genes.

A variant of biological reductionism is the Nietzschean claim that morality is an illusion and that its pretensions need to be unmasked if we are to be truly human. Friedrich Nietzsche's views of morality depended heavily on his exposure to Darwinian theories, but he was more aware than current sociobiologists tend to be of the fact that the reduction of morality to biology is actually the elimination of the truly *moral* sphere altogether.

It was common earlier in the modern period to use the existence of morality as an argument for the existence of God. We are not making so direct a claim, but our system does fit into the older pattern of assuming that if morality is to be justifiable at all, then it must be on the basis of a higher-level reality—in our case, theological. Thus, it is possible to compress our argument into the claim that the very existence of "the moral" provides data supportive of our theological claims. One has either to reduce the moral sphere to that of the prudential or the biological, or else provide some kind of explanation for it; a theological conception of reality provides one such explanation.

Upon expressing our argument in this manner, however, a problem arises: if the moral life is relevant evidence for a religious interpretation of reality, is it not the case that immorality and evil provide powerful counter-evidence? One might argue that we are building our proposal on the basis of carefully

---

2. See Bernard Williams, *Morality* (Cambridge: Cambridge University Press, 1993). Williams devotes a chapter to consideration of the "amoralist." He concludes that it is almost impossible to imagine a character who is truly human yet without any moral sensitivities whatsoever. Jeffrey Stout refers to a tribe often mentioned by anthropologists because of its anomalous immoral character, and quips that it is not inappropriately called the Ik. *Ethics after Babel: The Languages of Morals and Their Discontents* (Boston: Beacon Press, 1988), 18.

selected data; does it not crumble as soon as we look at the rest of the evidence?

We acknowledge the strength of this objection. The problem is exacerbated by the fact that the particular moral theory we endorse is more demanding than most and is also very much a minority view. Thus, behavior that others could count as moral falls outside the bounds of our theory. Yet we submit that it is both appropriate and necessary to be selective in deciding upon a domain of relevant data in the stage of theory formulation; as Thomas Kuhn has pointed out, a new theory or paradigm is "born in a sea of anomalies." Once the theory has been formulated, it is then necessary to address potential counter-evidence. A strong theory, as it develops, will turn the anomalies into convincing support.

A striking parallel can be seen in physics in the way that Newton's laws could only be discovered by ignoring the effects of friction (see chap. 3). All daily evidence contradicts Newton's first law (a body will keep moving at uniform speed), until a subsidiary hypothesis (the concept of friction) is introduced, which makes that law fit the apparently contradictory everyday experience. Attempts to build a theory of motion that focuses on ordinary experience (we need to push objects to keep them in motion) will fail to uncover the true nature of reality (their real tendency is to keep moving). This is a special case of the general concept of broken symmetry, which is central to much of modern physics, and is evident also in the physics of irreversibility (cf. chap. 3).

We take this as a model of the situation facing us in considering morality. One can focus on the good in humanity, or on the evil. One attains radically different views of the universe according to which of these one takes as more fundamental. We choose to view the moral as giving clues to the fundamental nature of reality; then we have to explain why selfish and evil behavior occurs, and is even the predominant feature in much of everyday life (the problem of evil).

An alternative is to view selfishness and evil as the more fundamental feature. In that case the problem is to explain why any generous or loving behavior occurs (the "problem" of good). One can initially choose either view (based on selected evidence) as the basis for a theory of ultimate reality, provided one then successfully deals with the apparent counter-evidence.

We have developed a system based on the idea that self-sacrifice is the central "law" of creation; therefore, a crucial test of this system will be its ability to deal with the problem of evil. Below we shall show that the existence of evil can in fact be turned from an anomaly into confirmation of our program. But here we are getting ahead of our argument. In sum, on the fine scale we claim that where empirical evidence is possible, we have provided sketches of the sorts of data available, noting some supporting evidence, as well as a major anomaly to be explained later.

3 MEDIUM-SCALE EVALUATION: PROGRESSIVE RESEARCH PROGRAMS

We have already, in the previous section, had reason to advert to the problem of assessing broadly comprehensive theoretical networks over against competing programs, each with its own set of relevant data. We claimed earlier that Imre Lakatos has made an important contribution to our understanding of the evaluation of competing research programs by providing his criterion of progress. A research program is *progressive* in Lakatos's terms when the following conditions are met: (1) each new version of the theory (core theory and auxiliary hypotheses) has excess empirical content over its predecessor; that is, it predicts some novel, hitherto unexpected facts, and (2) some of these predicted facts are corroborated.[3]

From this the contrary follows. A research program is *degenerating* when the change from one theory to the next accounts for the one anomaly or set of anomalies for which the change was made but does not allow for the prediction and discovery of any novel facts.

The choice of theories thus becomes a choice between two or more competing *series* of theories, and one chooses the more progressive of the programs. The choice is thereby made to depend on the programs' relative power to *increase* our knowledge.

This is an overview of Lakatos's position, but there are several points of refinement to be mentioned. The first is that "prediction" of "novel" facts can also mean "retrodiction" of facts that are already known but would have been considered irrelevant or impossible in light of the previous versions of the program.

Second, theories or research programs can support one another. That is, a theory (which might be the core of one program) may be inserted as an auxiliary hypothesis into another. In this case, progress for one counts as progress for the other. This is especially important for theology, where connections or clashes between theories (doctrines) are often a more important source of corroboration or of anomalies than are the data.

So there are actually several ways to provide progressive support for a research program: (1) by the prediction of facts that were previously entirely unknown and unexpected—a rare occurrence, according to Lakatos; (2) by

---

3. See Murphy, "Another Look at Novel Facts," *Studies in History and Philosophy of Science* 20, no. 3 (1989): 385–88 for a refinement of Lakatos's conception of novel facts.

relating to the theory facts that were already known but considered either irrelevant or contrary to it—often a move of this sort constitutes a dramatic victory for a program when the fact in question was seen either as an important anomaly for that program or as an important piece of evidence for its competitor; and (3) by the inclusion into the research program, as a new auxiliary hypothesis, another theory with a progressive track record of its own.

A specific instance, discussed earlier, of a progressive move for our theological program concerned the use of René Girard's theory of ritual violence to address anomalous texts concerning the point of Jesus' death. Recall that we endorsed John Howard Yoder's conflict model of the atonement, but we recognized that in so doing it was necessary to give some account of the scriptural texts that support the substitutionary theory. We claimed that the addition of Girard's theory as an auxiliary hypothesis not only removes the contradiction but turns the sacrificial language into positive confirmation for the core of the theological program. So this was an instance of both the second and third sorts of moves: the turning around of an anomaly, and the incorporation of another research program (with its own supporting data from anthropology and literature) into the original program.

As mentioned at the beginning of this chapter, it would be desirable but impossible to make a thorough assessment of each program incorporated into our total hierarchical system, comparing its degree of progress with that of each of its competitors. Since we cannot do so, it is worthwhile to look at the matter from a broader perspective.

If research programs can be nested (e.g., Girard's anthropological thesis within Yoder's theology), then it is reasonable to treat our entire scheme as a single, vast research program (with smaller nested programs) and to ask how it compares, in terms of Lakatos's criteria, with its competitors. We could call this a research program in Cosmology, where the upper-case C is meant to distinguish it from modern scientific cosmology, and to recall the broader, premodern sense of the term.[4]

The consequence of counting our entire system as a single, immense research program is that it will inevitably be more progressive than any of the subprograms of which it is constructed. It follows, then, from Lakatos's acceptability criteria that this large-scale Cosmological program will be more acceptable (more credible) than any of its components standing alone, and also more acceptable than any of the competitors of those subprograms stand-

4. See Stephen Toulmin, *Return to Cosmology* (Berkeley: University of California Press, 1981), for a comparable use.

ing alone (if we assume the subprograms and their competitors began with comparable amounts of empirical support).

Note that what we are saying using Lakatos's terminology is really no different from what a number of epistemologists and philosophers of science say about the value of scope and coherence in assessing a set of beliefs.[5]

The reference to coherence, however, raises a caveat. Lakatos recognized that, according to his definition, any research program could be made progressive simply by conjoining a previously unrelated thesis of any sort. He called this the "tacking paradox": "According to our definitions, adding to a theory completely disconnected low-level hypotheses may constitute a 'progressive shift.' It is difficult to eliminate such makeshift shifts without demanding that the additional assertions must be connected with the original assertion *more intimately* than by mere conjunction."[6] So, in other words, for our Cosmological program to count as more acceptable than any of its individual subprograms, there must be tight logical links from one subprogram to another. It has been the burden of the previous chapters to show that the theological and ethical theories treated here are indeed more intimately related to one another and to the sciences than by mere conjunction. In our judgment, we believe it is fair to say that the logical link from theology to ethics is very tight—in fact, the core of our Cosmological program is itself ethico-theological in nature. However, the connection from theology and ethics to cosmology and the other natural sciences is rather weak. This latter fact is unfortunate, in that the data on the natural-science side are "hard" and quite plentiful, while the social-science data relevant for support of the ethical program are, so far, more dubious.

We have argued elsewhere that while fine-tuning cannot be used alone as a new design argument, a theological program that can incorporate it as an auxiliary hypothesis thereby makes a progressive move.[7] Here we make the further argument that some theological programs can incorporate the fine-

---

5. See W. V. O Quine's holist epistemology in "Two Dogmas of Empiricism," in *From a Logical Point of View: Logico-Philosophical Essays* (Cambridge, Mass.: Harvard University Press, 1953), chap. 2; and Quine and J.S. Ullian, *The Web of Belief,* 2nd ed. (New York: Random House, 1978); Thomas S. Kuhn, *The Structure of Scientific Revolutions,* 2nd ed. (Chicago: University of Chicago Press, 1970); and also Basil Mitchell on cumulative case arguments in *The Justification of Religious Belief* (New York: Oxford University Press, 1981).

6. "Falsification," in *The Methodology of Scientific Research Programmes,* 46, see n.12, ch. 1.

7. See Ellis, "The Theology of the Anthropic Principle," and Murphy, "Evidence of Design in the Fine-Tuning of the Universe," both in Robert J. Russell, Nancey Murphy, and C. J. Isham, eds., *Quantum Cosmology and the Laws of Nature: Scientific Perspectives on Divine Action* (Vatican City State and Berkeley, Calif.: Vatican Observatory and Center for Theology and the Natural Sciences, 1993).

tuning in a more natural or intimate way than others. For instance, a theology in which human freedom is a marginal concept will not have the same resources for making this move; as we have argued, it is the link between freedom and intelligence that allows us to interpret the anthropic character of the universe as a manifestation of God's deepest purposes. A second and even more striking example is this: a theology that conceives of divine action as sporadic, interventionist, intrusive will have a hard time making use of the fine-tuning, for the fine-tuning suggests a "uniformitarian" and noninterventionist pattern of divine action—God achieves the divine purposes within the carefully planned system rather than by overriding the natural system. Or put another way, if God can be expected to create human beings *de novo,* without any natural antecedents, then the fine-tuning would have no theological interest. So we believe that our ethical and theological program is better suited than many to incorporate this hypothesis.

It is interesting to note that Lakatos developed the concept of a positive heuristic to guard against the tacking paradox: an acceptable program would develop systematically according to a preconceived plan; new hypotheses would not be added at random. Recall that while Yoder himself did not venture into the realm of cosmology, his theology is predicated upon the claim that the ministry of Jesus has cosmic significance: "In Jesus we have a clue to which kinds of causation . . . go with the grain of the cosmos."[8] Thus, it is fair to say that the positive heuristic of the program we have adopted from Yoder already included the demand to relate the theology and ethics to cosmology.

It is also fair to say that this program already contained projections for relations to at least some of the social sciences. Recall Yoder's claim for the possibility of a historiographical program in line with the core of his ethico-theological program. We have perhaps added more than Yoder envisioned by claiming empirical consequences in all of the social sciences.

So, in effect, we have constructed a cumulative-case argument. Each supporting strand is strengthened by the others, in that its incorporation into the whole makes the relevant interpretation of *its own* data more plausible. That is, apart from the system, the design hypothesis is no better supported by the fine-tuning than its competitors (e.g., many universes), but supplying the rest of the theological and scientific system tips the balance of evidence in its favor. The design interpretation of the fine-tuning then serves as support for the whole system. Similarly, this theology is better supported as an interpretation of the scriptural evidence insofar as it is more closely related to the natu-

8. Above, chap. 8, sec. 4.

ral or human sciences. And the ethical component is *much* more strongly supported than any "autonomous" ethic could imaginably be.

The consequence of the foregoing considerations for the evaluative task is thus to raise two questions: Are there any competing Cosmological systems with *empirical scope* comparable to ours? and, if so, Are the sub-programs making up these competing Cosmologies as intimately related to one another as ours?

Existing competitors can be classified loosely as theistic and naturalistic. Theistic competitors may include some based on other religions but, for example, there seems to be no fully developed Islamic competitor.[9] The only ones of which we are aware relate Christian theology (which usually includes at least some attention to theological ethics) to science. Most notable here, we believe, are the systems developed by Arthur Peacocke, Wolfhart Pannenberg, and Philip Hefner. We discuss each below.

Again we reach a point where a thorough evaluation of our system calls for more than can be accomplished here. We would have to lay out each competing Cosmology in as much detail as our own, and compare the degrees of support (or the amount of empirical progress, in Lakatos's terms). Because this is impossible here, we shall have to restrict ourselves to brief remarks.

3.1 Naturalistic Competitors

Naturalistic systems of similar scope include Marxism and various metaphysical systems developed out of science by writers such as Carl Sagan, Richard Dawkins, and E. O. Wilson.

Marxism presents an interesting case, in this era after the collapse of the Soviet Union. It seems that scholars no longer feel bound to take it seriously as an intellectual system since its social embodiment has shown to be unworkable. If this is the case, then it bears out our claim that an ethic's potential for social-embodiment (and that of its accompanying metaphysic) is an important ingredient in its evaluation.

If we expected the major readership for this volume to be scientists, we would have to pay a great deal more attention to competitors arising directly from the natural sciences. By this, we mean to refer to systems of thought such as Carl Sagan's. What Sagan puts forward is a peculiar mix of science and what can only be called "naturalistic religion." He begins with biology and cosmology but then uses concepts drawn from science to fill in what are

---

9. See P. Hoodbhoy, *Islam and Science: Religious Orthodoxy and the Battle for Rationality* (London: Zed Books, 1991).

essentially religious categories—categories, by the way, that fall into a pattern surprisingly isomorphic with the Christian conceptual scheme. He has a concept of ultimate reality: "The Universe is all that is or ever was or ever will be." He has an account of ultimate origins: Evolution with a capital *E*. He has an account of the origin of sin: the primitive reptilian structure in the brain, which is responsible for territoriality, sex drive, and aggression.

His account of salvation is gnostic in character—that is, it assumes that salvation comes from knowledge. The knowledge in question is scientific knowledge, perhaps advanced by contact with extra-terrestrial life forms who are more advanced than we.[10]

Sagan's account of ethics is based on the worry that the human race will destroy itself. So the *telos* of human life is simply survival. Morality consists in overcoming our tendencies to see others as outsiders; knowledge of our intrinsic relatedness as natural beings (we are all made of the same star dust) can overcome our reptilian characteristics.

The value of this example is to show that if one refrains from placing a recognizable theological system at the top of the hierarchy, there is an "empty space" that cries out to be filled by something. Sagan and others oblige by creating new scientistic religions.

Thus, a genre of writing is emerging that in one way or another attempts to fill this gap. We have several objections to such systems. First, they often use highly questionable grounding in science without alerting their readers to the speculative or contested status of the scientific evidence or theories. Second, they develop positions that go far beyond the bounds of science itself but attempt to attach the authority of science to those positions. Thus, they move far beyond the legitimate domain of scientific evidence without taking adequate account of the epistemological hazards involved in doing so.

An example is Frank J. Tipler's recent book, *The Physics of Immortality: Modern Cosmology, God, and the Resurrection of the Dead.*[11] An illustration of the overly optimistic use of science is his claim that life can exist forever in a universe that recollapses, and so one in which temperatures diverge to infinity as it approaches the final state. This is not based on any known physical structure that could support life under these extreme conditions. Also, Tipler relies in his argument on aspects of recent theories of quantum cosmology—a controversial area, where enormous extrapolation of present physical theories beyond the domain where they can be verified leads to methods and conclusions that cannot be claimed to be an established part of present scientific

10. See Thomas M. Ross, "The Implicit Theology of Carl Sagan," *Pacific Theological Review* 18, no. 3 (1985): 24–32.

11. Frank J. Tipler, *The Physics of Immortality: Modern Cosmology, God, and the Resurrection of the Dead* (New York: Doubleday, 1994).

theory. These proposals are the subject of debate and considerable skepticism within the scientific community, yet they are the foundation of key elements of the argument. There are many other such examples in his book.

As regards the extension of science outside its domain, Tipler claims that physics is omnicompetent and that nothing exists outside its purview. If true, this would imply, for example, that physics can determine the difference between great and mediocre poetry, can explain the social behavior of ant colonies, or can supplant psychotherapy—obviously unsupportable claims. In his attempt to apply science to religious themes, he has to resort to arbitrary argumentation that cannot be tested by any kind of physical experiment. Indeed, he introduces concepts such as the Omega Point that lie outside the domain of science, since they cannot be related in any way to experiment or observation.[12]

Similar difficulties emerge in D.C. Dennett's article, "Darwin's Dangerous Idea,"[13] which puts forward a scientism that claims to explain all. An example is his claim that algorithms are foolproof recipes that always work. In fact, major parts of modern computer science are concerned precisely with the issue of when algorithms do and do not work (the "halting problem"). An example of not appreciating the limits of science is his claim that through Darwinian evolution, excellence, worth, and purpose can emerge out of mindless, purposeless forces. But "excellence" and "worth," we have argued, are words that only attain meaning at higher levels of the hierarchy, and cannot be based on a scientific viewpoint alone. Thus, his scheme, in claiming to give an account of the evolution of values, introduces concepts that can have no place in a purely scientific worldview, yet that is what he claims to be presenting.

Richard Dawkins's idea of a genetic unit of cultural inheritance—a "meme"—would seem to be another idea that goes beyond what can be scientifically established.[14] His proposal faces numerous difficulties from genetics in that the fundamental premise of modern biology is that nothing we do or think can in any way alter the genes we pass on to our children. It is questionable from the cultural side as well.[15]

The fact that Dawkins believes science is in competition with religion and seeking to answer the same questions[16] suggests an exaggerated view of the

12. For a full critique, see W. R. Stoeger and George F. R. Ellis, "A Response to Tipler's Omega-Point Theory," *Science and Christian Belief* 7 (1995): 163–72.

13. *The Sciences* 35 (1995): 34–40.

14. *The Extended Phenotype* (Oxford: Oxford University Press, 1982).

15. See John Bowker, *Is God a Virus? Genes, Culture, and Religion* (London: SPCK, 1995), for further discussion.

16. Interview in *Sunday Times*, London, 30 July 1995.

domain of science: that it pertains to issues of good and evil and of ultimate meaning.

We claim that in general these schemes fail to tackle adequately not only the metaphysical issues underlying cosmology (cf. chap. 3), but also the crucial issue of the objectivity of the moral order. Sociobiology, however, is an exception in this latter regard, and is an important competitor for our system, in that it does attempt to give an account of morality—a bottom-up account.

"Sociobiology" designates a recent branch of science that attempts to explain morality in evolutionary terms. Originally this kind of view mainly explained aggressive behavior, but current interests focus on explaining altruistic (i.e., "moral") behavior as well.[17] In the terms of this study, it is an attempt to show that ethics can be entirely reduced to the biological level. If it were merely an attempt to show that there are biological or genetic factors that affect a person's ability to behave in moral ways it would be entirely unexceptionable, and in fact, according to our hierarchical model, it would be strange if there were not bottom-up factors to be considered in connection with the moral level, reaching all the way from the biological level.

The central problem with typical sociobiological projects is that they pretend to give an exhaustive account of moral behavior. But were they to show that "moral" behavior is genetically programmed, they would thereby show that it is not moral at all. That is, the very meaning of morality involves its voluntary, intentional nature. If it were possible to show that all of the characteristics our culture praises as admirable or condemns as blameworthy were simply the result of evolutionary selection, rather than the expression of a character shaped by deliberate choices, the consequence would be the denial of the realm of the moral, and, we might add, of that which is distinctively human. Note the correlations with Taylor's criticism, discussed in chapter 5, of naturalistic approaches to the social sciences in general.

Furthermore, if so-called moral behavior could be shown to be genetically programmed, this would undercut rather than justify moral prescriptions. And if the entire realm of the moral is shown to be an illusion, then anything goes. There are two pictures of possible outcomes. One is that we simply give up all language of praise and blame and simply do what we are programmed to do, or, if intelligent behavior (though not moral) is still intelligible, we might recommend courses of action that are more in step with

---

17. See, e.g., T. H. Clutton-Broch and Paul H. Harvey, eds., *Readings in Sociobiology* (San Francisco, Ca.: W. H. Freeman, 1978); Paul Thompson, ed., *Issues in Evolutionary Ethics* (New York: SUNY Press, 1995). For further critique, see Nancey Murphy, "Supervenience and the Non-Reducibility of Ethics to Biology," in Robert J. Russell, et al., *Evolutionary Biology: Scientific Perspectives on Divine Action* (Vatican City State and Berkeley, Calif.: Vatican Observatory and Center for Theology and the Natural Sciences, forthcoming).

what we know about evolution: killing or sterilizing those who have inherited more aggressive natures.

Thus, our general criticism of naturalistic metaphysical systems is that they will invariably end up reducing the moral to the nonmoral; that is, they will end up explaining away the phenomenon for which they intend to account. If our thesis in chapter 5 is correct—that moral systems require a higher level of assumptions, a theology, in order to support them—then ethics without theology will turn out to involve mere assumptions that cannot stand up to careful scrutiny (the problem of moral relativism) or else will be reduced to levels below. Since it is difficult to imagine a consistent and thoroughgoing rejection of the normativity of at least some ethical prescriptions, we expect that all naturalistic systems will turn out to be radically inconsistent; they will accept some moral principles and at the same time reduce morality to something else.

3.2 Theistic Competitors

The three theological systems we mention provide more aid and comfort than they do competition. The very notion that theology ought to be related to both natural and social sciences, and the arguments that they provide to that effect, can only help our cause. Thus, we are not enthusiastic about making invidious comparisons. Nevertheless, a few remarks are in order.

3.2.1 Wolfhart Pannenberg

Wolfhart Pannenberg has produced a series of writings comprising a remarkable program that aims at synthesizing Christian theology with the results of science. His work is well worth reporting here for several reasons. First, in contrast to many theologians of the current era, Pannenberg holds, as we do, to a highly *cognitivist* account of theology—that is, theology aims to provide an account of reality, not a set of symbols expressive of religious experience. Second, his methodology provides a comparable argument to the effect that theology and science are similar enough epistemologically to be related to one another, as well as a comparable argument concerning the structure of a science-and-theology synthesis. Finally, Pannenberg has in fact integrated some scientific material into his program, although we believe that the promise, so far, is greater than the delivery.

Pannenberg's theological method has been greatly influenced by recent philosophy of science: he affirms that hypotheses are acceptable insofar as they provide the best available explanation of the phenomena. Following Stephen Toulmin, he defines explanation as placing a phenomenon within a broader context that makes sense of it. This account is broad enough to apply to both the natural and human sciences. In the natural sciences a single event may be explained by placing it within the context of a natural law—that is, by showing it to be an instance of the law. The law itself is explained by situating it within the context of a theory, and the theory within the context of an "ideal of natural order."[18]

Similarly, a problematic passage in a text is understood by considering its relation to the text as a whole; the text is understood by placing it in its historical context. A historical event is explained by placing it within the series of events to which it belongs. Thus, we may envision the development of science, history, and theology as the development of a series of concentric spheres or circles, each circle providing a wider framework of interpretation, a broader horizon of meaning.

When in the process of explanation one reaches the "circle" representing the whole of reality, a further question arises: how is one to explain the fact that the whole of history *is* a whole? This is both a philosophical and theological question. Insofar as one answers it on the basis of a religious tradition's concept of "the all-determining reality," one is doing theology. Or, put the other way around, Christian theology is given scientific support insofar as it can be shown that its concept of God provides the best explanation for the whole of reality. The theologian's task is to provide a faithful reinterpretation of the tradition that makes apparent its value for understanding all available knowledge, including historical and scientific knowledge.

We might represent Pannenberg's view of theology in spatial terms as follows: Theology begins with two sets of concentric circles. One set involves the texts of the Christian Scriptures. Here texts concerning Jesus' resurrection are at the very center, surrounded by circles representing increasingly broad contexts required for their full understanding—most immediately, the rest of the New Testament. The apocalyptic worldview of the first century in turn forms an important context for understanding the New Testament. Beside this first series of circles is another, representing contemporary human experience and the ever-broadening contexts within which it is interpreted. At some point moving outward, we reach a circle that encompasses both foci. The Christian view of God, based ultimately on the fact of Jesus' resurrection, is represented by the outermost circle, intended to encompass and give meaning to all experience and to all other contexts of meaning.

In *Theology and the Philosophy of Science*,[19] Pannenberg suggests that the phenomenon of hope, an aspect of universal human experience, calls for explanation. Historically, two explanations have been available: belief in resur-

---

18. This is Stephen Toulmin's term. See *Foresight and Understanding* (New York: Harper and Row, 1961).

19. Trans. Francis McDonagh (Philadelphia: Westminster Press, 1976).

rection of the body or in the immortality of the soul. Within the context of modern science, the survival of a soul beyond the disintegration of the body is unreasonable. Thus, the phenomenon of hope cries out for a concept of resurrection to give it meaning. Therefore the apocalyptic worldview of the Bible provides a suitable context for the interpretation of this phenomenon, and the Christian and contemporary worldviews fuse at this point.

Although suggestive, Pannenberg's anthropological starting point in *Theology and the Philosophy of Science* was rather slight. In *Anthropology in Theological Perspective*[20] he has pursued further points of contact between anthropology and Christian theology; however, many in the English-speaking world would classify his anthropological work as philosophical rather than scientific. He has also investigated the relation between eschatology and some cosmological speculations regarding the future of the universe. Pannenberg's interests here have focused on the work of Frank J. Tipler, which we find questionable.

So, while we commend Pannenberg's program for its integrative goals and for its substantial arguments for the historicity of the resurrection of Jesus, and while we find its methodology intriguing, it has not gone beyond fairly tentative connections at scattered points with science.

Furthermore, Pannenberg has so far written only occasional essays in the area of ethics, on such topics as the relation between Christianity and politics, the theology of law, and on the Lutheran doctrine of the two kingdoms.[21] We suspect that if he were to develop a system of ethics compatible with his theological program he would place great emphasis, as we do above, on the importance of the *telos* of human life. He would argue, further, that the eschatological telos of the cosmos is already relevant for life today. In "Luther's Doctrine of the Two Kingdoms," he endorses the goal of the transformation of political conditions by the "powerful vision of the eschatological Lordship of God which already illumines the present world."[22]

While we expect that there would be some degree of overlap, therefore, between our account of ethics and a system developed in light of Pannenberg's theology, one deep difference emerges over the issue of pacifism. Pannenberg endorses the argument against Christian pacifism based on its (supposed) irresponsibility: "Christians who as a matter of principle reject the dirty work of politics and the use of armed force find themselves in the ambiguous position of being beneficiaries of those who take such tasks on themselves on behalf of the entire society, and thus on behalf of Christians."[23] He

20. Trans. Matthew J. O'Connell (Philadelphia: Westminster Press, 1985).
21. See *Ethics* (Philadelphia: Westminster Press, 1981), trans. by Keith Crim of *Ethik und Ekklesiologie* (Göttingen: Vandenhoeck und Ruprecht, 1977).
22. In *Ethics*, 130.
23. *Ethics*, 156.

concedes that there may be symbolic meaning when individuals or limited groups of Christians refuse military involvement; however, this cannot be a universal expectation for Christians.

What we have argued here is that the sciences are incomplete without, first, ethics and then theology. However, the contrary is implied: theology is incomplete without both ethics and cosmology. Most theologians intend to include ethics, but as James Wm. McClendon, Jr., notes, they are "forever leaving ethics till last, then leaving it out."[24] A less common claim, since the demise of the medieval synthesis, is that theology is incomplete without the natural sciences. This would seem to follow from our thesis regarding theology's position in the hierarchy of the sciences, but it would take another book to make good on the argument.[25]

3.2.2 Philip Hefner

Hefner's *The Human Factor: Evolution, Culture, and Religion*[26] develops a religious theory of the human person—a Christian anthropology—in light of both biological and cultural evolution. Hefner uses Lakatos's epistemology in an explicit way, so it is more accurate to say that he has set out to develop a *research program* in anthropology. The core of this program is the following:

> Human beings are God's created co-creators whose purpose is to be the agency, acting in freedom, to birth the future that is most wholesome for the nature that has birthed us—the nature that is not only our own genetic heritage, but also the entire human community and the evolutionary and ecological reality in which and to which we belong. Exercising this agency is said to be God's will for humans.[27]

Hefner bases his account of the nature of the human species on the fact that we have evolved by means of deterministic natural processes to the point of having genuine freedom. This freedom gives rise to moral responsibility, and our responsibility is to the natural process that gave rise to the species.

While Hefner claims only to attempt to incorporate the results of the natural sciences into his program, the contributions of social-scientific thought are marked. In particular, he makes use of a functional definition of religion (myth and ritual); he claims that religion is necessary in order to counteract antisocial genetic tendencies. But he parts company with reductionist accounts of religion in his claims that for myths to be effective they

---

24. *Ethics: Systematic Theology, Volume I* (Nashville, Tenn.: Abingdon Press, 1986), 42.

25. Pannenberg has already made a similar claim, however. If God is "the all-determining reality," then part of the task of coming to know God is to know about the "all." See *Basic Questions in Theology*, vol. 1 (London: SCM Press, 1970), 1.

26. Minneapolis: Fortress Press, 1993.

27. Ibid., 27.

must speak of what is real and, furthermore, that Christian myths (if properly reformulated) provide the best language for talking about reality.

A great deal in Hefner's system is supportive of our own, in particular, in his recognition that ethics provides an essential link between science and religion, and his claim that "Our *oughts* would have no real substance if they were not rooted in the *is*."[28] While the central focus of Hefner's ethic is concern for what is wholesome for nature, he gives a secondary place to an ethic of self-sacrifice and nonviolence. Finally, the connections he draws between intelligence and freedom, and between freedom and morality, support our contention that the anthropic universe is essentially a moral universe.

The differences between Hefner's system and ours are more a matter of focus than of direct disagreement. Most important is his account of the origin and justification of morality. Hefner means to draw his account of morality directly from science. "God talk" is then needed as a postulate to legitimize a morality derived from evolutionary theory. We, however, have argued that such a bottom-up account cannot actually justify a moral position. What is needed is a concept of the good for humankind drawn from an account of ultimate reality and thus from theology rather than from science. So we disagree over the basic direction of argument connecting theology, ethics, and science.

3.2.3 Arthur Peacocke

Arthur Peacocke has provided a vision for the integration of theology, the natural sciences, and the human sciences that is at least as helpful as Pannenberg's and more thoroughly integrated with the results of contemporary science. It has a somewhat broader theological scope than Hefner's. The outlines of Peacocke's system can best be seen in his recent volume, *Theology for a Scientific Age.*[29]

Peacocke's goal is to refurbish images of God in light of contemporary science. The first part of the book, much as ours does, provides an account of the general picture of the universe provided by science, including the evolution of life and of the cosmos itself beginning with the Big Bang. Since most theology is done against the background of an outdated mechanistic conception of the universe, Peacocke concentrates on aspects of the contemporary scientific worldview that differentiate it from its predecessor. For example, in place of discrete concepts of matter and energy operating within a temporal and spatial container, we now must conceive of these concepts as so closely interlocked that the "stuff" of the universe might better be de-

---

28. Ibid., 202.
29. Enlarged ed. (Minneapolis: Fortress Press, 1993).

scribed as "matter-energy-space-time." This stuff is organized into structures of varying complexity, from the inorganic, through the organic, to beings whose complex brains and nervous systems give rise to the phenomenon of consciousness.

Scientific and philosophical views held earlier in this century suggested that higher levels of reality could be reduced to lower levels, so that ultimately even human thought could be explained in terms of the laws of physics. In contrast, Peacocke develops his contention that reduction and analysis provide only a partial understanding of complex entities, which can only be fully described by employing concepts peculiar to their own level in the hierarchy and by considering causal influences exerted on the entities by their environments.

Peacocke's consideration of human life as the highest form of complexity yet to emerge from the evolutionary processes of the cosmos provides a transition to theology—humans alone among higher forms of life raise questions about the meaning of their existence and answer them by postulating another order of being conceived as the source of all other lesser being.

Peacocke works through two topics germane to the doctrine of God— divine attributes and God's interaction with the world—to see what enhancements or revisions are in order in light of the scientific advances just canvassed. With regard to divine attributes, he concludes from the interplay of chance and law in natural processes that, as creator, God must be seen as exploring through exploitation of random events the multitude of as-yet-unfulfilled potentialities of the created universe.

Peacocke draws upon the concept of top-down causation to provide a non-interventionist account of God's action. We can properly regard the world-as-a-whole as a total system so that its general state can be a top-down causative factor in or constraint upon what goes on at the myriad levels that comprise it. Add to this the panentheist idea that the whole world is "in God," and we can conclude that God acts in a top-down manner on the world-as-a-whole. This holistic mode of action and influence is God's distinctive means of shaping and directing events at lower levels to accomplish divine purposes. The closest analogy we have for such causation is the effect of conscious states (integrated mind/brain/body states) on the component parts of the organism.

In the latter half of the book[30] Peacocke examines the relations between contemporary science (including now the human sciences) and additional aspects of theology, such as revelation, religious experience, and Christian anthropology. He claims that Jesus, as both the "complete human being" and God's clearest self-expression, provides the answer to human beings' religious quest, understood as the quest for meaning.

30. Added to the enlarged edition.

We have already stated that in many ways we are in close agreement with Peacocke's work: An important presupposition of the book as a whole is that science and theology as disciplines are quite similar. We claimed above that Peacocke has contributed in an important way to the discussion of the relations between theology and the sciences by suggesting that theology be viewed as located at the top of the hierarchy of sciences—it being the study of the most all-encompassing system possible, that of God interacting with the spheres of nature and human society.

Peacocke offers a model for the relation of theology and science that differs from Pannenberg's concentric circles. We suspect that it does more justice to the independent character of the sciences and theology. That is, Pannenberg's model suggests that in order for a theological outlook to be justified, it must be able to *encompass* all of the results of all of the sciences. Peacocke's model suggests instead that theology must bear a relationship to the most complex of the sciences that is analogous to the relations among the sciences themselves. So, for example, biology need not be seen to encompass the whole of chemistry, even though it explains (and thus "encompasses") important parts of it.

While we agree in name with Peacocke's "kenotic" account of the nature of God, we disagree as to what this actually means. For Peacocke it involves God's acquiescence in ignorance of much of the future; Peacocke argues that the outcome of genuinely indeterminate processes is unknowable in principle. In addition, we believe that while his top-down account of divine action is an important part of any account of the relation between God and the world, it is not an adequate account, and needs to be supplemented with a bottom-up account of divine action through the quantum level.

Finally, Peacocke's system gives much less attention to the ethical dimension of human life, which we take to be an essential ingredient of any adequate account of reality. We suggest that were Peacocke to develop his ethical thought further, his noninterventionist account of divine action and the points of overlap between his kenotic doctrine of God and ours, together would demand a kenotic ethic such as ours. Were this the case, we would conclude that the differences between his system and ours were much less important than the similarities, and would see his work as support rather than competition.

4 LARGE-SCALE EVALUATION

Our arguments with Hefner and Pannenberg are essentially over issues of incompleteness: we claim that Hefner needs to supply a fully-developed concept of God in order to justify his ethical stance; Peacocke needs to develop a more robust account of ethics itself; Pannenberg needs to make more connections with the actual content of the empirical sciences. But individual thinkers cannot be faulted for what they have *not* written; the prize must not go to the most prolific.

This recognition leads us to raise the question of evaluation at yet another level of scale. Here we ask not about the comparative merits of the systems devised by individual competitors, but about the merits of large-scale traditions.

The concept of a *tradition* is a common one, but Alasdair MacIntyre has gone some way toward providing a technical definition of the term. A tradition is a historically extended, socially embodied argument concerning the interpretation and application of a (set of) formative text(s). As we pointed out in chapter 1, MacIntyre has also devoted considerable attention to the question how such traditions are to be evaluated over against their competitors. There are several ways in which one can argue for the rational superiority of a tradition. One possibility is to show that a tradition is able to reinterpret and incorporate its rival, but not vice-versa. A historical example was the incorporation (by Thomas Aquinas) of the Aristotelian tradition into Augustinian Christianity.

Another possibility is to show that one of the rival traditions has within it the resources to resolve its epistemological crises (brought on by the recognition of incoherence or by the inability to account for new experience), while its rival is unable to move beyond its own crisis. It may be possible to show, in addition, that the first tradition has resources within it to resolve the crisis into which its rival has fallen.

At this point, we intend to describe Western Christianity in terms of two rival traditions, which we designate (loosely) as the Anabaptist and Augustinian traditions. We claim that the central issues differentiating them are ethical: How central is ethics itself to Christian teaching? Is the ethic kenotic in character (and thus pacifist)? We then make the following argument:

1. Contemporary science presents a challenge to contemporary theology (just as Aristotelian natural philosophy did to the theology of the Middle Ages). Thus, both Christian traditions need to interpret and incorporate it. Our work represents a step toward the incorporation of science into the Anabaptist tradition, but there are a variety of contributions to the incorporation of science into the Augustinian tradition.
2. The Augustinian tradition suffers from longstanding and severe incoherence—the so-called problem of evil. Theological resources have been developed within this tradition that we believe are crucial for addressing the problem, namely, kenotic views of the character of God.

The dialogue with science has been helpful in advancing this strategy—what John Polkinghorne has named the "free process defense."[31] We argue, however, that these strategies are grossly incompatible with the Augustinian tradition's stance on Christian ethics.

3. Thus, while it may be possible to incorporate comparable amounts of current science into both Christian traditions, recent moves to address the problem of evil are helpful only within the Anabaptist tradition, since a similar move within the Augustinian tradition resolves one incoherence only to create another.

4.1 Theodicy

We noted above that evil stands as an anomaly over against our theological program—as it does for others. The attempt to reconcile this negative evidence with an account of the goodness and power of God has come to be called "theodicy." We argue in this section that while we are able to give a coherent accounting for evil, the Augustinian tradition cannot.

The centerpiece of an Augustinian theodicy is the free-will defense. God created all things good but mutable. First the angels rebelled and then Adam and Eve. Inasmuch as the whole human race was present in Adam's loins, all future humans inherited Adam's guilt. Suffering of all sorts, death, and ultimately consignment to hell are fit punishment for so great a sin.

Thus, moral evil, freely chosen, provides an explanation not only of the suffering humans cause one another, but also of suffering at the hands of nature. Says John Hick, "The theodicy tradition, which has descended from Augustine through Aquinas to the more tradition-governed Catholic theologians of today, and equally as we find it in the Reformers and in Protestant orthodoxy, teaches that all the evil that indwells or afflicts mankind is, in Augustine's phrase, 'either sin or punishment for sin.'"[32]

So it is sin that *justifies* death and all sorts of human suffering. But the ancients and medievals also had a *causal* account of how the once perfect universe came to have its "malevolent" features. In the fall of the angels, the great chain of command from God to lesser beings was broken. In that the angels were thought to play a crucial role in the governance of nature, those aspects of nature over which they have control have become disordered.[33] This disorder provides an account of animal suffering as well as of human misery.

31. See, *inter alia*, *The Faith of a Physicist: Reflections of a Bottom-Up Thinker* (Princeton: Princeton University Press, 1994), 83–85.

32. John Hick, *Evil and the God of Love*, revised ed. (New York: Harper and Row, 1977), 172–73, here quoting Augustine's *De Gen. ad lit.* 1.309.

33. Hick, *Evil and the God of Love*, 331–32.

Another theme relevant to reflections on evil is the notion of the *plenum,* or "the Great Chain of Being,"[34] which was used to explain the existence of entities that in their own right might appear undesirable. A universe in which all possible forms of being are actualized is a better universe than one that contains only the "higher" forms of existence.

This notion of the *plenum* is closely related to a theme in Augustine's writings of which John Hick is highly (and we think, rightly) critical. The "aesthetic theme" includes the view that a universe in which there is sin, but all sin is justly punished, is as good or better than a universe without sin—better that God should bring good out of evil than that there be no evil. Hick is critical of the failure of this view to reflect any sympathy on God's part for the suffering of sinners. He deems this conception of God and of God's relation to creatures "subpersonal."

In the modern period, developments in science and accompanying metaphysical and theological changes have reconfigured Christians' responses to evil and suffering. In place of the static *plenum* we now countenance an evolving chain of being. An evolutionary account of human origins contradicts the Augustinian view of sin as a heinous fall from original perfection. Hick has constructed a useful replacement for this view, with roots in the writings of Irenaeus (ca. 130–200) and Friedrich Schleiermacher.

In place of Augustine's account of biologically inherited original sin, Hick emphasizes the need for human development: sin is not so much the effect of mature, informed rebellion against God but more a manifestation of the race's childlike state of ignorance and weakness. But human sin contributes to a social environment that tends to perpetuate sin. Natural evils are permitted by God in order that the world be a vale of "soul making"; moral development is only possible in a world filled with the challenges of pain, temptation, and uncertainty.

Why does God require the race to go through this painful learning and developmental process? The answer is subtle but important. Virtue, moral character, cannot be instilled or implanted; by its very nature it must be acquired through a process of learning and testing. In addition, God's ultimate goal for human life is a relationship with God, and such a relationship cannot be coerced or created unilaterally.

There is much in Hick's theodicy with which we agree, and it is fully coherent with an evolutionary view of the development of the human species. No biological account of the transmission of original sin is necessary; and the idea of the creation *de novo* of morally perfect free beings is dismissed as incoherent.

---

34. A. O. Lovejoy, *The Great Chain of Being* (Cambridge, Mass.: Harvard University Press, 1936; 1964).

What is lacking is a replacement for Augustine's account of disorder in *nature*. Hick has a partial answer: God permits these things in order to create a morally challenging environment for human development. Yet the disorders of nature seem to go far beyond what is needed for human learning. In fact, if the amount and distribution of evils corresponded with our need for challenges and moral lessons, the problem of evil would not have arisen in the first place.

Biologists in the past century have added to the intellectual problem by pointing out that animal suffering and death preceded humans' coming on the scene by tens of millions of years. Thus, Augustine's and Calvin's accounts of their suffering as a result of our sin is implausible. Their suffering cannot be justified as leading to moral development for themselves or for the human race. The disorder and waste in natural processes long preceded human existence. Holmes Rolston notes:

> Suffering in a harsh world did not enter chronologically after sin and on account of it. There was struggle for long epochs before the human arrival, however problematic the arrival of sinful humans may also be. This has been Darwin's century and biology has been painting an ambivalent picture of nature. Nature is prolific and fertile enough, creative, and the panorama of life across the epochs of natural history is a good thing, a mysterious thing. This calls for a respect for life, perhaps even a reverence for life. But nature is also where the fittest survive, "red in tooth and claw," fierce and indifferent, a scene of hunger, disease, death. And nature is what it is regardless of human moral failings, indeed regardless of humans at all. . . . Nature is random, contingent, blind, disastrous, wasteful, indifferent, selfish, cruel, clumsy, ugly, struggling, full of suffering, and, ultimately, death.[35]

So the amount of suffering in and from the world of nature seems to go beyond any conceivable need of the human species.

We believe that the two most important changes regarding the problem of evil are, first, the change in conception of the governance of the universe—natural laws in place of angels—and the consequences of this change for understanding all of the major aspects of the problem of evil: sin, human and animal suffering at the hand of nature, and cosmic disorder. Second, there has been a widespread change in conceptions of God. In place of the impassible God of classical thought (to be affected by something outside oneself is an imperfection) we have various kenotic accounts of God's relations to

---

35. Holmes Rolston, III, "Does Nature Need to Be Redeemed?" *Zygon* 29, no. 2 (June 1994): 205–29; quotations, 205–206, 213.

creatures.[36] Some (such as Jürgen Moltmann) emphasize the notion that God suffers with and in creatures. Others (Ian Barbour, Arthur Peacocke, John Polkinghorne, and Diogenes Allen) emphasize that suffering results from God's voluntary self-limitation, not only with regard to human freedom (the free-will defense) but also with regard to other creatures.

Here the modern account of the governance of the universe and accounts of the character of God come together. The regularities in nature are necessary in order to have a cosmos (an order) at all. They are also a necessary basis for meaningful human action—we must be able to predict the effects of our acts. Yet, as byproducts of those inexorable laws, both humans and animals suffer through illness, starvation, and natural disasters.[37] The problem of evil thus shifts to the question why God does not cause exceptions to the (usually necessary) laws—why not occasional interventions, overruling natural processes when greater good will come from the exception than from following the rule.

It is the consensus among liberal theologians, as well as among scholars working in the area of theology and science, that God's action must be understood in a noninterventionist manner. We agree, claiming that God has apparently decided not to violate the "natural rights" of created entities to be what they are.[38] This means in part that God voluntarily withholds divine power, out of respect for the freedom and integrity of creatures. This means, as well, that God takes the risk and suffers the cost of cooperating with creatures whose activity violates or fails to measure up to God's purposes. This cost is accepted in order to achieve a higher goal: the free and intelligent cooperation of the creature in divine activity. This relation between God and creatures is one of God's highest purposes in creating. This mode of divine activity extends all the way through the hierarchy of complexity within the created world. Hence God cooperates with, but does not overrule, natural entities. We have argued that for this reason it is useful to conceive of God as acting at the quantum level, for here direct divine action is possible without violating determinate patterns of behavior of the entities in question.[39]

The crucial consequence of this view of noncoercive divine action at all

---

36. See Paul Fiddes, *The Creative Suffering of God* (Oxford: Clarendon Press, 1988); and our account above, chap. 8.

37. See Robert J. Russell, "Entropy and Evil," *Zygon* 19, no. 4 (Dec. 1984): 449–68, on the relation between evil and the second law of thermodynamics.

38. See Nancey Murphy, "Divine Action in the Natural Order: Buridan's Ass and Schrödinger's Cat," in Robert J. Russell, Nancey Murphy, and Arthur Peacocke, eds., *Chaos and Complexity: Scientific Perspectives on Divine Action* (Vatican City State and Berkeley, Calif.: Vatican Observatory and Center for Theology and the Natural Sciences, 1995, 325–57.

39. See Murphy, "Divine Action"; and George F. R. Ellis, "Ordinary and Extraordinary Divine Action," in Russell et al., *Chaos and Complexity*; and above, chap. 9, sec. 5.1.

levels of reality is that natural processes will be expressions not only of God's will but also of the limitations imposed by the creaturely natures of the entities with which God cooperates. At the human level, God's action is limited by human limitations but also by free choices in rebellion against God. At the lower levels of complexity, the issue is not sin, but simply the limitations imposed by the fact that the creature is only what it is, and is not God.

Earlier dualistic accounts of evil have identified the material aspects of reality with evil. While we reject this claim, we recognize that it was based on accurate observations that material beings are resistant to divine action. This is not evil in itself—it simply reflects the fact that the material is not divine—it is over against the divine. Yet this over-against-ness (what Simone Weil describes by a metaphorical extension of the term "gravity")[40] is in the process of being transformed, slowly and painfully, into the "image of God." The metaphorical expression in Genesis that God creates out of the *dust* of the earth creatures in God's own image, creatures enough like God to relate to God, has turned out to be closer to the literal truth than many have imagined.

So the aim of God, the creation of God-relating beings out of recalcitrant "matter" is achieved slowly and indirectly and painfully because the quality of relationship toward which God aims is not to be achieved by a process that violates that very quality. Therefore the process, too, must reflect noncoercive, persuasive, painstaking love all the way from the beginning to the end, from the least of God's creatures to the most splendid. Just as sin is a necessary byproduct of the creation of free and intelligent beings, suffering and disorder are necessary byproducts of a noncoercive creative process that aims at the development of free and intelligent beings.

We now make the claim that this kenotic answer to the problem of evil, this account of why God does not intervene in order to prevent evil and suffering, is consistent through and through with our program, including the theological and ethical aspects, as well as the use we make of cosmological fine-tuning. But it is radically inconsistent with any theological program whose *ethic* is not kenotic (nonviolent). We have argued that the justification for a Christian ethic is that human beings are to live in such as way as to become children of their heavenly Father. That is, our moral character is to be an image of the moral character of God.

The Augustinian tradition (including both its Catholic and Protestant developments), however, is the one that sponsors the just-war theory, and main-

---

40. See Weil, *Gravity and Grace* (London: Routledge, 1992 [1952]); and for a summary account see Diogenes Allen, *The Traces of God in a Frequently Hostile World* (Cambridge, Mass.: Cowley Publications, 1981), chap. 3.

line Christian ethics is largely committed to the principle that responsible Christians must sometimes do evil that greater good might follow. Terrence Tilley notes a connection between this ethico-political stance and Augustinian theodicy: Augustine's treatment of themes relating to the problem of evil is in fact part of the justification of an ecclesio-political system that arose in the context of the Constantinian church. The doctrine of original sin that justifies universal (and *apparently*) unmerited punishment also means that humans need to be restrained forcibly by political and ecclesial authorities.[41] Peter Brown, Augustine's sympathetic biographer, concedes that "Augustine may be the first theorist of the Inquisition."[42]

So the Augustinian tradition is a coherent whole, with its ecclesiology, its attitudes toward the use of political power to enforce church discipline, its social ethic, its doctrines of God, sin, and salvation. A kenotic account of divine action as divine restraint, as currently employed to address the problem of evil, can only be reconciled with great difficulty with other central theological doctrines, and not at all, we claim, with an Augustinian ethic.

In contrast, such an account flows directly from the core thesis of our theological program. Our program is part of a tradition whose root in the Radical Reformation was its rejection of the use of coercion (civil penalties, torture, execution) to enforce religious conformity.

In Anabaptist thought, the suffering of Christians is not generally punishment for sins, but rather redemptive participation with Christ in the expected consequences of obedience to God in the midst of a sinful world. It proclaims, "The Gospel of Christ crucified, how He suffered for our sake and was obedient to the Father even unto death. In the same way we should walk after Christ, suffering for his sake all that is laid upon us, even unto death."[43]

It is interesting to note that several of the original Anabaptist writers extended this account of human suffering to include "the Gospel of All Creatures." Hans Hut taught that the suffering of animals and the destruction of other living things conforms to the pattern of redemption through suffering, and in its own way preaches the Gospel of Christ Crucified.[44] The parallels with the writings of Holmes Rolston, whom we quoted in chapter 8, are striking.

So there has been present from the beginning a very different account of

---

41. Terrence Tilley, *The Evils of Theodicy* (Washington, D.C.: Georgetown University Press, 1991), 116.

42. Peter Brown, *Augustine of Hippo: A Biography* (Berkeley: University of California Press, 1967), 240.

43. Rollin Armour, *Anabaptist Baptism* (Scoudale, Pa.: Herald Press, 1966), 78; quoting Hans Hut, *Von dem geheimnus der tauf.*

44. Armour, *Anabaptist Baptism*, 82.

suffering in the Anabaptist tradition, intimately tied to an ecclesiology and a stance toward the world and its politics, and intimately tied as well to an account of God revealed in Christ Crucified. As we would now say, it is tied to a kenotic concept of the character of God. The kenotic ethic herein developed is *essential* to this system of thought.

A central move made in this book is to relate the core idea of noncoercion (which ties together a kenotic concept of God, a kenotic ethic, and an interpretation of suffering and evil) to the concept of fine-tuning. We claim that just as in the Anabaptist natural theology of the Gospel of all creatures, animal suffering testifies to the Gospel of Christ, similarly the fine-tuning of the cosmos can be taken up into a theology that sees God's noncoercive respect for the freedom and integrity of creatures to go all the way back to the initial design of an anthropic (intelligence- and freedom-producing) universe. Thus, while any theology can incorporate fine-tuning, fine-tuning can be more intimately related to a kenotic core theory than to a monarchical, authoritarian, or triumphalist model of God's character and action. The freedom of the creature is central to God's eighteen-billion-year project, not peripheral.

But if freedom from coercion is absolutely central to God's purposes, going all the way back to the beginning, then who are we, God's creatures, to attempt to coerce one another "that greater good might come"? Or, put the other way around, if God in fact permits us to intervene coercively (rather than persuasively) in human affairs, how ever can we explain a God who, with greater knowledge, power, and foresight, chooses not to intervene coercively in nature and history so that greater good—less suffering—may result?

4.2 *Epistemological Significance of Theodicy*

We pointed out in chapter 1 that, in general terms, hypotheses are justified by their ability to account for known phenomena. But this statement needs to be amplified because any number of hypotheses can be devised to account for an observation; similarly, a network of hypotheses can always be amended by the addition of auxiliary hypotheses in such a way as to make it consistent with any observation. Thus, the evaluation of theories or research programs depends on being able to show that the theoretical elaboration designed to account for an anomaly is not a mere verbal device but is actually integrally related to the core theory.

What we have done in this section is to address an anomaly, one that plagues all theistic systems, showing that research programs within our tradition are able to account for it in a unified way and in a way that follows directly from the core of the program, while the attempt to do so within the Augustinian tradition will inevitably introduce a new sort of incoherence. The theory of divine action explained here leads one to expect that the world's phenomena will not be direct expressions of the loving character of God; rather, God's character, God's plans, should be expected to be hidden by the effects of creaturely recalcitrance, in nature as well as in human life, in just the same way that the underlying inertial character of matter is concealed by the effects of friction. Note that this same account of divine action, including the emphasis on human freedom, makes it entirely reasonable to expect that there should be a variety of accounts of ultimate reality, many in conflict with our own. Thus, the minority status of our position does not in itself and automatically count against it.

In short, we have taken one of the most glaring anomalies faced by our system and have turned it into dramatic confirmation.

5 CONCLUSION

The second means, described by MacIntyre, of demonstrating the superiority of one tradition over its rivals is by its inclusiveness. It is a valid criticism of many traditional forms of Christianity (and of other religions as well) that they have been unable to incorporate the tradition(s) of modern science. This has been the focus of our project here, and we claim to have made a few significant advances in this direction, beyond those accomplished by others working on the relations between theology and science. We have provided a structure or model for understanding the relations among the natural and social sciences, ethics, and theology that sees them as hierarchically ordered and intrinsically connected. There are aspects of reality at each level that can be explained reductively, in terms of lower levels. There are also, however, boundary questions that can only be answered by turning to a higher level: Scientific cosmology raises boundary questions that can, appropriately, be answered theologically. The social sciences raise questions that can only be answered by turning to ethics. Ethical systems, in turn, raise theological questions.

We believe the point at which our project diverges most radically from other similar works is in the attention we accord to ethics. We have made several claims that are very much at variance with contemporary thinking: We have argued that morality has an "objective" basis in the nature of reality and that the discipline of ethics can be construed as the scientific study of this moral order. Further, we have claimed that, paradoxically, the ideal human life is one of self-renunciation, and that this involves centrally the renunciation of one's "legitimate right" to self-defense. It requires pacifism at the level of face-to-face encounters as well as the refusal to participate in state-sponsored violence, whatever the cost of that refusal may be.

This pacifist thesis is likely to be one of the most controversial of our claims. We see it as essential, however, both because it is needed for the overall coherence of the scheme, and also because of its practical importance in light of the situation currently facing humankind. It appears that the human race is at a critical stage of its evolutionary development: because of our technological progress we are faced with the necessity of making two ethical transitions. The first involves planetary management and environmental concerns. The stabilization of population is a key issue; however, the willingness to share economic goods is equally pressing. The second is the renunciation of force in international politics. Already the arms race has made available weapons of mass destruction; future developments will increase the danger. The long-term survival of the race depends on these two ethical advances, both of a kenotic nature. Thus, we see our project to be of more than mere "academic" interest.

Much remains to be done, however, both intellectually and practically. We hope that we have succeeded in stimulating interest in both social-scientific research and practical projects embodying the thesis that kenosis is the underlying law of the cosmos.

Index